StoryMaker
Catch Pack

Using genre fiction as a resource for accelerated learning

StoryMaker
Catch Pack

Using genre fiction as a resource for accelerated learning

STEPHEN BOWKETT

Published by Network Educational Press Ltd
PO Box 635
Stafford
ST16 1BF

© Stephen Bowkett 2003

ISBN 1 85539 109 0

The right of Stephen Bowkett to be identified as the author of this work has been asserted in accordance with Sections 77 and 78 of the Copyright, Designs and Patents Act 1988.

All rights reserved. No part of this publication may be reproduced, stored in a retrieval system or reproduced or transmitted in any form or by any means, electronic, mechanical, photocopying, recording or otherwise, without the prior written permission of the publishers. This book may not be lent, resold, hired out or otherwise disposed of by way of trade in any form of binding or cover other than that in which it is published, without the prior consent of the publishers.

Visual resources on the CD that accompanies this manual may be copied for individual classroom use.

Every effort has been made to contact copyright holders of materials reproduced in this book. The publishers apologise for any omissions and will be pleased to rectify them at the earliest opportunity.

Thanks are due to the following: A. P. Watt Ltd for the quotation on page 6 from W. B. Yeats, *The Celtic Twilight* (Prism Press 1999); Pearson Education for the quotations on page 23 and page 73 from Neil Postman and Charles Weingartner, *Teaching as a Subversive Activity* (Penguin Education Specials 1972; originally published by Pitman Publishing). On page 149 David Burroughs' illustration for *Roy Kane – TV Detective* by Stephen Bowkett (A. & C. Black Publishers Lt., 1998) is reproduced by permission of the publishers.

On page 156 the quotation from Kieran Egan, *Teaching as Storytelling* (University of Chicago Press, 1989) is reproduced by permission of the publishers, at whose request the copyright notice as it appears in their publication is reproduced, as follows:

'The University of Chicago Press, Chicago 60637
© 1986 by The University of Western Ontario,
London, Ontario, Canada
All rights reserved. Originally published 1986
University of Chicago Press edition 1989
Printed in the United States of America.

This book was first published in Canada by the Althouse Press, Faculty of Education, The University of Western Ontario, and is reprinted by arrangement.'

Managing Editor: Anne Oppenheimer
Design: Neil Hawkins – Network Educational Press Ltd
Illustrations: Annabel Spenceley
Illustration on page 56 by Stella Hender
Illustration on page 149 by David Burroughs

Printed in Great Britain by
MPG Books Ltd, Bodmin, Cornwall

Contents

Introduction		7
Acknowledgements		10
Section One:	The creative attitude	11
	Overview of Section One	12
Section Two:	The Big Picture for writing	35
	Overview of Section Two	36
Section Three:	A thinking toolkit	53
	Overview of Section Three	54
Section Four:	A bagful of story games	73
	Overview of Section Four	74
Section Five:	Reviewing, evaluating and planning creative work	185
	Overview of Section Five	186
Bibliography		207
Index		209

What is literature but the expression of moods
by the vehicle of symbol and incident?
And are there not moods which need
heaven, hell, purgatory and faeryland for their expression?
And are there not moods which will find no expression
unless there are those who dare to mix these together,
or even to set the heads of beasts to the bodies of men,
or to thrust the souls of men into the heart of rocks?
Let us go forth, the tellers of tales,
and seize whatever prey the heart longs for, and have no fear.

W. B. Yeats
The Celtic Twilight: Myth, Fantasy and Folklore

Introduction

Position and purpose

This pack is intended to complement the ideology of, and follow on from, the materials contained in *ALPS StoryMaker*. In *Catch Pack* too there is a substantial teaching manual linking the writing of fiction and literacy to creativity, thinking skills and the complex of ideas, principles and techniques that form the arena of accelerated learning. Some of the activities you'll find here extend and develop a number of those appearing in the previous book, although many are new. *Catch Pack* also follows the *ALPS StoryMaker* model by including accompanying fiction and a CD resource which adds depth and interactivity to the storymaking games.

◆ Emphasis

The stories in *Catch* and *Catch Minitales* are Fantasy, Science Fiction, Horror, and sometimes a mixture of all three. This reflects my own love of these genres and their current popularity, particularly perhaps where boys are concerned, in displaying an apparently insatiable appetite for all things scary, weird and wonderful. From an educational perspective, these linked genres – which I like to call 'The Three Sisters' – offer a rich conceptual framework where a great range of thinking tools can be discovered, applied and honed to greater effectiveness. Fantasy leads us swiftly into the world of myth and legend; deep currents that run through the global imagination and our own individual lives. Science Fiction raises awareness of the natural world and the greater universe, mapping out a staggering range of possible futures and allowing us to anticipate the consequences of our current actions. This capacity to 'preprocess' what-might-be is vital on every level: was it Pasteur who said that fortune favours the prepared mind? Even Horror has its place, being the dark thread that runs through the human psyche, sharing the power of Fantasy especially to tap into the huge range of our emotions through the mechanism of metaphor and symbol.

I often explain to people, with more than a touch of pride, that I got my O-Level and A-Level qualifications *because* of my passion for SF, Fantasy and Horror. They also provided 'safe havens' of increasingly familiar characters, motifs and scenarios that fuelled my adolescent fervour for writing stories – because here was something that took me out of my rather humdrum day-to-day existence into the most exotic of worlds. And I could travel with whomever I liked as I explored the universe of my own imagination. I was discovering myself as I found out more about the craft that came to be the focus my career. The authorship of such tales gave me a sense of authority and purpose in my life. Ironically, engaging with aliens and dragons and zombies in my head has over the years connected me in a profoundly meaningful way with 'the real world', and given me something worthwhile to do during my stay here. I have also met many

◆ INTRODUCTION

children on my travels who are going through exactly the same process. And I suspect that their love of the Three Sisters will, as it was for me, be their salvation.

◆ Using the materials

Having taught in classrooms for nearly twenty years, I have come to appreciate the value of practical, immediately usable resources. Ideally they should require minimal preparation, have few or no moving parts and work to good effect. These have been my aims in preparing *StoryMaker Catch Pack*.

◆ The manual

The *Catch Pack* manual has been arranged into the following sections:

1. The creative attitude
This summarises my thinking on what constitutes creativity, giving the reader a frame within which to practise the games that follow.

2. The Big Picture for writing
This addresses the key principles that lie behind writing as a means of human communication. The section also offers tips on the effective practice of writing creative fiction.

3. A thinking toolkit
This establishes the metaphor of a 'toolkit' of thinking skills, and begins to explore these through two core activities using imaginative exploration of pictures and a visual organiser of generic motifs. These core activities provide a sound basis from which to introduce all other storymaking games.

4. A bagful of story games
This is the meat of the manual – a menu of around fifty practical thinking/writing activities that can be used across the age and ability range. The games are arranged, broadly speaking, into sections on character, setting and plot, with the 'easiest' first and the more challenging coming later. But this should not prevent you from mixing and matching these games to suit your needs, using what works for you. All of them have educational value, which is outlined with the emphasis on accessibility.

5. Reviewing, evaluating and planning creative work
This section aims to give teachers and young writers a richer field of commentary for feedback and planning than the traditional emphasis on technical corrective marking. The ideas here link writing with confidence and self-worth, and make the vital distinction between personal achievement and politically motivated social measures of attainment.

6 **Contents and index**
Each section features an annotated contents page which is designed to provide a quick reference for linking any of the games with related activities in *ALPS StoryMaker* and also with the thinking skills that game aims to develop. The index is as extensive as I could make it, providing thumbnail definitions of the terms used in the main body of the text. The bibliography lists books that have been useful to me personally, and may provide some jumping-off points for your own further enquiry.

◆ The stories

- *Catch & Other Stories.* This collection of nine tales is a source of practical examples referred to throughout the manual, although the storymaking games can be used on their own, or with reference to any fiction.
- *Catch Minitales* – in two separate books: one of short Science Fiction stories and one of short Horror stories. This collection is not explicitly mentioned in the manual. The tales are under 1000 words long and can be read very quickly for pleasure and/or to illustrate many of the points made in the teaching materials. Each tale comes with an exploration sheet featured on the CD that allows the piece of fiction to be used effectively within the *StoryMaker* framework. Both books of stories are suitable for upper KS2 and 'across the bridge' into KS3 in terms of language level, subject matter and conceptual difficulty.

◆ CD resource

The CD aims to bring added depth and dimension to the storymaking games. Here you will find 'interactivities' that cannot be reproduced on paper and which satisfy the learning needs of more children as they explore the tales. The full text of both fiction collections is reproduced on the disk, together with author commentary and audio (in the case of *Catch & Other Stories*) and guidance for further exploration for the minitales. There is also a site map and hyperlinked index so that both teachers and students can navigate their way around the CD with the ease and assurance of a veteran space captain.

◆ Time

I have visited many schools to work with children and given scores of presentations of my ideas to adults. Sometimes the question of time constraints raises its head. All I will say here is that most of the storymaking activities can be broken down into bits that might take no more than a few minutes each to complete. Many of the games are cumulative, designed to allow children to 'step up to mastery' incrementally. They can be slipped between the cracks of the bricks that make up the National Curriculum. Also, the games develop thinking tools that can be applied elsewhere across the curriculum and beyond, in life generally – surely a worthwhile educational endeavour. Most important, for me, the activities in *Catch Pack* are fun and connect (or reconnect) the emotions to the intellect in a spirit of collaboration, co-operation and curiosity in exploring the world in which we live. Can anyone in the educational field deny the value of this process?

◆ INTRODUCTION

◆ Intention

It is my hope and intention that all of the material in *Catch Pack* will above all stimulate an excitement for exploration and enquiry that links the heart and the mind to the wider universe. When I explain the creative attitude to children I say 'Be nosy. Notice things. Ask questions.' That is the essence of being human and alive – to realise increasingly where and when and what we are, and to go beyond that and wonder why.

Acknowledgements

I wish to offer my particular thanks to The Team at NEP for their continuing support of my ideas, and to Anne Oppenheimer for her valued editorial expertise in bringing this project through to fruition.

I am also grateful to my friend Dave Newby who has patiently worked with me to produce the *Catch Pack* CD ROM, and to the artists whose talents have added such an important dimension to many of the current batch of storymaking games. Specifically I want to thank Annabel Spenceley for her vibrant cover art and very accessible illustrations in the *Catch Pack* manual. Thanks too to Stella Hender, wherever you are (if you read this, ring me!); also to Brian Towers for his stunning cosmic imaginings and fine sense of humour; to Russell Morgan and Chris Sellers for their animated contribution to the work; and to Russell Morgan and Chris Pepper for their splendid cover illustrations for *Catch Minitales* – Horror and Science Fiction respectively.

I also want to acknowledge the many Science Fiction, Fantasy and Horror writers whose visions have opened the doorways to many worlds. Their explorations have stimulated my imagination endlessly and have helped me to boldly go and make the kind of life I wanted for myself.

Finally, most importantly, I thank my wife Wendy whose love and support are unconditional. Hers is the best kind of teaching I know.

Steve Bowkett
March 2003

Section One

 # The creative attitude

 Wonder is the seed of knowledge.

Francis Bacon

Overview of Section One

Page	Activity	Story element	ALPS StoryMaker reference	Accelerated learning & thinking skills link
13	A Note on Creativity	All	Section 1 – The Creative Mind	See all of the AL links in 'The Creative Mind'
18	The Creative Climate	All	Affirmations pp.85–6; Fifty Positive Adjectives p.182	Emotional resourcefulness; self-determination; 'neurological levels' and the importance of a safe environment
21	The Logic Brain and the Artist Brain	All	Teaching Alpha p.273; Visualisation pp.273–287	Metacognition; attentional states; strategies for absorption, retention and recall of information
22–28	Manipulating Information; The Learning Arrow; Bisociations; Reframes; The Merlin Technique; Visual Organisers	All	The Creative Mind pp.11–45	See all of the AL links in 'The Creative Mind'
28	The Metaphor of the Story and Emotional Resourcefulness	All	Section 2: The Story Process – planning strategies; conscious construction of resourcefulness; Section 7: The Inner World of the Writer – motifs and meanings	Anchoring resources; modelling resourceful behaviours; cognitive distortions (unhelpful conscious filtering)
34	'IDEAS NOW'	All	Get an Attitude; The Write Attitude	Visual anchor for resourceful states

Section One

◆ The creative attitude

◆ A note on creativity

Read these statements carefully:

- You cannot teach creativity.
- Creativity demands high IQ.
- Creativity is a special talent of the few.
- Creativity is a province of the arts.
- Creative thinking flourishes in the absence of discipline, logic and factual knowledge.
- Creativity is not systematic – you must wait for inspiration to strike.
- Core skills such as literacy and numeracy need to be in place before creative thinking can flourish.
- Creative thinking is a 'right-brained' activity.
- Creative people tend to be highly intelligent but rather bohemian, vague, a bit odd.
- Creative people tend to look rather different from you and me.

Now tick the ones you think are true. When you have done that, consider these other statements:

- Work is play.
- Play can bring you money.
- Working hard and trying hard are not the same.
- Creativity is usually effortless.
- You can earn your living doing what you really want to do.
- Making a living and making a life are different.
- No pain, no gain.
- Experts are authorities.
- Authorities are experts.
- Enjoying the process is more important than measuring the result.

◆ SECTION ONE

Now rate each statement on a 1–6 scale, where 1 means *I completely disagree* and 6 means *I fully agree*. (See also 'Mediations' on p.140.) You will find my own opinions on the second group of statements on p.18.

Accelerated learning is also called brain-based learning, and derives its ideas and methodologies from insights gained through neuroscience and other fields. However, I am not particularly interested (in the context of creative thinking) in which parts of the brain carry out which functions, in the same way that I don't care which bits of my car's engine do what – all I want to know is which pedals to push to get me where I want to go. The activities in *Catch Pack* are designed to push pedals, to stimulate children's natural creative energy and focus it into the domain of writing genre fiction. The general purpose of this is to improve literacy skills, but the 'hidden curriculum'* is much more powerful and profound – namely, to train up children's creative attitude and equip them with a toolbox of thinking skills that they can use for the rest of their lives.

> * I came across 'the hidden curriculum' at college. The idea was only ever mentioned, not studied, and it intrigued me. The hidden curriculum is everything children learn about the world when they're at school, other than what is formally taught. This means, it seems to me, that only a fraction of what children learn at school is not part of the hidden curriculum! The great benefit of this principle for our purposes is that we can design materials that carry a raft of learnings built into apparently simple and enjoyable games. As teachers we appreciate the educational power of the activities we offer to children, and feel assured that they are learning anyway, in all kinds of ways that we do not need to labour or even make explicit.

Traditionally there has been a certain mystique surrounding the notion of creativity, coupled sometimes with fears that 'being creative' means chaos and noise and loss of control in the classroom, and unpredictable (if any) useful output. Before we get going with this book, I want to make it absolutely clear that:

- we are all naturally highly creative
- creative thinking is as organised and structured and systematic as any other kind of mental activity (if indeed there is any other kind of mental activity!)
- developing creativity can be taught as an educationally justifiable programme of activities in the classroom.

You will by now, I'm sure, have surmised that I regard all of the statements that opened this section to be completely untrue (my assessment of the second list of statements is on p.18). My belief – verified by years of writing experience – is that the creative attitude underpins meaningful education and that the ultimate goal of meaningful education is to draw out* children's natural creativity.

THE CREATIVE ATTITUDE

> * 'Education', from the Latin **educare**, 'to lead', and connected to **educere**, 'to draw out'. The sense of this for me is that we allow children to learn by leading them along ways that draws out of them the meanings they are making of the world. Although more artfully, as the old saying goes, 'Do not follow in the footsteps of the wise. Seek what they sought.'

Below is a model which summarises the points I've been making.

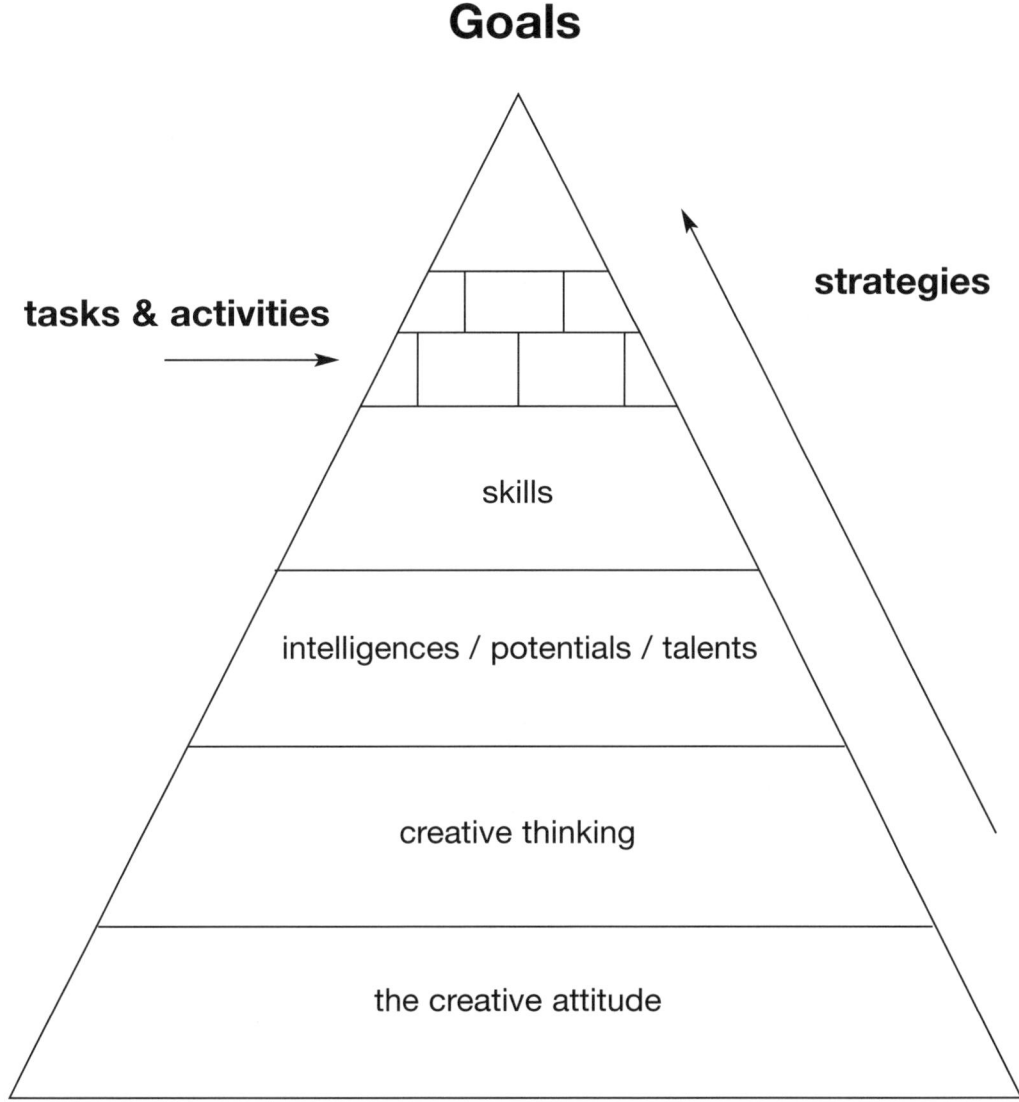

◆ SECTION ONE

The creative attitude is about being adventurous in manipulating information – I always think of it as *in-formation*, something that continues to be shaped inside the heads of learners: it is about being unafraid to have lots of ideas in order to have good ideas. The creative attitude also includes the drive to find explanations, build strategies, formulate plans, assess reasons and construct new solutions. This involves being thorough, organised and precise in one's thinking. The creative attitude also benefits from one being metacognitive – thinking about the thinking you do. I explain this idea by encouraging children to 'be nosy'. I tell them that you can be nosy by noticing things and by asking questions; you can be nosy by noticing things going on around you, and things going on inside your head; you can ask closed question to get precise answers, or open questions that throw out lots of possibilities. Noticing what goes on inside your head is the key to metacognition.

Creative thinking is the deliberate use of thinking tools (kinds of thinking) to shape information in desired ways. One useful definition of intelligence is just that – the ability to handle information flexibly. This mental activity 'bubbles up' through the range of potentials or talents with which we are born (see Howard Gardner's multiple intelligence model). Because of our upbringing and, increasingly, our own interests and choices, we tend to direct our creative energies into a few areas of talent rather than developing them all. We do this through practising the skills which allow the outward expression of our thinking*. The refinement of skill requires 'menus' of activities and tasks. These menus are learning strategies. Strategies are moveable feasts: I can mix-and-match activities to accelerate my journey towards my (fixed) goal. In my case this might be writing a book. In the case of children in school, our fixed goal is surely to allow them to become independent, creative, thinking individuals.

> * The writer P. G. Wodehouse was once asked how you become a successful creative writer. He said, 'You take your bum and you put it in a seat – every day.'

As teachers we can make our strategies more effective by establishing a balance between product and the process that creates it; between telling, showing and allowing children to *do*. Practically speaking, in the classroom this requires a balance between –

THE CREATIVE ATTITUDE

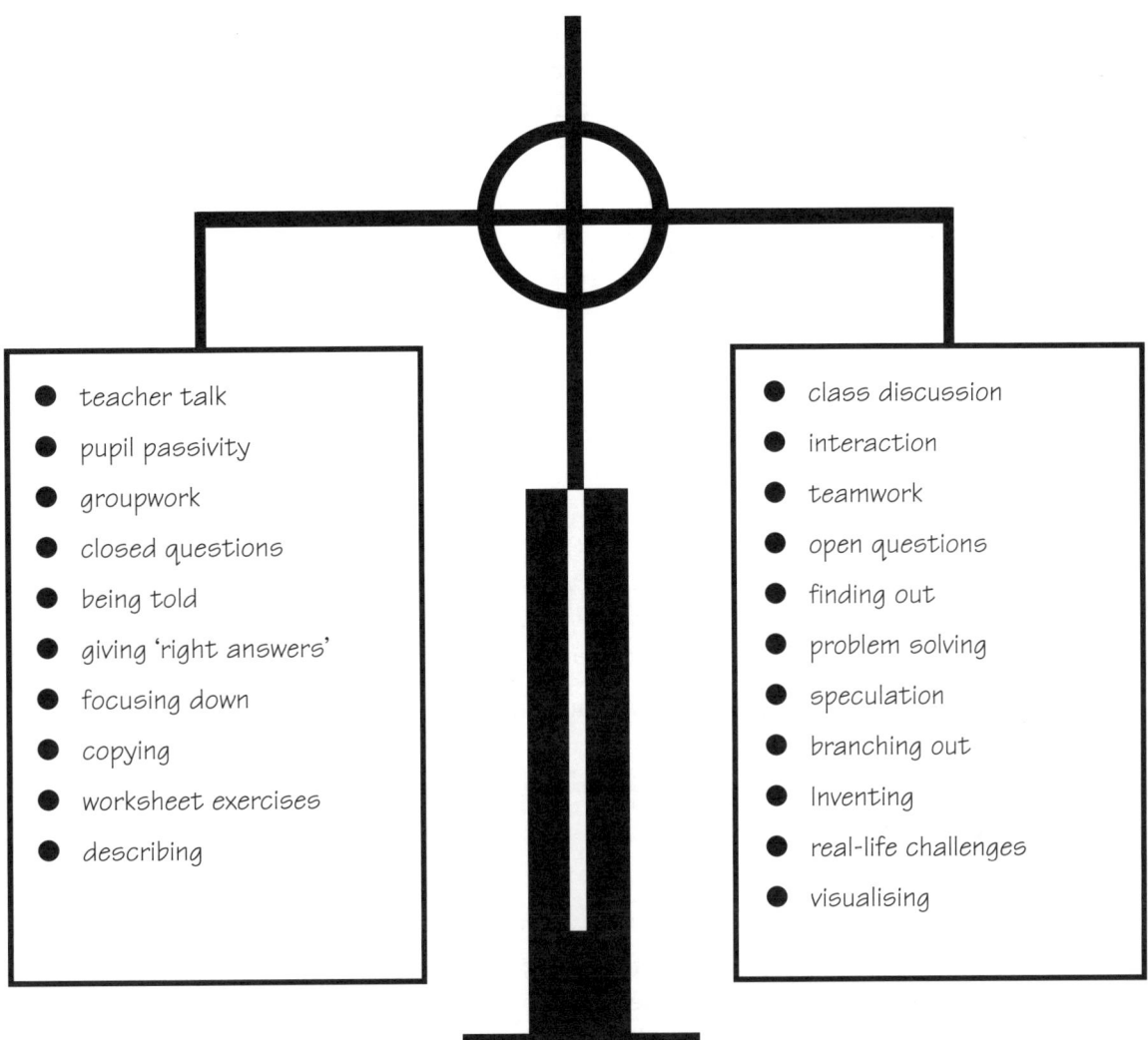

Within this framework our language should seek to support, encourage and draw out from children their emergent understandings of the world. And so we might say things like:

- That's an interesting idea.
- Tell me more about it.
- How did you reach that conclusion/point/idea?
- What other ideas might be useful?
- What other conclusions can you think of, I wonder?
- What other solutions might be possible?
- How will you decide which option to take?
- That's a good idea. I wonder how we will develop it?
- Just keep going and you'll soon be there…

◆ SECTION ONE

As someone once said, confidence doesn't come from having all the answers but by being open to all of the questions. My view is that the essence of children's creative thinking is being open to all of the questions, most of which they have generated for themselves.

> My opinions are:
>
> - Work is play – 6
> - Play can bring you money – 6
> - Working hard and trying hard are not the same – 6
> - Creativity is usually effortless – 6
> - You can earn your living doing what you really want to do – 6
> - Making a living and making a life are different – 6
> - No pain, no gain – 1
> - Experts are authorities – 1 (with exceptions)
> - Authorities are experts – 1 (with exceptions)
> - Enjoying the process is more important than measuring the result – 6 (the product is part of the ongoing process).

◆ The creative climate

Effective learning behaviour is supported by a creative climate. Review Alistair Smith's books (see Bibliography) for practical ways of establishing an Accelerated Learning classroom which, together with the attitude you espouse, generates an ethos – a spirit of working – that boosts children's creative thinking abilities. Broadly speaking, a creative climate includes the following factors (blocks to creativity are counterpointed in the right-hand column):

● There is structure and order at all levels.	Fear of change (especially unexpected change) can inhibit creative thought. Conversely, unchallenged routine and habit makes for sterile ground. Structure and order build the frame within which creative flexibility will flourish.
● Activities feature high challenge and energy and low threat.	Challenges are exciting. 'High' challenges are more exciting – i.e. those which push the limits of a learner's capabilities and take her into new areas of thinking. Low threat implies no fear of getting 'the wrong answer', and no fear of the consequences if an activity didn't turn out 'right'. As the saying goes, *good judgement comes from experience, and experience comes from bad judgement.*

THE CREATIVE ATTITUDE

• There is an acceptance and even celebration of personal differences. High expectations in teacher and learners are presupposed.	Creative breakthroughs often occur through bouncing ideas around between individuals. The 'sausage factory' model of education is not useful in this context. Expectations determine outcomes: high expectation does not mean the same as equal levels of attainment. Paul Ginnis (see Bibliography) talks about the shallow learning measured by standardised attainment procedures, and the deep learning that is expressed by individual achievement.
• Early and/or extreme value judgements are avoided. Self-evaluation is encouraged.	Early value judgements can prevent the appearance of a useful idea. More alarmingly, a judgemental climate based solely on corrective marking of work and comparisons between individuals might stifle the development of creative thought. One cornerstone of creativity is independence of judgement in the learner. Imposing principles, absolute truths* or previous models and paradigms without encouraging a questioning and challenging attitude towards them simply achieves the shallow learning which is the passive acceptance of received wisdoms.
• A positive approach to novelty is valued and utilised. Alternative solutions are always considered.	*If you always do what you've always done, you'll always get what you've always got.* Novel ideas are not right or wrong, but more or less useful in the end. Consider the vast number of breakthroughs in science and technology that have come about because someone wondered whether there might be a better way of doing things.
• Ambiguity and uncertainty are tolerated.	Change is the only certainty. Confusion, in the right environment, leads inevitably towards fusion – a coming together of parts to make the Big Picture.

---

* Is this statement true – 'the Earth is round'? Is it somehow 'more true' to say 'the Earth is spherical'? Science tells us that the Earth is an oblate spheroid (flattened at the poles, bulging at the Equator). This is more factually correct than saying the Earth is a sphere – but is it any more true? Is truth dependent upon one's personal reality any more than it depends upon 'consensus reality'? Supposedly, factual information in encyclopedias becomes obsolete at a rate of over 20 per cent a year. What is absolutely true today may be only partially true, or not at all true, tomorrow.

◆ SECTION ONE

◆ The logic brain and the artist brain

It has long been recognised that different areas of the brain are responsible for different functions. This understanding includes the notion that the left and right hemispheres of the neocortex (supposedly the most recently evolved part of the brain) are the physical locations for different kinds of thinking – the left cerebral hemisphere being the 'logic brain' and the right hemisphere the 'artist brain'. For our purposes what matters is that the whole range of thinking states and styles is necessary for creative thinking to be most effective, and that we can learn to exercise greater conscious control over the generally less well utilised 'artist brain', whose functioning tends to be relatively subconscious – occurring outside the realm of the conscious awareness – which is to say, we may not be aware of artist brain/subconscious thinking going on, but the *outcomes* of such processes pop into mind as ideas, intuitions, insights and hunches. Trust in and reliance upon this subconscious processing is key to the development of creativity. An important part of such reliance is the realisation that 'the Muse' is not vicarious, fickle or out of our control. We can train ourselves to shift between mental states to suit our particular thinking purposes.

These different mental states *feel* different. Broadly speaking, when we are consciously busy paying attention to the outside world, the functions of the logic brain predominate. When we 'tune out', drift off, defocus, lapse into daydream … then the artist brain is in the ascendant; the outside world may take on a kind of fuzzy ambience as our attention internalises and narrows to illuminate the thoughts that drift across our mind's eye. We can arrange for those daydreams to be pertinent to the problem we want to solve, the story we want to write, the information we wish to recall – as we begin to appreciate the power and usefulness of our vast subconscious resource.

Basically, encouraging children to 'be nosy' and notice what they're thinking about is the first step towards greater exploitation of the artist brain. Further, engaging children's attention with the magic of story – and reviewing what they saw with their mind's eye – develops this capability. See *ALPS StoryMaker* – 'Teaching Alpha' for more information.

◆ Brain waves

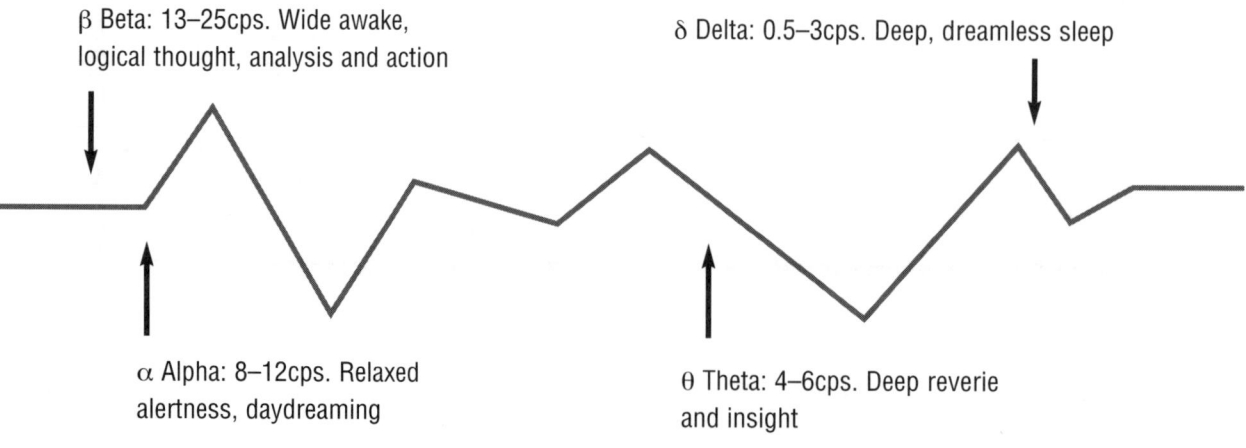

β Beta: 13–25cps. Wide awake, logical thought, analysis and action

δ Delta: 0.5–3cps. Deep, dreamless sleep

α Alpha: 8–12cps. Relaxed alertness, daydreaming

θ Theta: 4–6cps. Deep reverie and insight

The logic brain and the artist brain

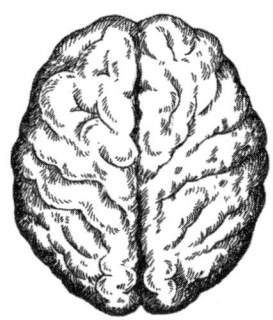

The logic brain is –

- categorical
- reflective
- deliberate
- neat
- linear/serial
- verbal
- sensitive to details
- literal
- deconstructive
- analytical
- focused attention
- single tasking
- 'sensible'
- censorial
- self-conscious
- ego-focused
- uses effort
- uses 'hard' thinking

The artist brain is –

- chaotic
- freewheeling
- intuitive
- untidy
- (w)holistic/associative
- nonverbal
- sensitive to patterns
- metaphorical/symbolic
- reconstructive
- inventive
- broad domain of attention
- multitasking
- reactive/impulsive
- accepting
- self-absorbed
- multifaceted
- effortless
- uses 'soft' thinking

◆ SECTION ONE

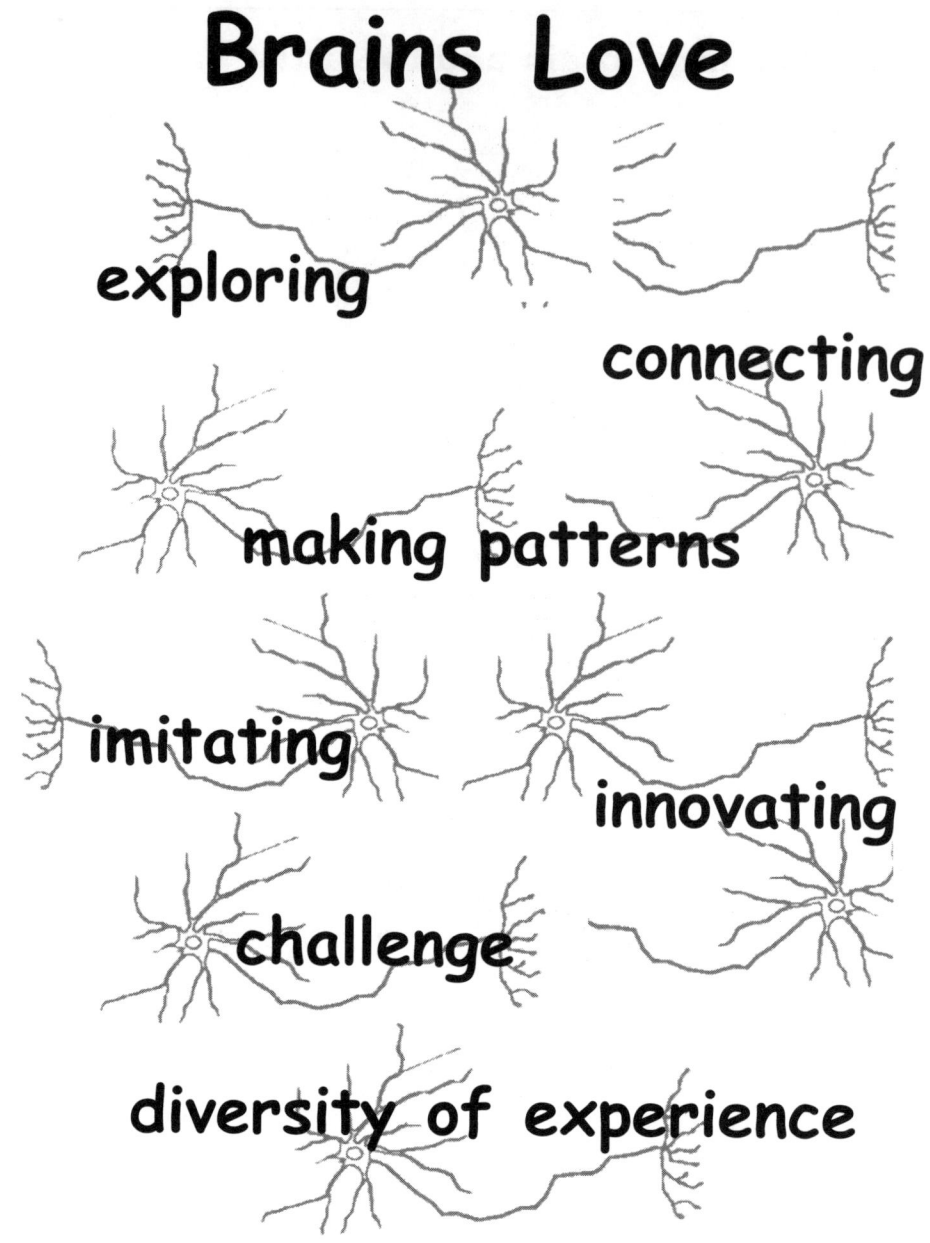

Brains Love

exploring

connecting

making patterns

imitating

innovating

challenge

diversity of experience

◆ Manipulating information

Information is constantly processed within the brain. We learn anyway, although it is advisable to take notice of the old wisdom, *Did you have ten years' experience, or one year's experience ten times?* We make sense of the world both through conscious thought and subconscious assimilation. Our own unique 'map of reality' is established largely at a subconscious level but can to a greater or lesser extent be accessed, reflected upon and modified with conscious thinking tools. The same cycle operates on a smaller scale with regard to our specific learning projects.

STORYMAKER CATCH PACK - USING GENRE FICTION AS A RESOURCE FOR ACCELERATED LEARNING

THE CREATIVE ATTITUDE

The mathematician Henri Poincaré devised a useful model for thinking about the creative process. He identified four main phases: *preparation, assimilation (or incubation), illumination* and *verification*. Each phase occurs across a continuum of formality, so:

informal ←――――――――――――――――――――――→ **formal**

preparation

assimilation

illumination

verification

- We prepare our thinking *informally* simply by living in the world, by 'meaning-making'* subconsciously, and by consciously reflecting upon how we represent ('re-present') the world to ourselves. *Formal* preparation involves specific systematic study and research.

- Assimilation is a continuation of the preparation phase, although consciously we can bring on the gathering up of ideas through the use of particular stimulus activities and so-called visual organisers (see below). Tony Buzan's famous mind maps constitute one kind of visual organisation.

- Illumination is the point at which ideas, connections and insights appear within our conscious awareness – the penny drops, the light goes on, suddenly we understand. Informally we might wait for the Muse to strike, or we can undergo a programme of training which makes light work of having illuminations more or less at will. The games in the *StoryMaker* manuals aim to do just that.

- Once we've had our ideas we can work on them consciously to get the best out of them. We can test them against our own internal experience (*Do I need to change anything to make this story even better?* – see also Section Five), and 'in the outside world' to verify their validity more generally.

> * 'Meaning-making' is a term used by Neil Postman and Charles Weingartner in the only college book I ever kept (and still have) – **Teaching as a Subversive Activity**. It has some wonderful chapter headings such as 'Crap detecting', 'The inquiry method', 'Pursuing relevance' and 'What's worth knowing'? Published in 1969, it seems to me that this book is just as pertinent to education now as it was then.

Practically speaking, all the phases of the creative process described by Poincaré occur all the time as an incredibly complex network of cycles within the mind.

◆ SECTION ONE

◆ The creative cycle

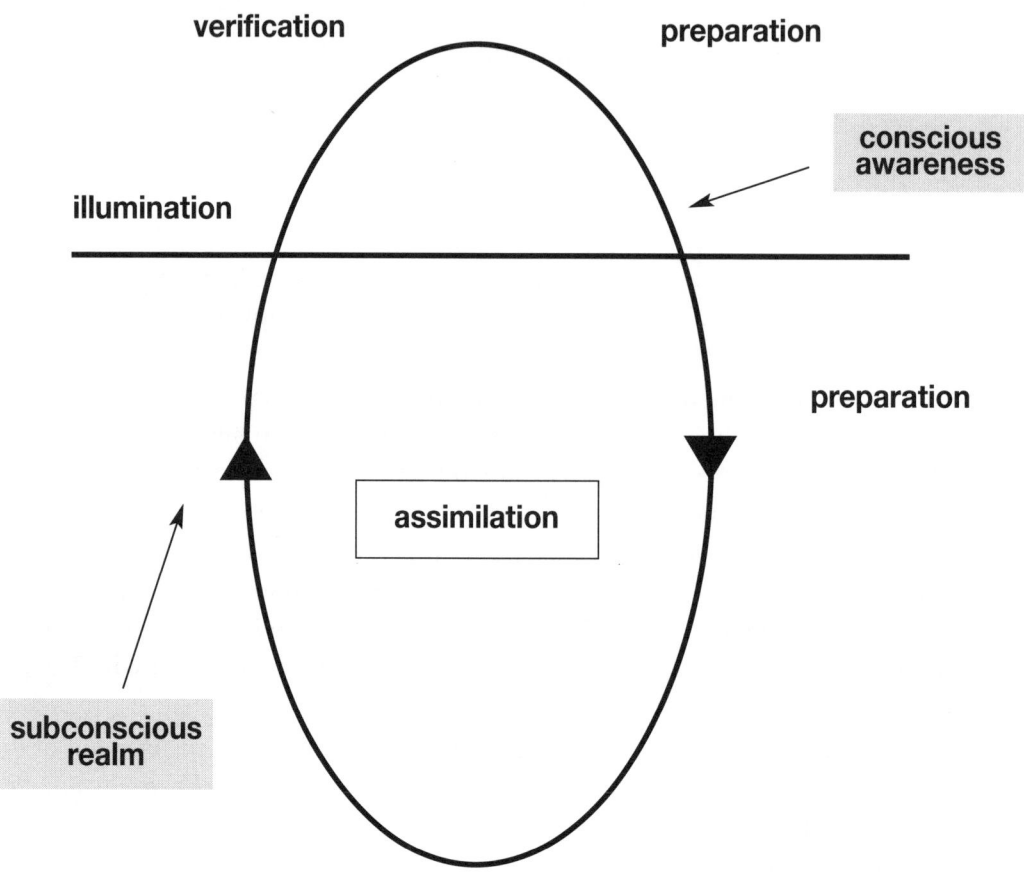

◆ The learning arrow

The endless cycling of information through the mind is the true 'learning curve'. When it is applied to the development of a specific skill or completion of a project, to me it resembles more of a 'learning arrow' that moves from a state of conscious incompetence – where we try hard to do it, and do it poorly – to a state of nonconscious competence – where we are 'in the flow' and accomplish the task effortlessly and with the minimum of conscious interference. Note here that we may need to work hard to achieve our goal, but working hard and trying hard are emphatically not the same thing.

THE CREATIVE ATTITUDE

The learning arrow — from puzzlement to mastery

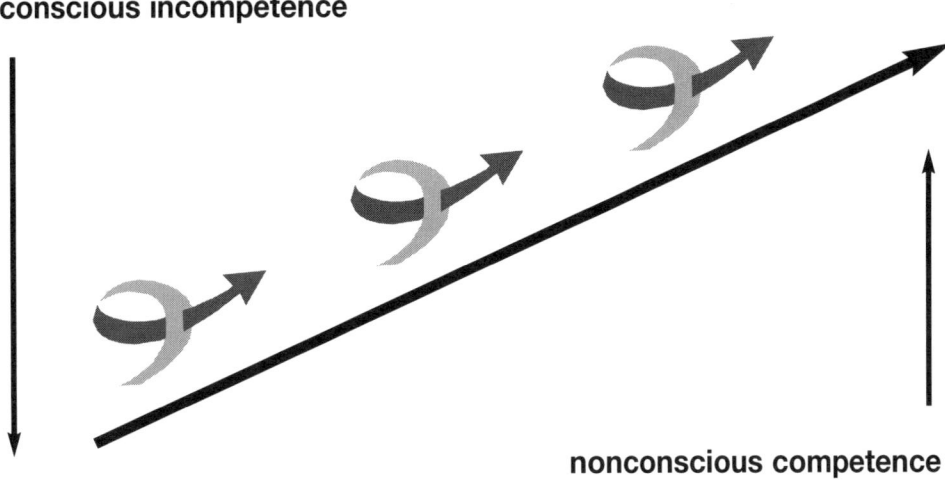

◆ Bisociations

These are creative links or associations between two previously unrelated items. A bisociation constitutes one of the most basic creative thinking skills. Brainstorming, it seems to me, is a kind of blanket bombing of a given topic to see if any items 'stick together' in a useful way. Successful bisociations are usually the outcome of 'seeing with new eyes' so that, for instance, a bisociation between adhesive and sawdust gave us chipboard, and a bisociation between a skateboard and a yacht led to the invention of the land yacht. Once you have introduced the idea to children, encourage them to notice which machines and other everyday objects are the product of bisociative thinking. (See also '6×6 Fantasy Grid', p.65).

> Marcel Proust said that 'Voyages of discovery consist not of going to new places, but of seeing with new eyes.'

◆ Reframes

We often think predictably – which is to say, predictably to ourselves as much as to other people. A mindset is a structure of predictable thinking (I always think of 'minds set' in a concrete way!). A reframe is any means we utilise to change the structure of our thinking, to allow us to see with new eyes.

◆ SECTION ONE

A simple reframe is to lead someone's expectations along a predictable path and then change direction unexpectedly. Many jokes are reframes of this kind (Person A – 'Did you know that God is black?' Person B – 'Is she?'). So too are 'twist in the tale' stories. A clear reframe of this kind is to be found in the story *She Bites*, where the reader expects Eleanor to be a vampire or, less likely, an ordinary girl. Part of the art of storytelling, of course, is to keep the reader guessing and then to come up with a shock ending, a sudden reframe.

Reframing language can lead to a change of behaviour so that, for example, reading 'information' as 'in-formation' can flip us over into a new way of seeing. Similarly, thinking of 'intuition' as 'inner tuition' evokes the notion of the subconscious part of one's mind being a resource of wisdom and guidance. A lovely reframe you can use if a child says to you 'Please Miss/Sir, I can't do this…' is 'Well, pretend you can and let me know when you've done it.' If the child doesn't think too hard about what you've said, (s)he'll most likely go away and do it. Wordplay of all kinds can kick up some interesting and powerful reframes, since redefining words can redefine perceptions of reality.*

> * Not so long ago I was talking with a lady who told me that she'd felt guilty for years about not visiting her (now deceased) mother very frequently in her final years. I pointed out that a judge defines guilt as the intention to cause harm, followed by the action of harming. This was a revelation to my companion. She said that thinking of it in that way was 'like a weight off my back'. The redefinition allowed her to be free of guilt, although, she said, she was sorry she had not seen her mum more regularly.

More complex reframes (in structure, not necessarily ones that are harder to achieve) involve more general 'pretending you can'. Being a character, object or place in a story can allow you to take a new perspective, both on the story and perhaps in life (see 'Pseudonyms', p.49). 'Thinking outside the box' is a common expression for the idea of stepping beyond the bounds of one's usual (and automatically maintained) structures of perception. In this context, every piece of art is a reframe: stories take us inside the author's mind, allow us to inhabit a different world and, if the writing is powerful enough, to come away changed.

Reframing is a powerful tool and can be developed to a high degree of sophistication. To find out more, see Bandler, in the Bibliography.

◆ The Merlin Technique

The Merlin Technique is a well-known game for solving problems and/or having ideas by seeing things in new ways. Imagine that a problem/idea can be transformed by the wave of an imaginary (or imaginative) wand. Standard waves include enlarging, reducing, stretching, reversing, switching positive-to-negative (or vice versa) and eliminating. So, if I wanted to get more mileage out of the idea of *She Bites*…

THE CREATIVE ATTITUDE

- **enlarging**
    - This could be a novel.
    - All the girls in Eleanor's extended family are vampires.
    - All the girls in the school turn into vampires (at certain phases of the moon).
    - The whole town transforms once every full moon (maybe with exceptions).

- **reducing**
    - Eleanor – or whoever – transforms only briefly and has lapses about what's happened.
    - The story could be a mini-saga (50 words only).
    - Colin's little baby sister transforms.

- **stretching**
    - This could be a series of stories!
    - Eleanor's transformation is progressive. Each time it happens, she turns into something a little more dreadful.
    - Colin becomes her confidant and is drawn progressively into her dark world.

- **reversing or positive-to-negative** (these two are sometimes not the same)
    - Eleanor transforms into an angelic creature.
    - Colin is the one who transforms (though the reader is led to suspect that it will be Eleanor).
    - The reader's sympathies are guided towards Eleanor and away from Colin's plight.
    - The story begins with Eleanor's transformation. The earlier part of the tale is told as back story (extended flashback) or several shorter flashbacks.

- **eliminating**
    - People start to disappear from school/around the town.
    - Even though Colin doesn't have proof of Eleanor's monstrous true self, he decides to destroy (eliminate) her.
    - In a world of vampires, non-vampires are the freaks and need to be eliminated.
    - Monster-Eleanor and Colin join forces to eliminate a greater evil.

Out of Merlin's magical spray of ideas, a few usable ones will usually appear. The ones that don't seem to go anywhere are not forgotten, but put by for later – when they may combine creatively with other ideas in new and as yet unsuspected ways.

◆ SECTION ONE

◆ Visual organisers

Throughout *Catch Pack* a number of templates will be offered as devices for the arrangement of information. These visual organisers can stimulate further thinking and aid understanding, retention and recall. Note that although they are presented within the context of storymaking, they can be used flexibly across the curriculum. Where appropriate, applications in other subjects will be mentioned.

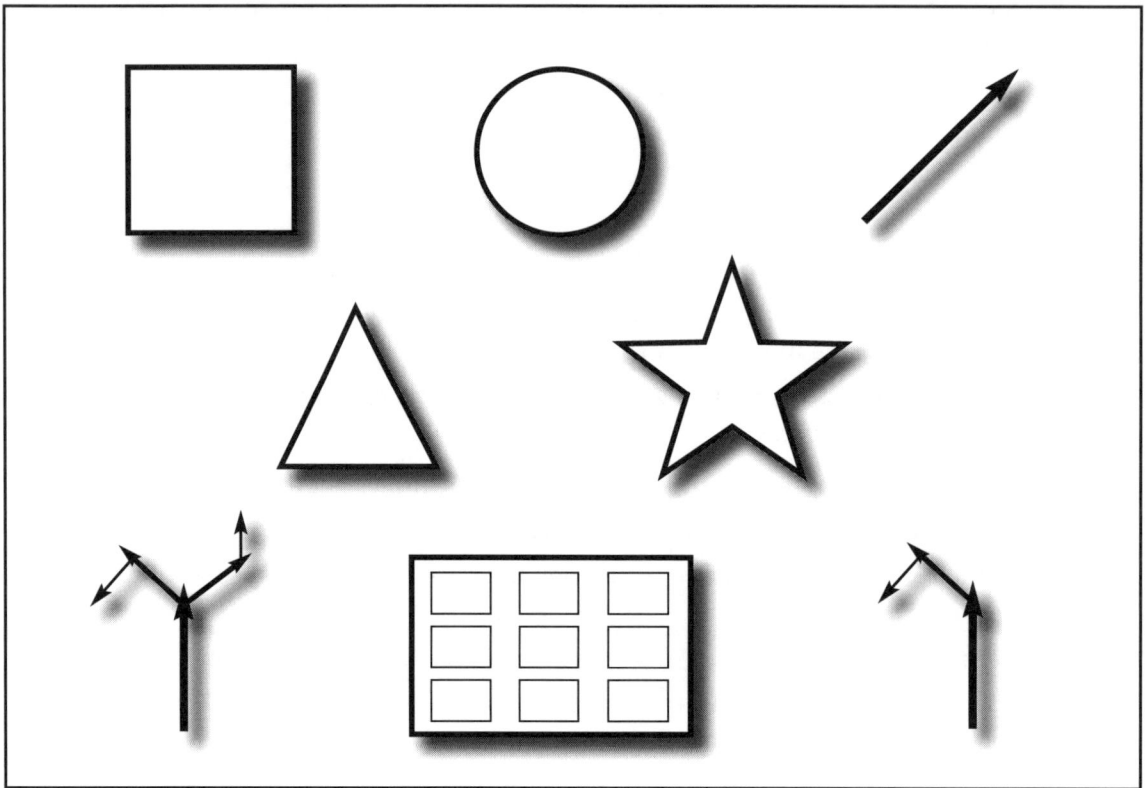

◆ The metaphor of the story and emotional resourcefulness

As a young boy I was painfully shy and severely lacking in confidence, a state which lasted well into my twenties. I think that part of the appeal of writing for me was that I could withdraw into the world of my stories and turn my back on the trials of the real world. This is escapist fiction in its deepest sense! Interestingly, as I look back now, I never suffered what has been called 'the dread of the blank page'. I have encountered this many times, however, in both children and adults: a fear of committing yourself to paper, a feeling almost of panic at the prospect of filling up that huge white sheet with meaningful words. Clearly, confidence is an important issue in creative writing.

I started submitting novels to professional publishing houses in my mid-twenties. The rejections came thick and fast and each one hurt a lot, especially when accompanied by what I considered petty, negative or unjustified criticism. It would have been so easy, in such a demoralised state, to conclude that I was no good at writing and pack it all in… Except that the practice of writing had given me qualities I had not suspected in myself. The perseverance needed to write a novel sustained me now, together with a certain independence of judgement: I knew that my stories were OK, of a publishable standard, and I came to realise that their acceptance or rejection depended largely on the editor's (or editorial reader's) opinion. These were crucial insights in terms of my own emotional development, which is why when I teach or write about creative writing I like to offer practical activities and techniques – *and an attitude* that will carry you through to success.

More recently I have come to appreciate the power of metaphor, and particularly the metaphor of 'the story'; there can be few more important notions than 'the life story', after all. This idea can be developed and used to help deal with the trials and tribulations of life, and below I have listed some of the 'sub-metaphors' that stem from the big idea of the life story. If you choose to use them you might simply offer them as pieces of advice (metaphors tend to be appreciated subconsciously anyway, even if you don't consciously make the connection). Or you can make them explicit to children to help develop in them the emotional qualities and strengths that every true education should nourish.

The metaphor …	… unpacked
Effective authorship allows us to read between the lines.	Emotionally resourceful people are aware that communication amounts to more than is said. Metaphor, innuendo, facial expression and body posture are all aspects of communication. Such people also recognise that they are responsible for what they say, but not for what others hear.
A good author does not copy other writers' ideas, but gains inspiration and insight from their work.	An old proverb says 'When someone points at the moon, the fool looks at the finger and the wise one looks at the moon.' Similarly, 'Do not follow in the footsteps of the wise – seek what they sought.' Our journey is our own. We may consider others' advice, but our own independence of judgement is our true strength. Incidentally, read 'insight' as 'in-sight': we look inside to find something out. And 'to inspire' means 'to breathe life into' and comes from the same Latin root as 'spirit'.

◆ SECTION ONE

A story can be a piece of back-fence gossip or a creation myth.	The oral tradition of storytelling includes a concept called 'The Ladder to the Moon'. This is a hierarchy of stories that links the Earth to the heavens, from 'earthy' everyday snippets to the timeless myths of cosmic origins. The idea allows us to keep in mind that sense of a grander purpose as we go about our mundane tasks. This is a highly nourishing perspective. (For more see *ALPS StoryMaker*, p.292)
The work shows you how to do it. (Estonian proverb)	Rules work best when they are embedded in good practice. The act of creative writing gives you a sense (nonconscious understanding) of what works well and what doesn't. Simple labelling, the naming of parts – that activity so abhorred by the poet Henry Reed – does not of itself lead to understanding. Having faith in the process of writing allows natural learning to occur.
Pedantry is the last refuge of those with no story to tell.	Strict insistence on accuracy inhibits the creative process. Pedantry reinforces the walls of the box. Creative thinking often works beyond the box, but recognises that the box exists (and that it has been put there by somebody else). Often the creative bending of the rules leads to innovation and breakthrough.
The creation of a story rarely happens in the same order in which it is told.	'The beginning, the middle and the end' is the outcome of a creative process of generation and organisation of ideas. Creators of fiction (and often fact) do not routinely start at the beginning. More broadly, the solutions to a problem need not be found by thinking first of possible solutions. Recognise that creativity is messy and that the trick is not to have lots of ideas but to know which ideas work best.
Effective writers are the captains of their own author-ship (and expect the crew to follow instructions).	Independence of judgement is a key quality. That judgement is based upon experience, reflection and intuition – using all the tools in the thinking toolkit. In other words, our conscious decisions and judgements are in part the product of subconscious processing and response. (For more about conscious–subconscious interactions, see *Imagine That!* and *Self-Intelligence* by Stephen Bowkett; see Bibliography)

THE CREATIVE ATTITUDE

A good author runs away with her imagination, and not the other way round.	Creative thinking is organised, systematic and self-disciplined. Creativity is messy, to be sure, but this is flexibility within a structure. Letting your imagination run away with you means a lack of control and random access to the pool of ideas that lie in the subconscious mind. 'Training the brain' and accelerating learning involves keeping the spirited horse of the imagination on a tight rein.
Creating a story brings us to many points of decision, and at each point there are many possibilities.	A written story usually looks linear, and we have a sense that it could only have been conceived in that way: a good story seems so natural. Time and routine deceive us into thinking that life itself is linear and predictable. At worst, a feeling of inevitability can be overwhelming. Realising that there are always options open to us, choices and decisions to be made, gives us strength and empowers us to act with greater purpose and determination.
Everyone's story is different, and yet all share common themes.	We can feel connected to 'the human condition' while realising that our individual lives are our own. My story is *my* story: I can take advice from anyone I choose, but the pen on the paper moves by my hand.
Stories are a translation of inner meanings.	Fiction (especially) represents the inner world of the author. In a sense, all stories are talking about aspects of the writer's personality. We can learn from our own tales if only we bother to reflect. Also, stories made public represent the author to the world. Therefore we should take pride and care in offering them up to be read.
Out of nothing comes nothing.	Authors who consistently produce stories are in the minority. If you don't attempt to write, no meaningful story will emerge. Self-determination, inner motivation and discipline are the strengths that support the writing process.

◆ SECTION ONE

A good story by its very nature is an emotional experience.	As writers we aim to generate feelings in the reader. Often this means experiencing those feelings for ourselves as we create. The best stories teach profound truths which connect us to our feelings and to the world. Effective authors have more than a sense of audience – they have a sense of how they want to make their audience feel.
Conflict is the primary energy of a story, which gives it purpose and direction. Resolution is a story's natural outcome.	Human beings have been called 'bundles of contradictions'. We have conflicts between and within ourselves. If we allow conflict to run on unchecked, we find ourselves on a negative downward spiral to destruction. Realising that the outcome of conflict can be resolution gives us a more useful sense of direction. Similarly, confusion ('con-fusion') is a signpost on the road to fusion.
Make-believe is essential to human endeavour.	Make-believe in one sense means making beliefs. Beliefs form the support structure that sustains us in the world – or they can cage us in. Beliefs are written in thought, not stone; they can be reflected upon, reassessed, modified. The act of fantasising, of imaginatively entering other realms of possibility, frees us from the prison of limiting beliefs.
The story is not the whole thing.	Most writers understand that what they put in a story is the tip of the iceberg – they know far more about the world of the story than they express. By the same token, creative self-exploration gives us greater choice and control of the scripts we present to the world as part of our life story.
Doing it by the book usually means doing it by somebody else's book.	Authors write their own books, 'seeking what the wise have sought'. Unthinking obedience to rules leaves one limited and vulnerable. Sound, intelligent reflection on rules pays more respect to those rules (and the rule-makers) and frees us up to be creatures of choice and independence.

THE CREATIVE ATTITUDE

There are three Golden Rules to successful creative writing – and nobody knows what they are. (Somerset Maugham)	We naturally try to relate information to our own situation. Rules make most sense when they seem personally relevant. Discovering the rules through experience lies at the heart of education. It is the experience which gives meaning to the rules. As the saying goes, *'Good judgement comes from experience – and experience comes from bad judgement.'*
All stories are laden with metaphor.	Human beings have been called 'meaning-making' creatures. We are hard-wired for interpretation. Working on the assumption that 'what we get is more than what we see', the world can take on a new and deeper significance.
Stereotypes are generalisations used unthinkingly.	The area of communication known as Neuro-Linguistic Programming (NLP – see Bibliography) points out that we filter information in our minds, such that the 'map of reality' we carry in our heads is not the territory but our interpretation of it. Three major filters are those of deletion, distortion and generalisation. Generalisation gives us a useful shorthand for viewing the world – we don't need to reprocess the concept of traffic every time we cross the road – but the downside is that we may become less sensitive to uniqueness and individuality. We also tend to interpret (automatically) a current situation in the light of past experience. Again, this has positive and negative value. Emotions with a subconscious origin can colour our present perceptions. Simply noticing what is going on around us (Cherie Huber, see Bibliography) and being sensitive to uniqueness helps to break the link between observation and opinion (see 'Picture exploration' p.55, for more notes on this), leading to a richer, fresher experience.
Redrafting is subject to the law of diminishing returns.	My own opinion is that practice never makes perfect: practice makes better – and better. Going over old ground again and again delays venturing into new areas. Creative people always have new projects clamouring for attention, and the case can be made that there is more learning value in moving on than rearranging tiny details in something that is essentially completed.

◆ SECTION ONE

The purpose of 'back story' is to inform the current action.	People talk about carrying their emotional baggage about with them. I say, unpack those bags, clear out what's not required, and travel light.
Effective writers use the close of a chapter to anticipate further adventure.	The close of a chapter is just that, the end of an episode which informs what is to come, but which is itself over and done with. Similarly with the chapters of our lives – we've put the full stop there and turned over the page.
The only valid criticism is that which allows the author to improve.	Any other kind of criticism is the critic's baggage. P. G. Wodehouse claimed that he never read his reviews, he weighed them. To be inflated by praise is the same as being hurt by negative criticism. In both cases you are being controlled by the comments of others. Reflect for yourself on whether others' opinions allow you to improve.
The story isn't over till it's over.	'Every child is an artist. The problem is how to remain an artist once (s)he has grown up.' *Pablo Picasso*

◆ IDEAS NOW

Use acrostics to help children remember ideas or lists – see p.126 for an example in connection with 'gathering treasures'. To reinforce the creative attitude, use the IDEAS NOW acrostic – and encourage young thinkers to make up other versions. A colour 'IDEAS NOW' poster is available on the CD resource.

Inquisitive
Daydreamy
Excited
Attentive
Sensitive
Nosy
On-the-ball
Wondering
*

Section Two

 # The Big Picture for writing

 Learning is fuelled by the embodied belief that patterns do exist, can be found, and are worth discovering.

Guy Claxton

Overview of Section Two

Page	Activity	Story element	*ALPS StoryMaker* reference	Accelerated learning & thinking skills link
37	The Big Ideas in English	All	Section 2: The Story Process	Chunk size; logical-sequential details set against a Big Picture overview
38	The Writing Process	Planning; good practice	Help me to Write a Story; reviewing	Reflective dialogue; visual organisers for planning; role modelling; deliberate use of perceptual filters
39	The Writing Pyramid	All	The Tale Unfolds; themes	Chunk size; visual organisers for analysis and synthesis; peripheral learning devices
41	The Knowledge Pyramid			As above – using the visual organiser as a way of making sense of factual information
43	Themes, Ingredients and Motifs	Structural elements of stories	Themes and Motifs; The Confidence to Write	Chunk size; hierarchical structure
46	Story Staircase	Structural elements of stories	As above	'Top down–bottom up' strategies for understanding; stepping up the challenge
47	The Learning Journey	Narrative structure(s)	Plotting; Story Maps and Tracks	Accelerated learning cycle; the creative process using the whole brain
49	Pseudonyms	Writing for different purposes; What's in a Name?	Audience; Purpose in writing	Role modelling; perceptual positions; anchoring resourceful states
51	The Importance of Application	All – good practice	Intention–Output–Effect; Scoring Goals; Story Organiser	Motivational techniques; resilience (as one of the '5Rs'); states of 'flow'; self-actualisation and peak experience

Section Two

◆ The Big Picture for writing

◆ The Big Ideas in English

The writer and educational trainer Richard Dunne asserts that in every subject domain (field of knowledge and understanding) there exists a backdrop of 'big ideas' against which learning experiences within a subject can be – and need to be – set. His contention remains that much of what goes on in classrooms consists of individual learning experiences that sometimes fail to be connected with the underlying concepts and principles of the subjects concerned. Dunne maintains that experiences need to be 'pushed into the big ideas' so that they make better sense, and so that the underlying concepts themselves can be increasingly defined and described. One implication of Richard Dunne's work in this area is that when children understand core principles for themselves, they will then be able to 'connect the learning' automatically and in a far more meaningful way.

It seems to me that English as a subject underpins many others because its raw material is language and communication. Some of the big ideas underpinning the subject, then, must be:

- awareness of self-talk, including the power of insights from etymology
- an understanding of the metaphorical/figurative nature of language, and the realisation that English is laden with metaphor
- an appreciation that literature represents a range of individual views of the world – all attempts at 'meaning-making'
- a realisation that subject vocabularies are frames within which students view the world
- an understanding that language is a process and that mastery is achieved by actively engaging in it
- an understanding that language, being a product of human thought, changes as the human world changes. We all own language and contribute to its ceaseless development.

Literacy is an ongoing key issue in education. My view is that literacy – defined in the dictionary rather obviously and not that helpfully as 'the ability to read and write' – is more importantly about decoding content as part of a deeper meaning-making process. Linguistic intelligence, as Howard Gardner thinks of it, is the capacity we have to do this capably and creatively. Once children become familiar with the Big Ideas in English, they will have a sound basis of understanding that sets individual learning experiences against the greater canvas.

◆ SECTION TWO

◆ The writing process

Often when I work with children I explain that there are three parts to making a story. Usually their hands go up before I've explained and I'm told 'the answer' – the beginning, the middle and the end. This allows me to point out that I said 'making a story' not 'writing a story'. The three parts to *making* a story are:

- thinking time
- writing time
- looking-back time

The most effective kind of thinking time is what I call 'systematic daydreaming', which is the Alpha state (see p.20), when you defocus your attention and notice ideas drifting across your mind. When, as a writer, you are actively engaged in storymaking, then the flow of ideas will be largely about the project in development. Also, that same state creates selective perception – things you notice around you are often uncannily relevant to the story in your head.

The key to effective writing time is *regularity of practice*, irrespective of the amount that is produced at each session.* Regular writers develop a word-by-word and sentence-by-sentence sense of what works and what doesn't: when something doesn't work, you get insights about why, and how to fix it.

> * The American SF writer Harlan Ellison was once being interviewed about his working method. The interviewer asked how much writing Ellison produced each day. On being told that the daily output was 500 words, the interviewer commented that didn't seem like much for a day's work. Harlan Ellison replied rather stonily, 'Yes, but they're the **right** five hundred words each day.'

Looking-back time, for me, focuses on two key questions:

- Is there anything I need to change to make this piece of work the best it can be at present?
- What have I learned through writing this piece of work, which will lead to the next piece being even better?

I always want explicit answers to these questions, so a certain amount of honesty and integrity is required. Also, these guidelines help to demystify the process of redrafting. Some writers, it's true, redraft several times, while others simply 'tweak and polish' the first draft (informed as it was by thorough thinking time). Redrafting is not about writing the story out again more neatly with the spelling and punctuation corrected, as some people think is the case.

Going on in the background of the storymaking process are the two phases of gathering ideas and organising ideas. Both phases require a full toolbox of thinking skills; both require the use of the logic brain and the artist brain, with the focus of attention moving freely and artfully between the two.

The process of writing

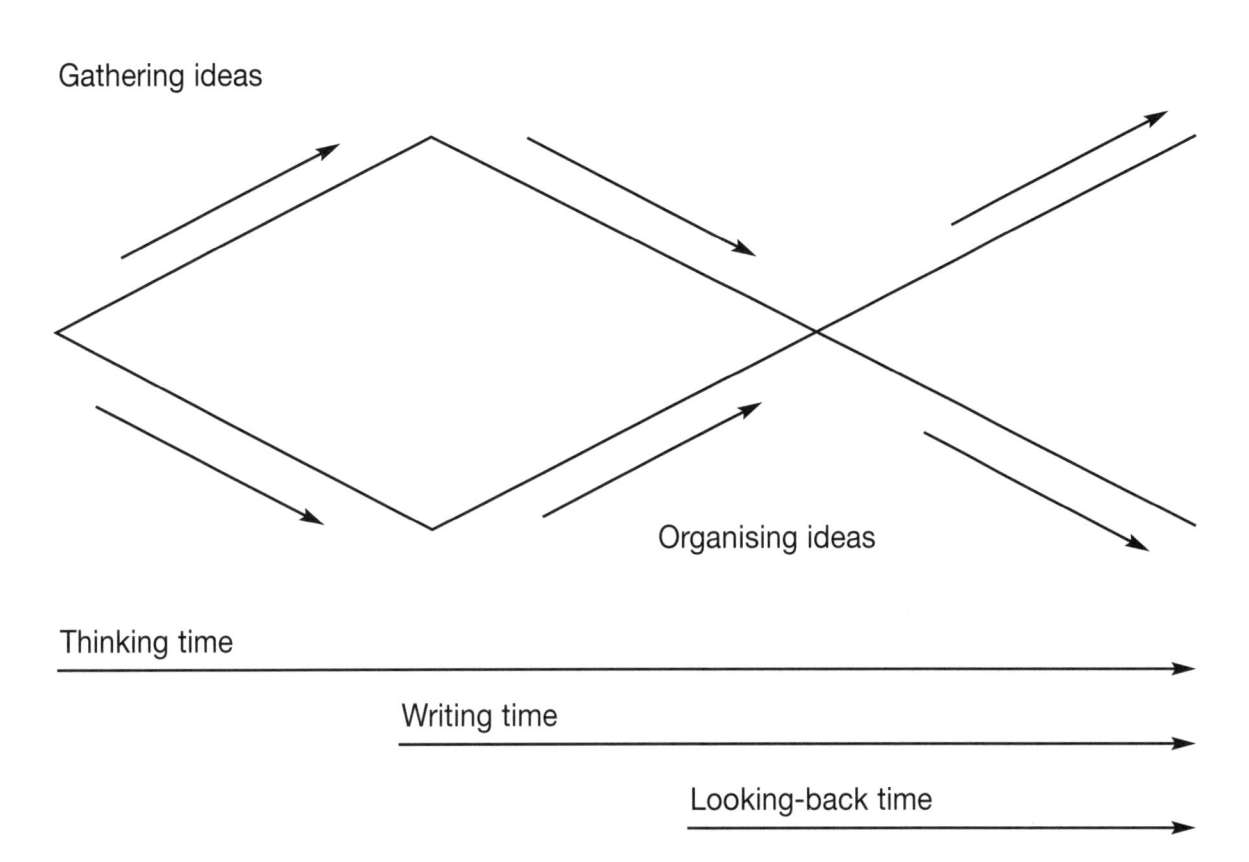

Gathering ideas

Organising ideas

Thinking time →

Writing time →

Looking-back time →

◆ The writing pyramid

The process of storymaking is in many ways a microcosm of the kinds of thinking we need to do in real life. Even as we compose a story at the level of word-by-word detail, we keep an overview in mind of what the whole story is about. In other words, with a small leap of the imagination we move from looking at the logical-sequential structure of words and sentences to the 'Big Picture', that is, the entire concept. These two ways of looking form two major ways of learning, and although children may tend to favour one above the other, to give them an understanding of and practice in both increases their learning power substantially. The writing pyramid uses a basic visual organiser to show at a glance the layered structure of a story*.

> *Note that we are talking about structure here, not content. Look at 'Themes, ingredients and motifs' (p.43) for ideas about putting flesh on the bones.

◆ SECTION TWO

When considering the whole story, young writers need not concentrate on 'making up sentences' or thinking about the correct word to use – their task is simply to gain an impression of what the whole thing is about. At the top of the pyramid the emphasis of attention and concentration will be on which particular words to select in order to make a sentence or part of a sentence meaningful. This is much smaller-scale thinking, though clearly just as important in the long run as having a coherent map of the whole project.

Take time to notice how many, if not most, children compose their stories. Be nosy. Ask them. Often young writers will be trying to 'make it up as they go along' – they'll be attempting to create the basic narrative structure and think about which words to use in this or that particular sentence. Even when they are encouraged to write a plan first, children will still be flicking between big-picture mode and word-by-word (logical-sequential) mode. Use the writing pyramid to help them apply the right thinking to these tasks…

Initially you might want to introduce only the top and bottom of the pyramid – the level of the whole story and the level of words in a sentence. Ask children to sum up a story they've written or read in one sentence. Now look at, say, the opening sentence of a story and discuss why the writer has chosen those particular words – what impressions did (s)he want to create in your mind? What other words might have been chosen? How would these other words alter the pictures, etc., in your mind?

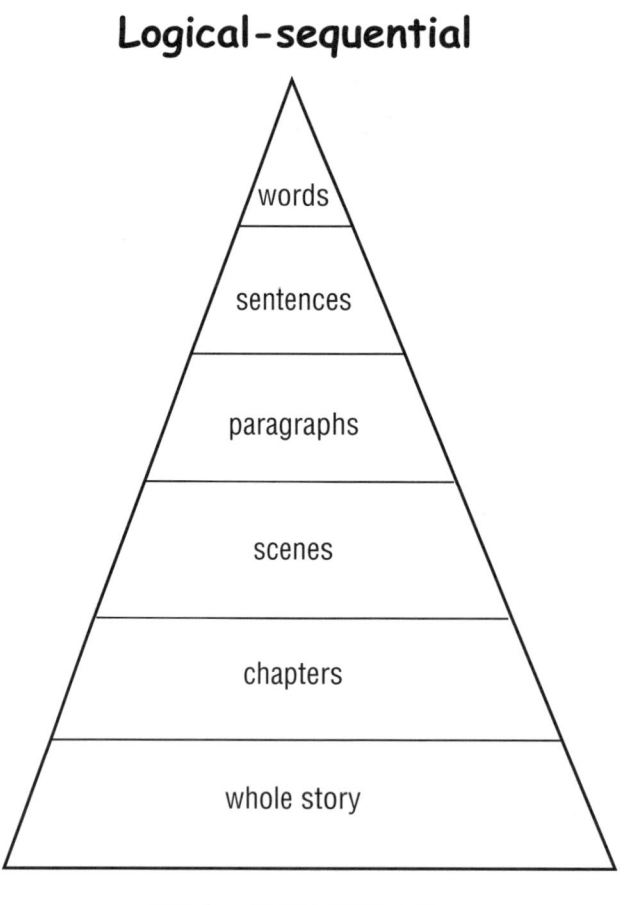

Logical-sequential

- words
- sentences
- paragraphs
- scenes
- chapters
- whole story

Big Picture

Subsequently allow children to see the detail between the extremes. When they talk about stories, point out to them the level at which they are thinking. So, in the case of the story *Dragon's Egg*, Anika might say that it's about a boy who finds a strange egg in the woods and he can't decide whether to stay at home and wait for it to hatch, or go out with his friends. This is the Big Picture. Make that explicit to Anika. Duane might say, 'I like the bit where Austin and Kev go to Rowland's Wood and find the egg.' Duane is talking at the level of scenes. Tell him so. Beyond introducing these ideas into casual conversation about stories, you can set particular tasks to familiarise children with the writing pyramid…

- Ask children to break down a story in the following way:
  - Tell me what the whole story is about in one sentence.
  - Decide how many scenes there are in the story and tell me about each one in a single sentence.
  - Choose some paragraphs in the story that you think work really well. What is the main idea the writer is telling you about in each of those paragraphs?
  - Look at the opening/closing sentence of the story (or of a chapter). What pictures do you think the writer is trying to make you see? What feelings do you have as you read this sentence?
  - Choose a few words from the story that you think work well (or words that are unusual, or that you haven't come across before). From the way the writer uses them, what do you think they mean? Check what the dictionary says about these words.

- Use the pyramid template as a planning device. Adapt it to suit your own purposes. (You may want to leave out the level of chapters, for example, if the children are writing very short stories.) Supply the children with A5 pyramid blanks and ask them to write their plan on those. Suggest they:
  - sum up the whole story in a sentence; sum up each scene in one sentence
  - explain the main idea in the opening/closing paragraphs
  - write the opening sentence; define a favourite and/or particularly effective word.

- Use the template as a peripheral learning device – see *ALPS StoryMaker*, p.243.

- Use this visual organiser in other contexts – see *ALPS StoryMaker*, p.174, and below…

◆ The knowledge pyramid

The pyramid visual organiser can also be used for delivering factual information. We make sense of the world by structuring ideas in our minds. Giving children the *structure plus the ideas* allows them to access the information more effectively – this is the basis of mind mapping.

◆ SECTION TWO

```
              /\
             /  \
            /'gee\
           / whiz \
          /  data' \
         /----------\
        /  key ideas \
       /--------------\
      / elaboration of \
     /    key ideas     \
    /--------------------\
   / supplementary information \
  /------------------------------\
 /     'What if?'                 \
/  (manipulation of knowledge)     \
------------------------------------
```

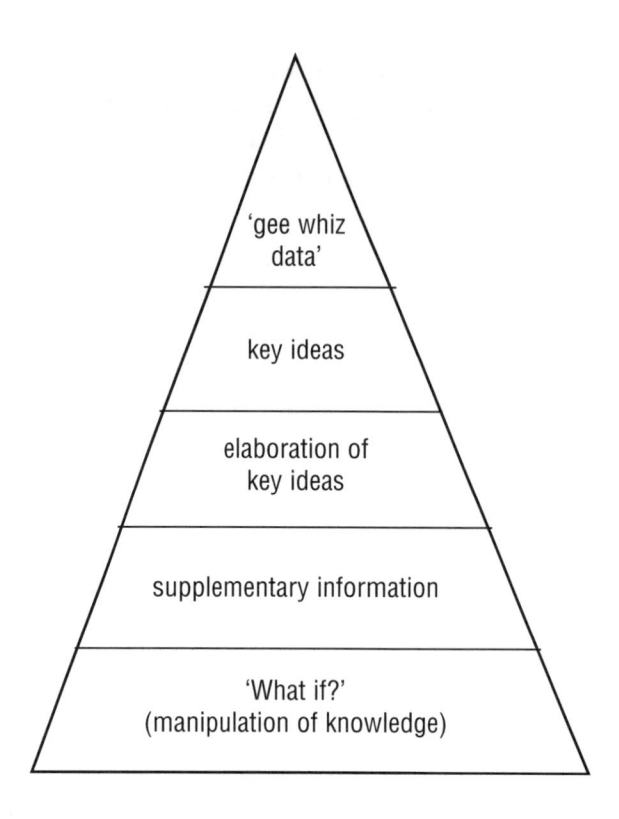

Catch children's interest with what Americans call 'gee whiz data' – a piece of information that opens the doorway to the world of the topic you're exploring.* Next, explain the key ideas of the subject and/or topic simply and succinctly. Use mind maps and other visual organisers to ensure that these key underpinning concepts are clear in children's minds. Now add some detail and elaborate upon the basic ideas. If time permits, offer children supplementary information – other facts and ideas that broaden out their understanding of the topic and relate it to other areas. Finally, most important, set some tasks which give children the opportunity to *do something* with the knowledge you've delivered, rather than just having them remember it; or, as Richard Dunne would say, 'Push the learning experience into the Big Ideas that underpin the subject.' One easy and effective way of doing this is to play the 'What if?' game (see *Imagine That!* p.86). So, if your topic is dinosaurs, say, 'What if dinosaurs had never become extinct?' You will find very quickly that children are using the concepts and vocabulary you've taught them. They will also be crossing topic domains, talking perhaps about ecology, food chains, predators, the difficulties we would face with live dinosaurs in the world, the morality of exploiting animals, etc.

> * My lifelong interest in space and space flight was fired when I found out, age 8, that the bright star I kept noticing moving across the sky was a 100-foot-diameter metallised plastic balloon – the communication satellite Echo 1.

When children are familiar with this use of the template, they can use it as a planning device for their own essays. Incidentally, newspaper editors and journalists use the same structure for news items – headline, catch line, opening paragraph that defines the topic, further explanations, eyewitness accounts/editorial comment, etc. Editors tend to cut from the bottom up if there is a lack of space on the page.

The knowledge pyramid still makes use of the conventional way of delivering a lesson – objectives, content, method, evaluation. A radically different model, using the structure of stories for teaching facts, is proposed by Kieran Egan (see p.103).

◆ Themes, ingredients and motifs

A story is a sophisticated organisation of ideas on a number of levels. Traditionally as teachers we put our emphasis on looking at the structure of chapters, paragraphs, sentences and words. By shifting our focus a little we can give children further insights into the way stories are built and allow our students a valuable means of planning and evaluating their work. This template visualises the point:

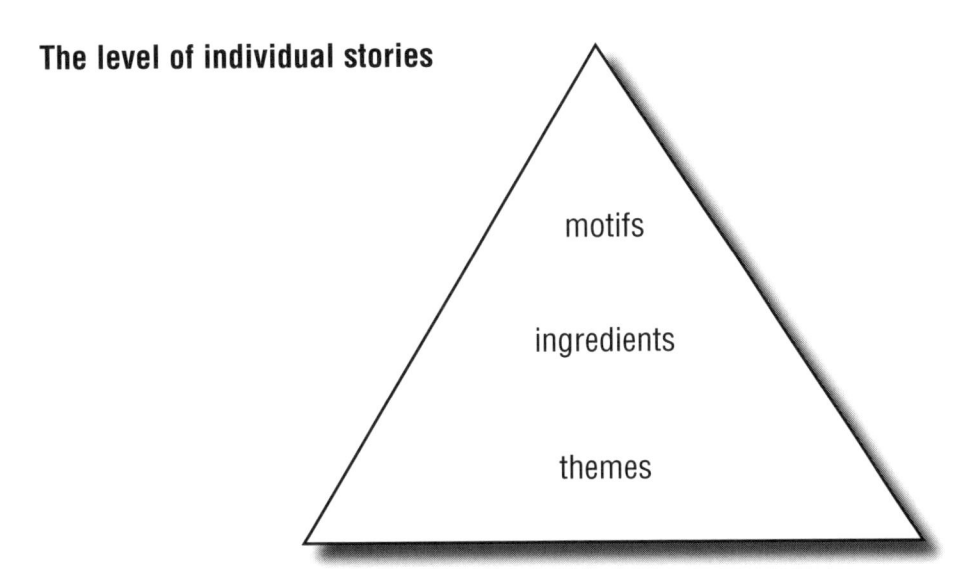

The level of individual stories

```
          motifs

        ingredients

          themes
```

The level of all stories

Themes

These are the 'big ideas' that underpin all the other components of a story. They are the basic building blocks of 'story' – yet themes are also dynamic. I often think of them as currents in the swiftly flowing stream of human consciousness, with stories as the leaves being carried along with the flow. Great literature expresses themes that span the species, and links 'the human condition' to individual lives. All well considered stories more or less explicitly deal with themes that run through the author's life also, in terms of loves, hates, fears, wishes, dreams. One way of introducing children to the concept of themes* is to look at the essential meanings of folk- and fairy tales, parables and proverbs, where lessons are taught (subtly through story telling) that are often more widely applicable in life.

◆ SECTION TWO

> * Kieran Egan, Professor of Education at Simon Fraser University, asserts that even very young children must have an understanding of themes in order to make sense of fairy tales. To comprehend Cinderella, for instance, children at some level must 'know' about jealousy, love, coincidence and justice. See Bibliography.

The grid opposite (top) outlines some of the themes that crop up in my own stories. Interestingly for me, I realised I was writing about these things way down the line, after a number of novels had been published. In one form or another, these themes have relevance to my own life. The writer Tom Chetwynd (see Bibliography) identifies a number of themes which run through general and personal mythologies: *hazardous crossing; quests; journeys of discovery; underworlds containing treasure; otherworlds; disguises that are removed; initiations* – see also 'The learning journey', p.47, and 'The deeper structure of stories', p.156.

Ingredients

These are the general components of most or all stories. They are smaller then themes but larger-scale than motifs. The most familiar core ingredients of any story are characters, settings and events. Other key components can be: problems, secrets, excitements, conflicts, mysteries, dangers, treasures (i.e. something precious. This does not need to be a physical object, but might be a feeling, an insight, a positive act, some words that are spoken, etc.).

Motifs

I regard motifs as the 'constituent features' of a story on a smaller scale than 'ingredients'. Motifs are combined to express, say, the central problem within a story, or to establish a setting, or to develop character. Motifs also help to 'locate' a story within a genre or narrative tradition. A motif, therefore, might be an object, a set piece of action, a character type, some dialogue, a descriptive detail, etc.

The following tables help to clarify these ideas in relation to *Catch & Other Stories*.

THE BIG PICTURE FOR WRITING

1. **Themes** found in *Catch & Other Stories*

	She Bites	Gurney	Catch	Dragon's Egg	Brag	Nanoman	The House That R'ork Built	The Forever Man	Burning
Unexpected power		★	★			★		★	★
Transformation	★	★				★			
What you see is what you get – or is it?	★	★	★	★	★	★	★		
Destiny – choice or chance? Accident or design?			★					★	★
The creative balance of good and evil		★			★	★		★	★
You get nothing for nothing. There's always a price to pay		★	★					★	★
The balance point between innocence and experience							★		
Small beginnings causing major outcomes							★		★
Daring to defy / crossing the line / forbidden areas				★	★	★		★	★

2. **Motifs** in *The Forever Man*

Character type	Dialogue	Setting	Descriptive detail	Object
Rob – bored and sometimes angry teenager	'Where is the horse's head?'	Patchley Woods, mysterious, unexplored	Great stretches of beech and oak fill the valley.	
Darren Phipps – 'the boffin', thick-lensed spectacles	'By half-past nine Aldebaran will be up.'	The third week in October – nearly Halloween	The brilliant light in the woods	Darren's binoculars. He gazes at the stars.
Simon Greaves – 'a thin grey kid from a children's home'		Kenniston – 'anytown'. Uptown Kenniston, very middle class	'Imagine a frontier bordering many lands…'	The centaur, symbol of the other-wordly
The odd partnership		The Lodge – forgotten magical house	The Lodge lies at the very centre of the woods.	A barbed screen of brambles
The Forever Man – wizard-like	'The hooves of centaurs are not to be taken lightly.'	We went out into the night with its high gusting winds	The night outside was windblown and dark.	

STORYMAKER CATCH PACK – USING GENRE FICTION AS A RESOURCE FOR ACCELERATED LEARNING

◆ SECTION TWO

◆ Story staircase

Some people are naturally Big Picture learners – they like to understand the whole context of the learning in order to make best sense of its individual components. Others are logical-sequential learners, who prefer to see how pieces of information fit together as they build towards an understanding of the bigger picture. Both learning styles need to be accommodated within the classroom. Storymaking provides a safe and enjoyable arena in which to familiarise children with the skill of seeing both the parts and the greater whole.

A story staircase serves to link small details with the thematic underpinning of the work.

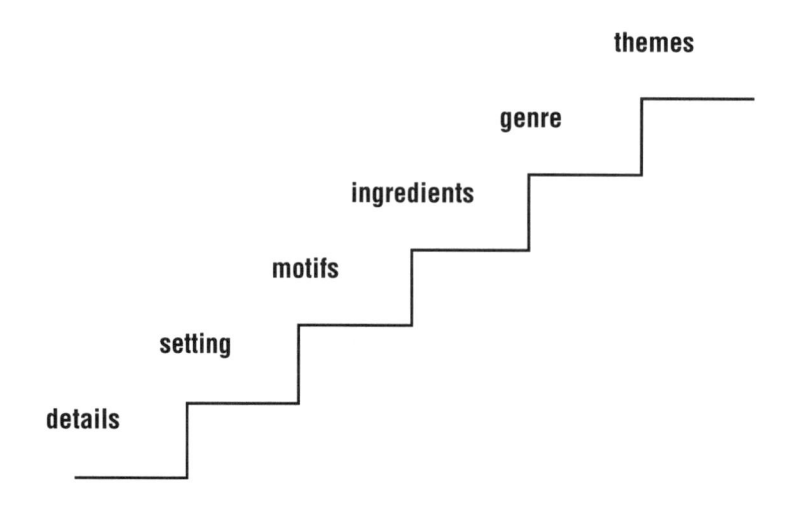

```
                                    themes
                             genre
                      ingredients
               motifs
        setting
details
```

Here is an example of how this works practically, with reference to the illustration called 'Asteroid Patrol 2050' on the CD resource.

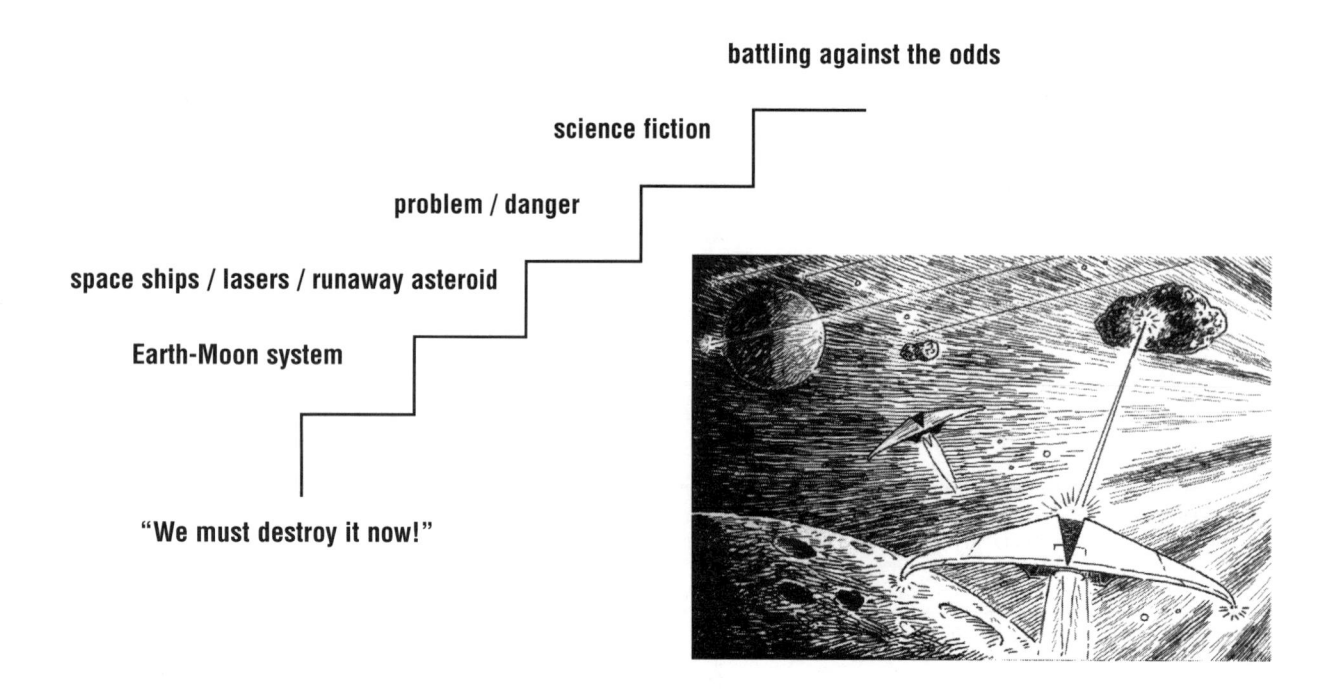

```
                                    battling against the odds
                             science fiction
                      problem / danger
space ships / lasers / runaway asteroid
Earth-Moon system
"We must destroy it now!"
```

STORYMAKER CATCH PACK – USING GENRE FICTION AS A RESOURCE FOR ACCELERATED LEARNING

◆ Bottom-up top-down staircase

The same idea can be applied when delivering factual information. The 'Bottom-up top-down staircase' acts as a device for categorising and contextualising information in a logical, meaningful way:

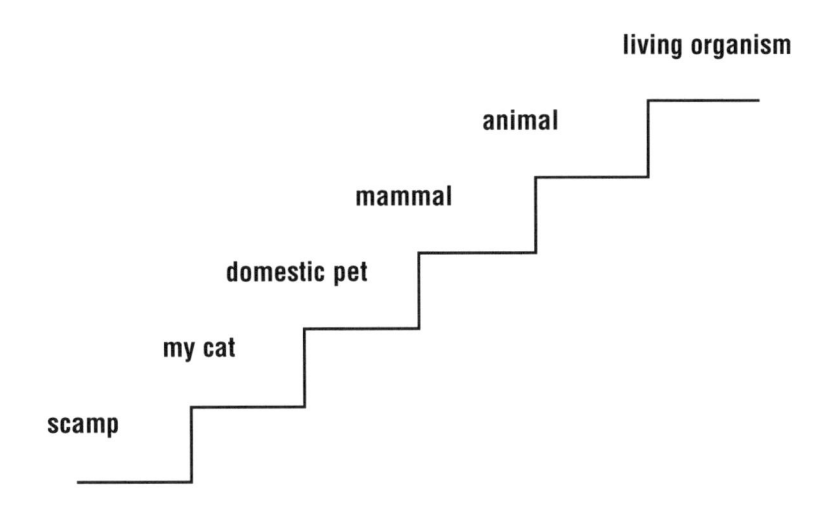

```
                                    living organism
                              animal
                       mammal
                domestic pet
         my cat
  scamp
```

◆ The learning journey

Someone once said that knowledge is a quest and not a commodity. That simple emphasis epitomises the creative attitude. In similar vein, Howard Gardner maintains that 'coverage is the death of understanding'. The metaphor is apt, for to cover is also to hide or make obscure, while the cover of a book marks the limits of the content within. Or perhaps this is going too far, and deep down we, as professional teachers, know that formal education is not the end of learning, and that our primary goal is to make children familiar with the rich and diverse capabilities of their own minds, so that their quest may continue lifelong.

For me this notion links the central ideas of this and my other books with my love of ideas and language and a personal search to understand myself and my purposes in life. The author and consultant Robert Dilts puts structure to this journey when he talks about the 'neurological levels' on which we build our realities (see *ALPS StoryMaker*, p.175 and Bibliography). The most profound level of being, the spiritual level,* is the level at which we ask the biggest questions – Who am I? Why am I here? Where am I going? What is behind the universe I see?

> * By 'spiritual' neither Dilts nor I mean 'religious'. Spirituality is our capacity to wonder about ourselves and our individual lives within the context of the universe we perceive. It also implies the drive to see our lives and the universe as purposeful in one or many ways. One can be a spiritual being without subscribing to any formalised religion. For much more about this see Zohar and Marshall in the Bibliography.

◆ SECTION TWO

Finding the answers takes us inevitably on a learning journey which, as T. S. Eliot might say, brings us back to the point where we began, but wonderfully transformed. With this in mind you might consider the usefulness of the following model as you use the techniques in the *StoryMaker* books…

The learning journey

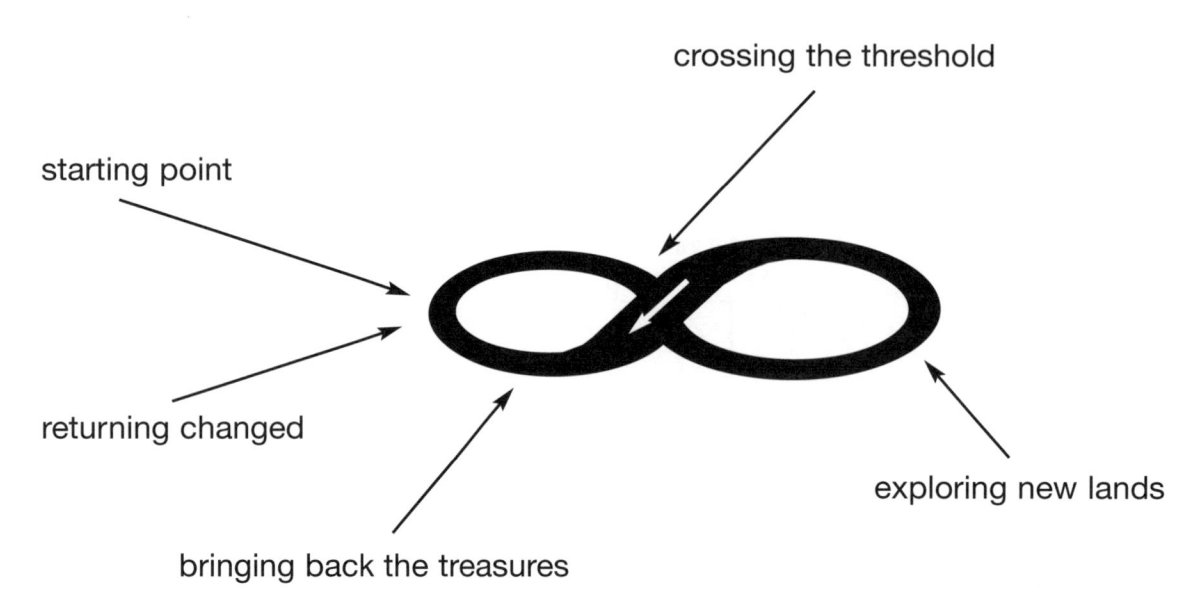

```
                              crossing the threshold
                                      ↓
    starting point
         ↘
           ↘        ∞
         ↗
    returning changed                 ↖
                                       exploring new lands
              ↑
    bringing back the treasures
```

Our learning journey begins from the point at which we become aware that knowledge is a quest and not a commodity. When we journey, we do so with a plan of where we might like to go, but realising too that life's circumstances can take us in unexpected directions to new places and adventures. When we journey, we accept that everything we experience is part of the learning. We will go to the limits of our 'comfort zones' and cross the threshold into new lands, which we explore with the thinking toolkit that epitomises the power of our minds and the essential qualities we carry with us. The meanings we make in our explorations are the treasures we bring back to our new starting point – now – the only point in time and space that we can influence directly. And now we realise that we have changed: we realise that the quest has made us more resourceful, more resilient, more responsible ('able to respond') human beings.

This is the journey on the grand scale, one that spans our whole life story. Interestingly, and not coincidentally, the structure of the learning journey as it is suggested above is also the shape of the 'mythic journey' to be found at the heart of the world's myths, legends and folk tales. It comes as no surprise to learn that the ∞ shape is the template behind some of the most influential and popular movies ever made – see Stuart Voytilla's *Myth and the Movies* for further explanation of this fascinating idea. It is also worth pointing out that ∞ is the mathematical symbol for infinity (endless potential).

More practically, on a day-to-day level, the 'lazy eight' shape echoes the accelerated learning cycle…

THE BIG PICTURE FOR WRITING

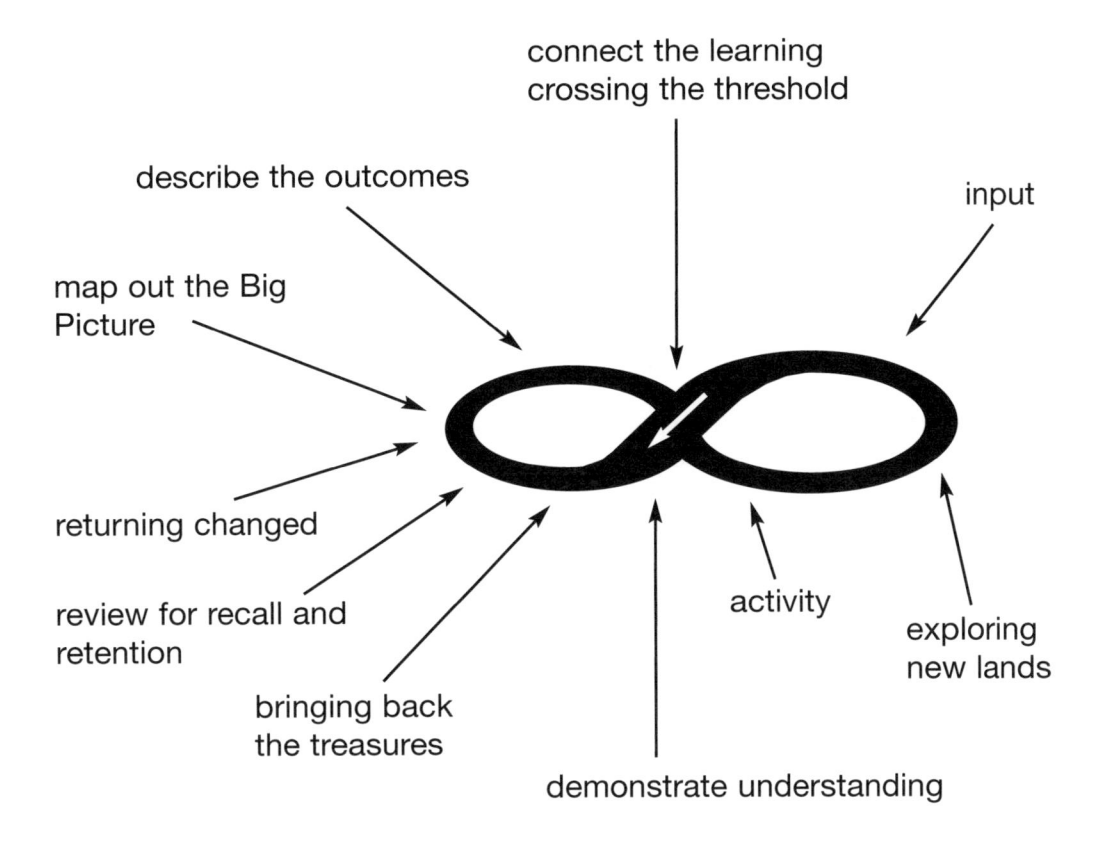

- connect the learning / crossing the threshold
- describe the outcomes
- input
- map out the Big Picture
- returning changed
- review for recall and retention
- bringing back the treasures
- activity
- exploring new lands
- demonstrate understanding

For more information see, for example, Alistair Smith and Nicola Call, *The ALPS Approach* (see Bibliography).

◆ Pseudonyms

I must start this section with an anecdote. During my long, though perhaps not especially illustrious, writing career I've been involved in all kinds of projects. As a result of writing a children's Horror novel some years ago I had the opportunity to write adult Horror fiction, and was told that if the first novel was accepted I would land a three-book deal – a significant contract for me.

I set to work, but try as I might I somehow couldn't bring myself to write the gritty, gutsy, explicit kind of stories that were called for. I felt that this wasn't to do with a lack of capability or determination. But there was a definite block, and it was only after some time that I realised what it was – I wouldn't want my mum or my work colleagues to see this stuff in the bookshops! The insight surprised me, yet I knew this was the reason. Furthermore, I decided that because I also wrote for children, I wouldn't want young readers to see my name associated with emphatically adult material.

◆ SECTION TWO

My answer was to write under a pseudonym.* And I must emphasise here that this amounts to a kind of role play – you assume the persona that goes with the name. This may be, and probably is, an aspect of your own personality mixed in perhaps with behaviours modelled on other people. I mention this because it is the central point of the technique that I'm explaining.

> * I sent the first Ben Leech book away and the editor quickly sent it back with a rather brusque letter stating that the idea was derivative, the characters were flat, the sex and violence were gratuitous – in short, she loathed the book and would have nothing to do with it. I felt crushed.
>
> My agent at the time suggested that we submitted the book elsewhere without changing a word. The editor swiftly replied enthusing about the sparklingly original idea, the well drawn characters, the insightful use of sex and violence as a way of exploring the story's central themes, etc., etc.
>
> This was a useful lesson about the assessment and evaluation of creative work!

And so Ben Leech was born. He was the Edward Hyde to my Doctor Jekyll. Ben could think and write the things that Steve Bowkett did not feel comfortable with. Ben dared to explore the darker realms of Steve's imagination and had the courage to meet what was there and bring it out into the open*. Frankly, I found this to be a very refreshing and even liberating experience. And I got my three-book deal.

> * People have wondered how I cope with Ben Leech in my life. But I'm not crazy – are we, Ben?

Elsewhere in *StoryMaker Catch Pack* I talk about editor caps (p.124) and the 'Disney Strategy' (p.123). These utilise the same basic principles as the pseudonym technique. In its simplest form, the pseudonym technique invites a child to write under a different name. If a child believes she doesn't have the confidence or imagination or ability to write, let her pretend to be someone who can.

- You might say, 'Well, for today you're Jacqueline Wilson and you can write the same kind of brilliant stories that she makes up all the time.'
- Or establish a Jacqueline Wilson (or whoever) cap, badge or writing chair. When the child wears the cap or badge or sits in the chair she suddenly finds she can do her best writing easily.
- Combine pseudonyms with 'Gathering treasures' (p.125). Use well known/well written books as the kinaesthetic anchors to allow children to exploit their latent capabilities.

STORYMAKER CATCH PACK – USING GENRE FICTION AS A RESOURCE FOR ACCELERATED LEARNING

- Invent a Wise Writing Wizard – give him/her a name. Encourage children to write letters to the 'story oracle' addressing the problems they have. Then get the same or other children to pretend they are the WWW and reply to those letters. Build a resource bank of pertinent replies.
- A variation of the technique above is the 'Writing agony aunt'. Establish a fictional character who is the class's writing expert. Children can post their writing problems to her and receive a personal reply shortly afterwards. The agony aunt can be made up of older children, or those who are acknowledged as being very capable writers, or members of staff – or all of these.

◆ The importance of application

As I hope that many of the activities in this book will demonstrate, there is a vital difference between working hard and trying hard. The network of beliefs, skills and strategies that we call 'creativity' operates in its early stages completely inside the head, within the subtle realm of ideas – preparing to have them and then noticing them when they 'pop into mind'. The Muse is not mysterious, it's just that its work goes on behind the scenes. For this process to operate most effectively we need to maintain the attitude of 'IDEAS NOW' – see p.34. Once we consciously recognise the outcomes of subconscious activity, then we can begin to express and develop those ideas in the direction of the fixed goal of our completed project, in this case a finished piece of written work.

Trying hard to have ideas is fruitless. It's like riding a rocking horse. You put lots of energy into it but you get nowhere, and after a while it's *boring*. Using the whole mind, which offers a greater range of mental tools than just conscious intellectual effort, leads to the ongoing generation of ideas and their systematic and effective development.

For that process to work we need to apply ourselves to the task. This book and my earlier *ALPS StoryMaker* aim to make thinking and writing fun. The activities themselves hope to motivate. But without *self*-motivation focused by application and regular practice, all the skills associated with creative writing will not develop optimally. Paradoxically, self-motivation makes practising easier. Regular engagement with the task can and does become more and more of a joy. Certainly, as far as writing is concerned, concentrating for long periods of time as you reach (not stretch or struggle) for the right words is tiring. But a completed piece of work that you have enjoyed brings enormous satisfaction.

The writer P. G. Wodehouse was once asked how one becomes a good writer. He replied, 'You take your bum and you put it on a chair – every day.' There is no other way. The only thing, ultimately, that will make a child a better writer is for that child to sit down and put pen to paper. If he loves doing that, so much the better.

◆ SECTION TWO

The application pyramid

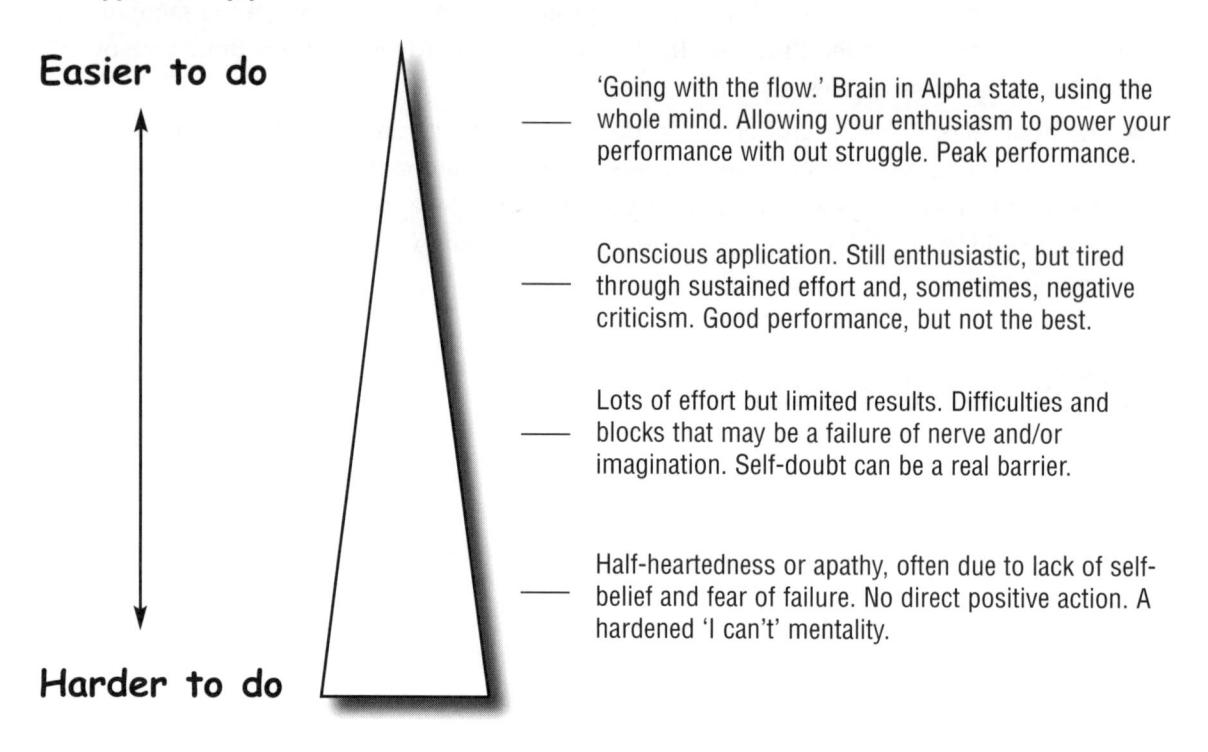

Easier to do ↕ **Harder to do**

— 'Going with the flow.' Brain in Alpha state, using the whole mind. Allowing your enthusiasm to power your performance with out struggle. Peak performance.

— Conscious application. Still enthusiastic, but tired through sustained effort and, sometimes, negative criticism. Good performance, but not the best.

— Lots of effort but limited results. Difficulties and blocks that may be a failure of nerve and/or imagination. Self-doubt can be a real barrier.

— Half-heartedness or apathy, often due to lack of self-belief and fear of failure. No direct positive action. A hardened 'I can't' mentality.

The writer Ian Fleming said that 'Effort is desirable for its own sake. Those who succeed through their own endeavours are heroes', or, as the psychologist Abraham Maslow termed them, 'self-actualising people'. We can support and guide the child on her learning journey, but it is she who must put one foot after the other, again and again and again.

◆ Use everything

Many people ask me (as all writers must be asked, I suppose) for advice on 'becoming' an author. I invariably tell them 'Do it because you love it' and 'Use everything'. This means being determined that everything you do and everything that happens to you will make you a better writer* – negative criticism, rejection, frustration, anger, doubt – all of these things can make you stronger and better and lead you to fulfil any particular potential. I tell children whenever the opportunity arises that I truly believe that what they can be is already inside them. Tolerate no sabotage!

> * Beware what I call 'the Wordsworth Syndrome'. This begs the question, 'When you write a thousand words, do you get a thousand words' worth of experience, or one word's worth of experience a thousand times?'
>
> Quantity and quality are not the same. We learn by reflecting on what we've done and making conscious decisions on the matter. Another way of looking at it comes in the form of the old saying 'Good judgement comes from experience, and experience comes from bad judgement.'

STORYMAKER CATCH PACK – USING GENRE FICTION AS A RESOURCE FOR ACCELERATED LEARNING

Section Three:

A thinking toolkit

> The mind is a wonderful thing. It switches on as soon as you wake up and doesn't switch off again until you get to school.
>
> *Irish proverb (modified)*

Overview of Section Three

Page	Activity	Story element	*ALPS StoryMaker* reference	Accelerated learning & thinking skills link
55	Picture Exploration	All – initial generation of ideas for plot, character and setting	Picture Work; Mind's Ear	Awareness of sensory modes; techniques for developing attention and concentration; raising awareness of different thinking skills
58	Submodalities	'Vivid particularities', the importance of small details	As above; Visualisation	as above
59	Mix-and-Match Senses	Word and sentence level descriptions		Synaesthesia; perceptual filtering
61	Lensing	Genre Overlap; character point-of-view	Lensing	Perceptual filtering; bisociations; problem-solving across knowledge domains
64	Fantasy Grid	Genre; motifs	The Landscape of Genre; Structure and Function	Bisociations; logical-sequential reasoning; kinaesthetic anchoring; training the Alpha state
70	Six Big Important Questions	Early generation of ideas	The Inner World of the Writer; Six Big Important Questions	Systematic questioning as an exploratory tool; reasoning; reflection; tolerance of ambiguity

Section Three

◆ A thinking toolkit

◆ Picture exploration

Aims

- to increase children's attention and concentration skills
- to raise awareness of visual/auditory/kinaesthetic sensory modes of imagination
- to raise awareness of 'thinking tools' such as observation, deduction, speculation
- to create a safe frame to encourage 'risk-taking' behaviour
- to give children a means to develop character, setting and plot for storymaking.

Introduction

This is a core activity requiring minimal preparation: it's easy to use with children across the age and ability range and can be revisited if time is a limiting factor. You will see from the notes below that 'Picture exploration' begins with a 'low challenge – low threat' task, with the challenge steadily increasing the safe and supportive framework of the activity itself and the creative climate of the classroom. The artwork is by Stella Hender. This and other pictures can be accessed directly by going to the 'Photocopiable pages' section of the CD resource.

This is what you do…

- Show your group a picture such as the example given. Ask them to notice anything in the picture and mention it to you – if they see it they can tell you about it.
- Collect **observations** and praise that behaviour.
- Some children might offer a **deduction/inference** such as, 'Well, I think it's autumn.' Ask what clues they've noticed in the picture that lead them to this conclusion. Distinguish between a pure observation and a deduction (a likely conclusion derived from observed evidence).
- Some children might offer a **speculation**, such as, 'Well, I think there's a big dog up the street and it's frightening the cat.' Point out that they've noticed the cat ('Well done!') and they've hooked a 'maybe' on to it. Mention that you can often attach lots of maybes to observations. Now ask for some more – maybe a dog is frightening the cat, or…?

◆ SECTION THREE

Illustration by Stella Hender

STORYMAKER CATCH PACK – USING GENRE FICTION AS A RESOURCE FOR ACCELERATED LEARNING

- Some children might offer a **value judgement**, such as 'I think it's an ugly cat.' Praise them for noticing the cat and point out that they've also given you an opinion about it. Always distinguish between a pure observation and a value judgement, adding that an opinion is a personal set of feelings that other people might not share.

- As ideas peak and then fade, say, 'If this picture was in colour, what **colours** would there be?' Collect ideas and value them. Ask children to give you a bit more information as they become familiar with this exercise – 'So what do you think is the difference between the brown of the tree and the brown of the leaf?' Draw language out of them through encouragement and guidance.

- If a child offers an unlikely or silly idea – 'the cat's purple' – mention that good storymakers always have good reasons for the ideas they put into a story. The reader has to *believe* the story. Suggest that if the child can offer a logical and believable reason why the cat is purple, then you might include it in the story the group is making.

- As ideas peak and fade, ask what **sounds** the children hear in the picture, and go through the same process as for colour.

- As ideas peak and fade, say that you'll count up to three, and on the count of three you can all jump into the picture and **be there**. Then the children will be able to notice something new, that they haven't noticed before. Once you are in the picture, associated with it, concentrate on **kinaesthetic** impressions: smells, textures, temperatures, size, shape, weight, etc. Draw out details by focusing the children's attention on their (by now visualised) scene.

- Allow individuals to explore at some length, if this does not slow the pace of the activity for others. A child might say something like 'I can hear voices coming from the room with the light on.' Invite the child to 'float up' to the window in the picture and go into the room. Ask about the details he sees, hears, can touch, etc. If you are actively creating a storyline by now, ask the child questions which build on this framework.

- There will come a point where children's ideas and story-scenarios diverge beyond the point where whole-class work is practical. Split the class into smaller groups/individual work, or switch to one of the games extensions and links.

Extensions and links

- Encourage children to ask the Six Big Important Questions (see also p.70). Emphasise that there is no need at this stage to come up with answers – they can be supplied as a follow-up activity later. Examples might include:
  - **What** is the cat's name? What is frightening the cat? What does the garden behind the wall look like?
  - **Where** does the cat live? Where does the gate lead? Where did the firework come from?
  - **When** in the day is this event happening? When did the cat last eat something? When will someone walk by?
  - **How** long has it been since the newspaper was dropped on the ground? How old is the cat? How will the cat get home?

◆ SECTION THREE

- **Who** might be in the room with the lighted window? Who is setting off the fireworks? Who owns the cat?
- **Why** is the cat scared? Why are the two walls made of different kinds of stone? Why doesn't the cat run away?

● Coins for decision-making. Tell the children they can ask questions about any aspect of the picture and the imagined scenario it has generated. These will be yes–no questions and a flip of a coin will decide the answer – heads for yes/tails for no. Demonstrate the idea a few times… 'Is it a dog that's frightening the cat?' 'Are the people in the room with the lighted window going to be important to the story?' 'Is the cat lost?' And so on. Children will generate large amounts of information using this safe and easy technique. Once again remind children that the questions they ask must contribute positively to the story.

● 'A trip around town' – see *ALPS StoryMaker,* p. 284. Have children 'locate' the picture on a map of a (real or fictitious) town. Using the visualisation techniques they are learning and/or flipping a coin, have them add detail to the locality.

● 'People are like onions' – *ALPS StoryMaker,* p. 174. Combine coin-flipping and discussion to produce character profiles of people imagined in the picture, featuring physical attributes, personal qualities, details of background, etc.

◆ Submodalities

We learn about the world using all of our senses. The most involving learning experience will be multisensory. When we represent ('re-present') our understanding of the world through our own imaginations, one sensory mode tends to predominate: when I'm writing a story I 'see the movie' playing in my mind's eye. I need to make a gentle effort of will to hear the characters' voices or the sounds around them, as I do to create a clearer impression of smells, tastes and textures in the world the characters inhabit. As a writer I want my created world to be as vivid as possible for myself and my readers, and I notice as I write that my visual sense is the strongest.

Children's preferred sensory mode will show (note the visual reference!) in their written and spoken language. This indicates their preferred way to learn: a strongly visual child will tend to feel more comfortable absorbing information visually, and so on. Exploring the smaller details – submodalities – of all of the senses will create the opportunity for children to expand their range of learning channels. The pay-offs can be dramatic –

- exploring submodalities develops sensory acuity (see *Self-Intelligence*)
- thinking in different sensory modes can be applied to new learning experiences such as spelling and retention and recall of other information (see Dilts and Epstein in the Bibliography)
- increased awareness of all senses allows children to notice and use details more effectively (see for example 'One unique detail' in *Imagine That!*, and 'Vivid particularities' on p.192)
- see also 'The mind's ear' in *ALPS StoryMaker,* pp.192–193.

Note: The submodalities chart can be accessed directly in the 'Photocopiable pages' section of the CD resource.

Seeing	Hearing	Touching
point of view	sounds/words	place
colours	direction	hard/soft
brightness	distance	size
depth	loudness	texture
clarity	soft/harsh	weight
movement	length	temperature
speed	speed	how long
size	continuity	shape

◆ Mix-and-match senses

Aims:

- to extend children's ability to describe sensory impressions
- to develop a technique that can be used for the description of feelings and issues (initially within the context of generating characters, but ultimately for use by the children in 'real life').

Introduction

One way of increasing the effectiveness with which children move between the sensory modes is to encourage them to represent one sense in terms of another. This kind of perception is known as synaesthesia. Mozart was supposedly a highly developed synaesthete and perceived music as cascades of colour. Indeed, music has been described as 'the perfect Rorschach stimulus for … meaning in reverie'. In other words, our daydreams and stream-of-consciousness thinking as we explore ideas creatively can be given an added dimension through music. For a more thorough discussion of synaesthesia, see *Stone Age Soundtracks* (Paul Devereux) in the Bibliography.

This is what you do...

- Perhaps the first use of the technique of mix-and-match senses will come during the 'Picture exploration' activity. Suppose you have 'stepped into' the picture with the group and are asking what smells the children are aware of…

◆ SECTION THREE

> **Abbie:** I can smell the smoke from the fireworks.
> **Ben:** I can smell the smoke from the bonfire.
> **You:** So how will you describe the differences between the smell of these?
> **Ben:** Well … the bonfire smoke is, um, stronger and it stings your eyes more. I don't like it much.
>
> *(Notice how Ben switches to another sensory impression as he starts to struggle over describing the bonfire smoke smell. He also gives a personal opinion in the absence of further impressions of the sort that you want).*
>
> **Abbie:** I think the firework smell is stinkier!
> **You:** OK, let's pretend that the firework smell is a colour. What colour do you imagine it would be?
> **Ben:** It's blue!
> **You:** What's blue?
> **Ben:** The smoke.
> **You:** Pretend the smell itself has a colour…
> **Abbie:** Purple.
> **You:** What kind of purple?
> **Abbie:** Kind of dark with black streaks in it. And sparkly bits.
> **You:** OK, and what about the smell of the bonfire smoke?
> **Abbie:** I see green in it – fuzzy green.
> **Ben:** [*not to be outdone!*] Well it smells red to me, but maybe there's some green in it too…

Extensions and links

- Extend the activity by exploring submodalities (the smaller details of a sensory impression). In the example quoted, Abbie in particular has already started to do this by talking about the generally purple smell having dark streaks in it and sparkly bits. Ben concedes later that the bonfire smoke, red overall to him, has some green in it too.

- Encourage the use of this technique across a range of storymaking games. If you are exploring a character's voice, for example, say, 'If you could feel this voice, what would it feel like?' Be aware that our language is already rich with such trans-sensory references. We talk about someone having a rough or gravelly voice; we describe moods and feelings in terms of a colour – feeling blue, being green with envy, etc. While making children more aware of these and acknowledging their day-to-day use, encourage children to be more individual in their thinking. If Abbie is describing envy in terms of colour, it may not be green that she sees in her imagination. Allow children to be original in their thinking.

- Select a piece of instrumental music. Say to the class, 'This music is a person. When I play the music you can see that person and hear that person's voice, and learn all kinds of things about that person's life. Here we go…' Subsequently, gather ideas and encourage children to scribble notes of their impressions.

- Use music in the same way to evoke impressions of feelings, landscapes, animals, etc.
- See 'Dealing with feelings' in *Self-Intelligence* for using these techniques to develop emotional resourcefulness.

Use this grid to relate different sensory modes, e.g. to describe a particular sound in terms of colour, or vice versa.

	sight	sound	smell/taste	touch/movement	feeling
sight	■				
sound		■			
smell/taste			■		
touch/movement				■	
feeling					■

◆ Lensing

Aims:

- to develop children's awareness of genre within storymaking
- to demonstrate that perception is selective, but can be controlled to an increasing degree
- to practise the skill of 'moving elements between domains'.

Introduction

One of the key aspects of creative thinking is to see in new ways. 'Thinking beyond the box' generates multiple possibilities and accelerates innovation. To think beyond your own box it is sometimes necessary to go to someone else's box, be nosy, have a good look around, notice things, ask questions and bring back some ideas that can be applied to your own situation or problem. The technique of 'Lensing' mirrors this process within the safe frame of storymaking.

This is what you do...

- Run the 'Picture exploration' activity with the group, to the point where you are about to flip coins to answer questions. Then say, 'Let's imagine this is going to be a thriller and mystery story. What's in the picture already that helps us to make that kind of

◆ SECTION THREE

story?' This prompts children to interpret what they see in the picture, as it were through the lens of the idea that this is now a scene from a mystery thriller.

- Encourage the group to ask questions as though they were exploring the mystery thriller genre. Guide them in their understanding of the motifs (constituent features) they would find within that genre.
- Subsequently, use the same picture as the basis for stories from other genres – Fantasy, Science Fiction, Horror, etc.

Note: See also 'Bisociations' on p.25.
See *ALPS StoryMaker*, p. 228 for a variation of the 'Lensing' activity.

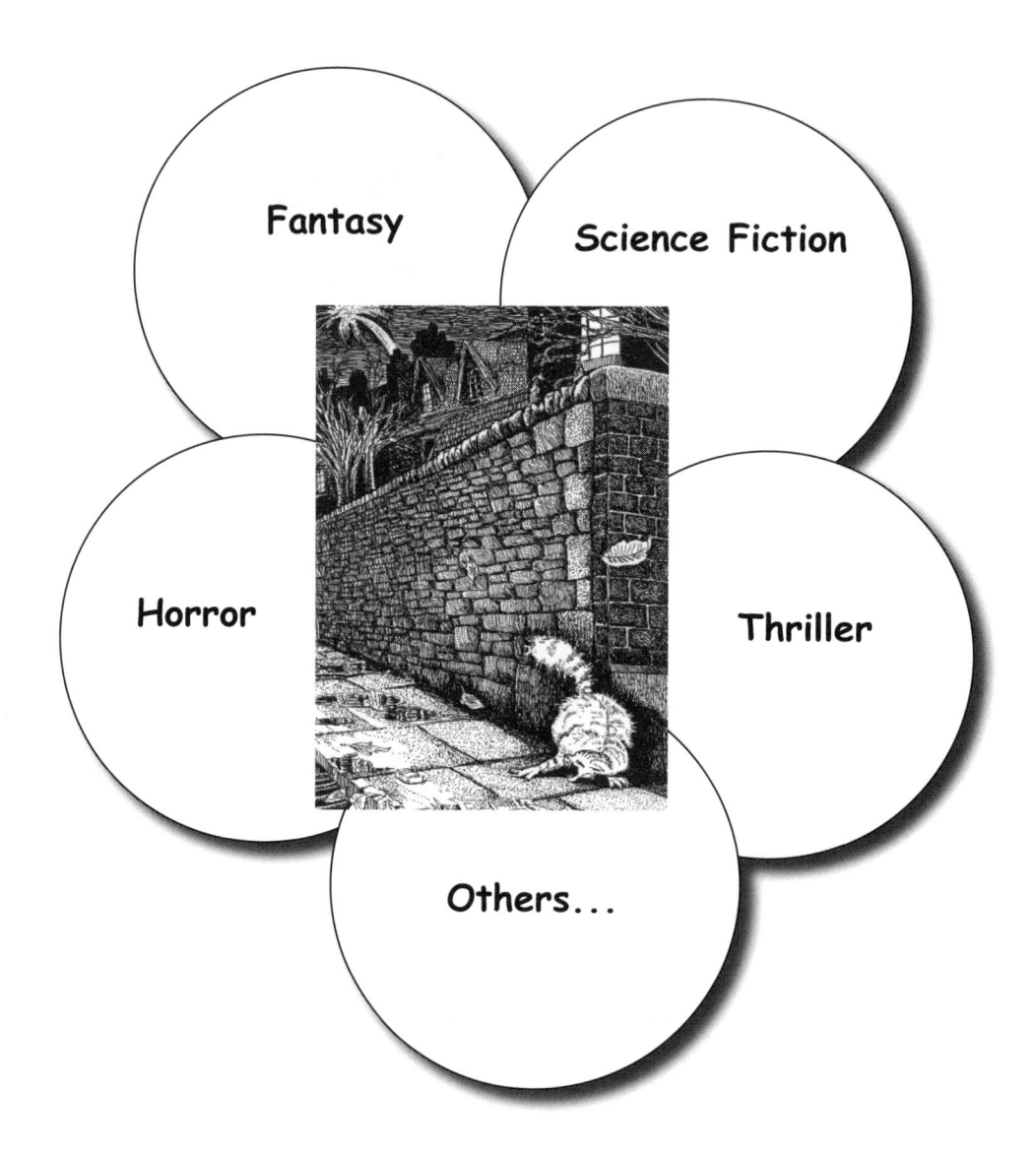

Fantasy

Science Fiction

Horror

Thriller

Others...

- See 'Genre overlap' in *ALPS StoryMaker*, p. 222. In this activity, circles of card represent different genres. Slide the cards one over the other so that they overlap. What mixtures of motifs might be found in these overlapping areas? Use the chart opposite to begin practising the technique. Take two dice and roll them together to pick an item from each column. Put the three items together. What ideas spring to mind?

	Fantasy	SF	Horror
2	wizard	spaceship	vampire
3	dragon	planet	graveyard
4	elf	ray gun	ghost/spirit
5	giant	robot	laboratory
6	wand	moon	werewolf
7	spell	computer	thunderstorm
8	ork	technology	zombie
9	princess	alien	potion
10	magic jewel	time travel	skeleton
11	sorceress	giant insects	forest
12	high tower	mutants	witchcraft

The first few rolls I made produced these mixtures:

- *ork – ray gun – witchcraft*
- *spell – time travel – zombie*
- *ork – moon – potion*

The first combination didn't trigger any ideas in my mind; that's OK, because you need to have lots of ideas to have good ideas. The second combination threw out the notion that an evil wizard found a way of bringing dead warriors through time to help him take over the kingdom. The third combination sparked the idea that an ugly ork-like creature fell in love with the beautiful princess. He believed that the only way she could fall in love with him was if he drank an enchanted potion to make himself handsome. However, the potion contained five rare ingredients, one of which was a special dew produced only by the light of the full blue moon…

- Apply the technique of overlapping domains to the 'real world': when NASA scientists were given the challenge of designing small, reliable, tough, unmanned rovers to explore the surface of Mars, they talked to entomologists whose knowledge of insects helped the technologists to solve their problem. Use the card circle game in this way. Identify a problem in one area of human endeavour: gather ideas in another area and

◆ SECTION THREE

bring them back to address the difficulty. Remember, you need to have lots of ideas to generate some good ideas. Consider these as starters...

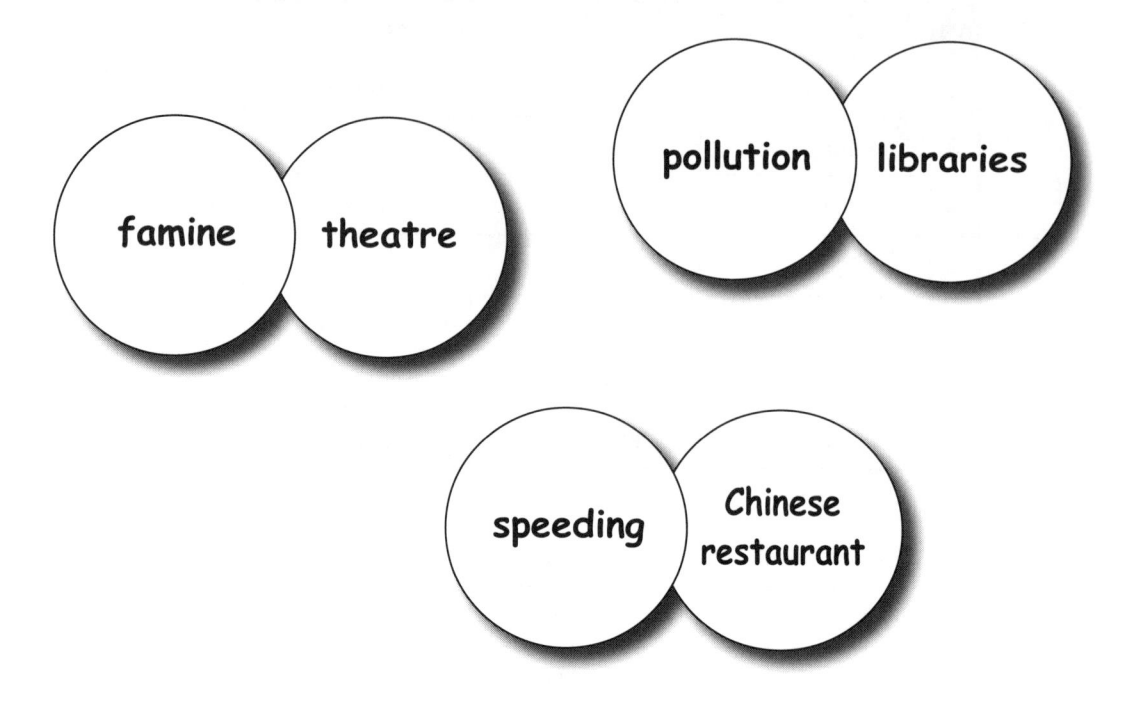

- famine / theatre
- pollution / libraries
- speeding / Chinese restaurant

◆ Fantasy grid

Aims:

- to raise awareness of the notion of genre (in this case Fantasy) and the motifs which help to define genre
- to introduce a visual organiser that can be used in a variety of ways, for storymaking initially and then in other applications.

Introduction

The human brain naturally links things in order to make sense of the world. We can exploit this 'meaning-making' imperative to boost creative and innovative thinking. When two disparate items are brought together imaginatively a new and often useful idea can emerge. This process is known as *bisociation*. Bisociations have brought many useful artefacts into existence... Sawdust and wood shavings were once linked with glue, and chipboard was born; a sailing dinghy and a surfboard combined to produce the windsurfer; more glue and scraps of notepaper brought us Post-It notes. Look around and notice what other everyday items are the products of bisociative thinking.

A THINKING TOOLKIT

This is what you do...

- A 6×6 grid is used here to enable items to be chosen at random with dice rolls. If a 36-box grid seems too daunting for children, cut it down to 5×5, 4×4 or whatever size suits your purposes.

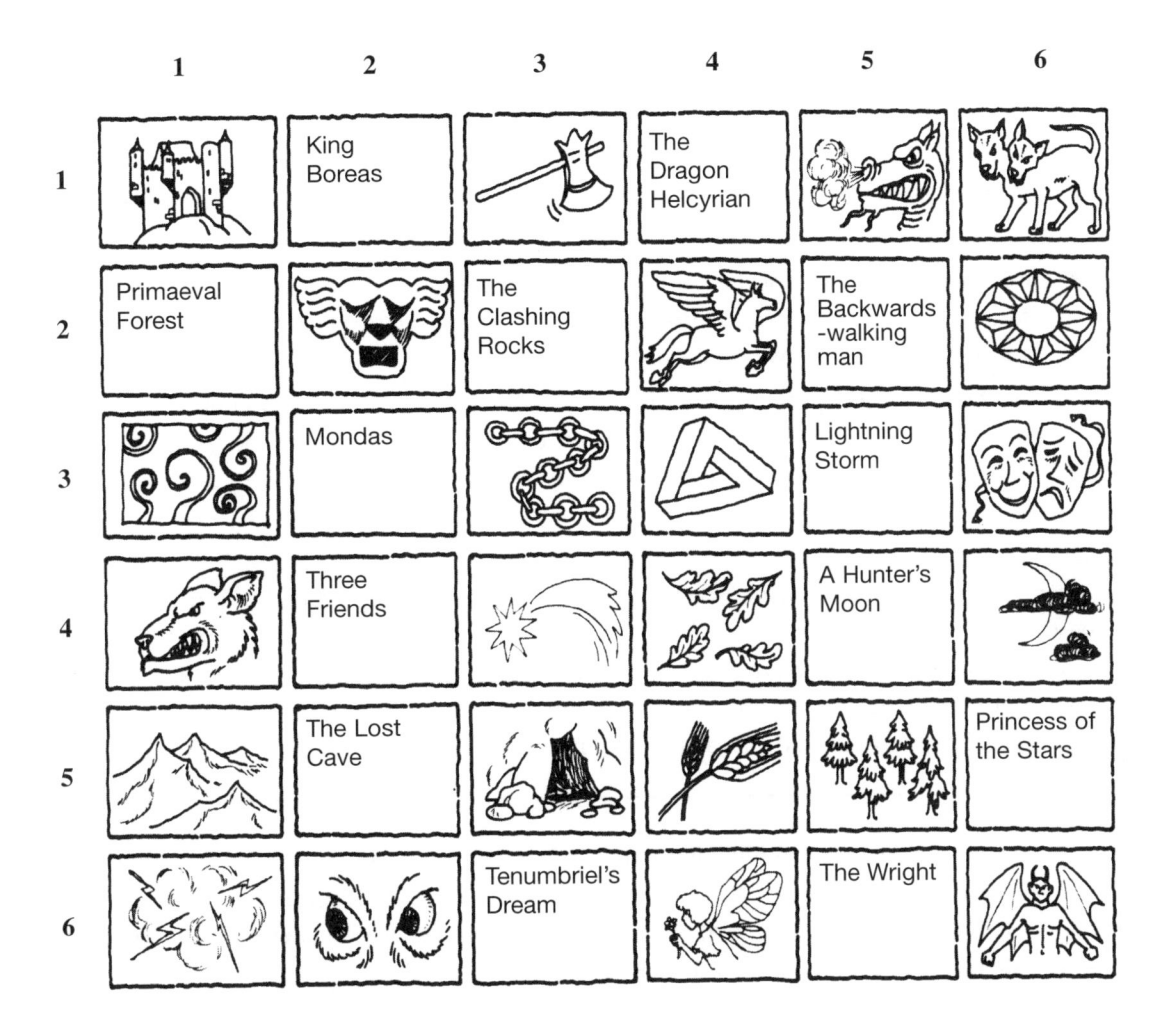

	1	2	3	4	5	6
1	(castle)	King Boreas	(axe)	The Dragon Helcyrian	(dragon head)	(two-headed dog)
2	Primaeval Forest	(winged mask)	The Clashing Rocks	(pegasus)	The Backwards-walking man	(rose window)
3	(swirls)	Mondas	(chain)	(impossible triangle)	Lightning Storm	(comedy/tragedy masks)
4	(wolf)	Three Friends	(shooting star)	(leaves)	A Hunter's Moon	(crescent moon)
5	(mountains)	The Lost Cave	(cave)	(wheat)	(pine trees)	Princess of the Stars
6	(lightning)	(eyes)	Tenumbriel's Dream	(fairy)	The Wright	(winged demon)

- Explain that all of the people, places, creatures and objects in the grid are part of a Fantasy world. Other items can be added later, as required. Many of the items are *motifs* – constituent features that help to define the genre. Motifs can often have a metaphorical or symbolic value (a symbol being something greater than the thing it represents). A dragon, for instance, might be 'only' a large winged reptilian animal that breathes fire; but symbolically in the world of Fantasy and myth it can be a guardian and protector, and also the force of evil against which goodness battles (and traditionally wins). Other activities such as Gathering Treasures and the Story Stone (below) make use of the Fantasy grid and will help children to understand metaphor and symbol.

◆ SECTION THREE

Game 1:

The simplest 6×6 grid activity is to roll the dice to choose two items at random and cascade ideas about how they might be linked. Roll twice to select each item: the column first (across the top) then the row (downwards). So, let's suppose the dice throws up King Boreas (2/1) and A Hunter's Moon (5/4). How might they be linked?

- The king likes to go hunting at the time of the hunter's moon (maybe to try to catch the dragon!).
- The hunter's moon happens only once every so many years, and something dreadful appears to hunt down the ruler of the kingdom.
- At this time King Boreas has a chance of tracking down and finding the magic crystal that can save his kingdom.
- Years ago at the time of the hunter's moon, the evil Mondas took King Boreas's daughter away to a secret realm. Now is the king's chance to retrieve her, if he can find the path that glows by moonlight…

Simple connections like this give glimmerings of possible storylines and also help children to map out in their imaginations the world of the genre through the items on the grid; playing with ideas helps them to become more familiar and authoritative with the Fantasy genre.

Game 2:

Begin in the bottom left-hand corner of the grid. Roll the dice once and pick the item indicated. Roll the dice again, move on and select a second item. Link them. Roll for a third item, then a fourth, and so on, zigzagging your way across and up the board as you would in a 'Snakes and Ladders' game. Construct a storyline as you go. Anticipate that the last item, on the top row, will suggest the resolution of the tale. Here is an example.

- (rolled 1) **thunder and lightning** – (rolled 5) **a demon**: An evil demon appeared one day in a terrible flash of light – (rolled 3) **wheat**. He said to the people of the land, 'You have ignored me for too long. Now I will blight your country and destroy your crop, unless you can bring me my heart's desire!'

- (rolled 6) **shooting star**: The king of the land saw a shooting star that night and it gave him an idea. Next morning he took the demon all of the sparkling jewels he had stored in the treasure house, but that was not the demon's heart's desire. With a flick of his claw the demon destroyed a third of the country's wheat.

- (rolled 1) **leaves**: The king's first son thought that the demon would like wood for building a shelter and for fuel, so he commanded the woodsman to chop down some trees and take the wood to the place where the demon sat waiting. But the wood was not the demon's heart's desire, and with a flick of his claw he destroyed another one-third of the country's wheat.

- (rolled 3) **comedy/tragedy masks**: The king's second son thought that perhaps the demon was unhappy, so he decided to mount a great entertainment. He brought all the dancers and clowns and singers he could find to cheer up the demon. But the demon was not amused, and with a flick of his claw he destroyed all of the remaining wheat in the land. 'And now I will begin to destroy your cattle and sheep and all the other animals you farm, unless you bring me my heart's desire!'

- (rolled 3) **chains**: Now the king was angry. He sent his soldiers to destroy the demon, but the creature was very powerful and with a blast of sulphurous breath he put all of the soldiers into a deep sleep.

- (rolled 6) **winged horse**: The king's advisers met to discuss this serious matter. They thought that perhaps the demon needed a companion and so they brought their land's rarest and most beautiful creature – a winged horse – before the waiting demon. But the demon was not pleased and with a huge beat of its leathery wings it sent the winged horse whirling away into the sky. 'Now I am all out of patience!' the demon declared with a snarl. 'Unless you can bring me my heart's desire when I am next visited, I will unleash my fiery temper and desolate your entire kingdom!'

- (rolled 2) **jewel**: The king was in a terrible state. He had no idea how to appease the demon. His only daughter, a little girl of only eight summers, happened to see this problem in a different light. 'You have been looking for the demon's heart's desire all over our country,' she said to her father. 'But maybe that heart's desire is already inside him.'

- (rolled 4) **axe**: Neither the king nor his advisers had any idea what she could mean, but the little girl had read many stories about demons and dragons and monsters of many different kinds, and she knew what lay behind the thunder and the lightning and the fire. Borrowing an axe from one of the king's knights, the little girl walked over the meadows to where the demon stood glaring beneath the heat of the sun. She strode up to him showing no fear (although she was rather nervous inside), and flung the axe at his feet. 'You have done our land and people dreadful damage and we still cannot bring you your heart's desire. Use the axe to desolate this kingdom – start with me if you like – and ask yourself then if you have gained what you truly wish for.' The demon looked upon the small child and after a long deep silence he shook his great head. 'Slaying you would give me no peace. Destroying your kingdom would still leave me angry!' 'Is it peace you wish for, then?...' But the demon was already nodding, as though realising this for the first time. 'Then why not settle here awhile among those shady trees. Get out of this harsh sunlight and I will bring you some water to cool you down.' The demon found himself following this suggestion, but then he turned back and looked into the eyes of the child and saw no trickery there. 'I have wronged you but you show me kindness. I have withered all of your crop.' The girl shrugged her shoulders and sighed. 'Yes, but I have my heart's desire too. I am alive and I can cool myself with water and the shade of those nearby trees. As for the wheat, once the seed is planted the fruit will always grow back.'

◆ SECTION THREE

This is a first draft attempt, which emerged as the dice was rolled. It requires some 'tweaking and polishing', but it illustrates the point. I have played the zigzag game on dozens of occasions with groups of all sizes and we never fail to produce a workable storyline.

When I play the zigzag game with a whole class I flesh out some of the story for them. Afterwards I split the class into smaller groups of three or four and ask them to roll another story, this time working back down the board from the top left-hand corner.

Variation: Combine the rolling of the dice to choose icons in conjunction with story ingredients (p.175) and/or structural elements of the story that you want the children to use. Also see 'Storylines', p.169.

Dice roll – link the item you pick with…	structural element …	story ingredients (you do not have to use them in this order)
First dice roll	Strong opening sentence: introduce a major character.	Problem
Second roll	Set the scene. State the story's central problem. Introduce an important protagonist.	Conflict
Third roll	Begin the solving of the problem. Maybe introduce secondary characters.	Mystery
Fourth roll	Plot development. Move the story on. Perhaps introduce a complication.	Danger
Fifth roll	A crisis for the main character(s). Build up towards the story's climax.	Excitement
Sixth roll	The climax – usually fast paced. Many of the characters meet and conflict here.	Danger
Seventh roll	The story's resolution. Tying up loose ends. Perhaps a 'twist in the tale'.	Treasure (something precious)

Game 3: Story stone

This game allows children to access a state of 'quiet alertness' that is characterised by the generation of alpha waves in the brain (see *ALPS StoryMaker,* p.273 'Teaching Alpha'). In this state your attention is more evenly balanced between what's happening outside and the thoughts drifting across your mind. Being able to switch into this state at will gives you a powerful tool for creative thinking and for the absorption, retention and recall of information.

A THINKING TOOLKIT

I have also called the use of this technique 'systematic daydreaming', which gives you an idea of what's involved.

- Demonstrate the activity first so that the children can model your behaviour. Use a small polished pebble in conjunction with the Fantasy grid (initially – when the children are more practised in this technique they'll be able to apply it to any character, place or object they wish).

- If you write with your right hand, hold the story stone in your left hand (or vice versa). Explain that the stone allows you to 'notice the ideas that float to the surface of your mind' – in other words, the stone will give you better daydreams about the story you are creating. Now pick an item from the Fantasy grid. Explain that when you place the stone in your writing hand you can be the thing you've chosen. The audience can ask you questions about your chosen character (or object) and *without any effort at all* you'll be able to answer those questions. (This point is crucial. If you find yourself applying conscious effort to try to answer the questions, you will have switched from alpha to beta state and will no longer have such rich access to stream-of-consciousness ideas.)

- Now pick your character. Place the story stone in your writing hand and allow yourself to relax. Say 'OK, now I'm... – What do you want to know?' (Example follows.)

Steve:	OK, I'm the two-headed dog. What do you want to know?
Anika:	Why have you got two heads?
Steve:	Well, once long ago all dogs had one head, but we could never decide about things – we were always in two minds about what to do for the best... And so the Princess of the Stars gave us two heads until we can learn to agree within ourselves.
Thea:	What do you eat?
Steve:	My left head loves meat and my right head prefers nuts and fruits. We plan our meals so that we are both satisfied.
Duane:	What are you scared of?
Steve:	Well, dragons can be scary and very fierce. The demon-bat is our worst enemy. In fact, it likes to hunt two-headed dogs for food, so we steer clear of it if we can.
Tommy:	Are you married?
Steve:	No, I'm still too young. Maybe one day I'll find someone and fall in love and we'll have lots of two-headed puppies.
Laura:	What is your name?
Steve:	[*looks at grid*] I am called Mondas...

I want to emphasise the importance of your demonstrating the story stone to the children first. They must see that you are relaxed and easy in your answers. You are literally 'making it up as you go along', but with the quiet confidence that your subconscious mind will supply all the information you need. I usually tell the children

◆ SECTION THREE

that I've learned a lot too, in this case about the two-headed dog. This phenomenon has been described as 'How do I know what I think until I hear what I say?' It is linked to pole-bridging (see *ALPS StoryMaker,* p. 33 and p. 115), muttering one's understanding, bringing the subconscious flow of ideas into conscious awareness as you speak them.

Within a very short time of starting this activity, you'll find that the children's questions reflect the new information you've just given them. They will be in the same alpha state as you are, all of you involved with and focused on the character you've picked. Note that this activity is *not* hot-seating. That technique as I understand it is to say the first thing that comes into your head in response to a stimulus word. 'Story stone' is a more elegant technique that yields a richer field of information: your conscious and subconscious are working in a more balanced and extended way – more of a dance than a knee-jerk reflex.

Extensions

❶ Use the story stone to explore characters, objects and settings from other books, including non-fiction. Because the technique draws information up from the subconscious, it allows you to review, reassess and rework your previously gained knowledge and understanding.

❷ With this in mind, consider allowing your group to use story stones *as you introduce a new topic*. Because the children are in alpha state, they'll be aware of the information you're delivering and the sense they are making of it at that moment. In other words, they'll be combining the new ideas with what they already know. Similarly, when you review topics and revise for tests, let the children have their story stones* to access the Alpha state.

> *One teacher I met gave each child in her class a small pebble – their own personal story stone. She explained that she had touched each one with the 'class story stone' that she kept in her desk. And so, if a child lost her stone, another could easily replace it once it had touched the class stone.

◆ Six Big Important Questions (revisited)

Aim:

- to raise children's awareness of questioning as an exploratory tool.

Introduction

Surely no one involved in education denies the importance of asking questions. The *ethos* of questioning lies at the heart of any meaningful learning process. Intelligence has usefully been defined as the capability to handle information – being aware that the word implies information, understanding that is still being formed inside the head of the learner. Ideas, facts, data therefore fuel intelligence. Questioning demonstrates purpose and direction in the quest for understanding – 'quest' and 'question' having the same etymological root, 'to seek'. In this vital sense, to ask a question is not an admission of ignorance but a desire to know more so that intelligence can be more fully developed.

The 'Six Big Important Questions' are

What? Where? When? How? Who? Why?

See p.55 ('Picture exploration') and *ALPS StoryMaker,* p. 250 for specific applications. Encourage* children to adopt a questioning approach to knowledge, for this defines and enhances the creative attitude. The example I quote in *ALPS StoryMaker* (p. 15) concerns Paris being the capital of France. Notice the difference between the sterile delivery of a fact – Paris is the capital of France – and the rich field of language and ideas generated by the questioning approach and subsequent exploration of possibilities:

- Why do you think Paris is the capital of France?
- How can we find out why it is?
- Who decided that Paris should be the capital of France?
- How are the capitals of countries chosen?
- Where is Paris and does this help to explain why it is a capital city?
- When was Paris made a capital?
- What qualities does a place need to have to be a capital?

> * Encourage – to en-courage, to give courage to.

And so on. You can raise the profile of questioning in a number of ways:

- When introducing a topic, split the class into six groups. Allocate each group on one of the big-question-words and ask them to generate as many questions as possible using that word as it relates to the topic.
- The writing activity related to *Nanoman* on the CD resource focuses on questioning as a way of exploring text.
- Also use questioning as a way of generating ideas for stories. The picture overleaf is titled 'Asteroid Patrol 2050' – a full-size colour version can be found on the CD. Have children think of questions relevant to the picture, then map out possible answers. A worked example follows.

◆ SECTION THREE

- ★ What first alerted people to the danger of the asteroid?
- ★ What will the spaceship pilots do if this plan fails?
- ★ What if the asteroid breaks into lots of smaller pieces?

- ★ Where did the asteroid come from?
- ★ Where are the space fighters based?
- ★ Where could people find shelter if this plan fails?

- ★ When will the asteroid strike if it's not destroyed now?
- ★ When will the pilots know if they have succeeded?
- ★ When will the order be given to evacuate moonbase?

- ★ How fast is the asteroid travelling?
- ★ How was it detected?
- ★ How can the people on the moonbase survive if pieces of the asteroid crash down?
- ★ How can I make this story even more exciting?

- ★ Who decided on this plan to stop the asteroid?
- ★ Who are the pilots of the patrol ships?
- ★ Who gave the order to strike?

- ★ Why was the attack left until the asteroids were so close to the moon?
- ★ Why are the ships using lasers instead of missiles?
- ★ Why are there only two ships?
- ★ Why is the attacking pilot aiming just there?

STORYMAKER CATCH PACK – USING GENRE FICTION AS A RESOURCE FOR ACCELERATED LEARNING

Section Four

A bagful of story games

> The ability to learn is a function of one's capability for perception change.
>
> *Neil Postman & Charles Weingartner*

Overview of Section Four

Page	Activity	Story element	ALPS StoryMaker reference	Accelerated learning & thinking skills link
77	Twenty Questions	Early generation of ideas; insights about character, setting		Systematic logical questioning; reasoning skills; evaluation of information; sequencing and categorisation
80	Venn Diagrams	Genre	Title Match; The Landscape of Genre; Genre Mix-and-Match	Domains of knowledge; frameworks of understanding; categorisation
81	Nameplay	Names of characters and places	Genre; What's in a Name? The Scribe's Road; Wordbuilder	Reframing; developing insight into language
86	Alphabet Roll	As above	As above	As above
87, 88	Dragonslayer; Princess of the Stars	As above	As above	As above
88, 89	Stereotypes and Character Types	Character; vivid particularities	Character; Getting to Know You; Character Stew; People are Like Onions; The World Inside; One Unique Detail	Insight and development of interpersonal intelligence; raising awareness of generalisation
90	Design-a-Monster	Character design and development	Character; Classification Patterns; The World Inside	Classification and sequencing; Decisionmaking; Chunking down
97	Add-a-Bit	As above	As above	As above; philosophical enquiry
99	How Tall, How Strong?	As above; exploration of setting; exploring the meanings of words	People Are Like Onions; Treasure Mapping	Mediations; philosophical enquiry
102, 103	Monster-Maker; Monster as Metaphor	Character design and development; awareness of stereotyping; 'generic monsters'	as above; Literal and Metaphorical Functions	Mediations; metaphorical thinking linked to interpersonal intelligence
105	Character Grid	As above	Genre; Structure and Function	As above

Page	Activity	Story element	ALPS StoryMaker reference	Accelerated learning & thinking skills link
107–113	Thumbnails; Diamond Ranking; Living Graphs; Advanced Thumbnails	Summary of character and/or setting	Empathy; Gathering Treasures	Manipulation and consolidation of information; mediation; sequencing and interpreting information; values thinking
114–117	Context Sentences and Connective Prompting	Mapping 'the world of the story'; storylining; using time spans and scene changes flexibly	The Creative Mind; Connective Prompting (to overcome limiting beliefs)	Contextualising; logical linking
117	Fortune Cookie Phrases	Plotting; themes		As above; time-lining; planning and decision making
120	Consequences	Motifs; story elements	Plotting; With Good Reason; Predictions	Cause-and-effect thinking; future mapping
122	Odd-One-Out	Motifs; characters		Brainstorming; reasoning skills; sequencing and prioritising information
123	Personas	Characters; editing and review	The Inner World of the Writer; Uniquely Me; The Write Attitude	Modelling behaviours; feedback techniques
125	Gathering Treasures	Exploring the qualities of motifs; characters	Gathering Treasures	Developing emotional resources; metaphorical thinking
128, 129	Ideas Wheel; Story Darts	Exploring motifs; storylining; themes		Bisociations; exploration; synthesis
130–134	Story Circles; Start Anywhere	Plotting; links with themes; strong beginnings	Spider-web Daydreaming	Pole-bridging; Big Picture thinking; bisociations; metaphorical thinking
135–142	Story Maps Revisited; Dice Journey	Plotting; story ingredients; motifs	Dicework	Mind mapping; sequencing; synthesis; mediations; decision making; problem solving
143	Jigsaw Town	Settings	Maps and Tracks	Visualisation; consolidation of information; mind mapping
144	Story Tray	Settings; plotting		Kinaesthetic learning

Page	Activity	Story element	ALPS StoryMaker reference	Accelerated learning & thinking skills link
145	Story Tree	Plotting; character motivations	Story Tree	Outcomes thinking; mind mapping; decisionmaking
147	Mystery Mapping	All		Visual organisation of information; sequencing and prioritisation; problem solving; speculation and inference; questioning
151	Concept Mapping	Relationships between characters, settings, events and motifs	Story Maps	Mind mapping
154	Other Worlds	Genre; motifs and elements of stories	Genre	Far transfer of knowledge between domains
156–166	The Deeper Structure of Stories; A Melange of Motifs	Themes; plotting; narrative structure	Motifs and Meanings; Story Symbols	Metaphorical thinking; life themes; decision making
167	The Idea as Hero	Themes; plotting; narrative structure		Metaphorical thinking
169	Storylines	Narrative structure	Time Spans	Organisational skills; logical thinking
175	Story Ingredients	Plotting	The Tale Unfolds	Visual organisation of information; sequencing and prioritisation; speculation; problem solving
179	Mix-and-Match Grids	All		

Section Four:

A bagful of story games

◆ Twenty questions

This is a quick-fire game that develops logical response and can also be used for review and philosophical enquiry.

- Choose an item from the 6×6 Fantasy grid (overleaf) and invite the children to ask questions to narrow down the possibilities until they can conclude which item you've selected. Notice if or to what extent the questions:
  - follow on logically one from the other
  - demonstrate that the children have remembered information gleaned previously.

Your aim is to hone children's questioning skills, such that the questions are more general at the outset and more specific towards the end. This corresponds to the state of having less information at the beginning and more later on.

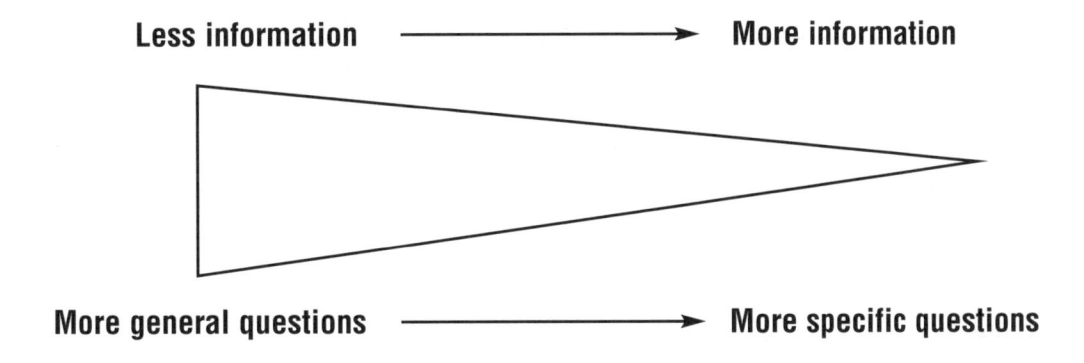

Less information ⟶ **More information**

More general questions ⟶ **More specific questions**

- Discourage direct naming and guessing. Ask children to support their choices with the evidence that's been gathered. Point out that the more evidence you have, the less of a guess you need to make.
- Use the game (sometimes anyway) to explore some of the issues that the questions will raise – see the example below.

◆ SECTION FOUR

- Extend the game by using 'Thumbnails' (see p.107) that this or another group have previously created.
- You can also play 'Twenty questions' in the library. Select a book, write its title down, and have children work out your choice. This version allows you to review genre, alphabetical order, the Dewey Decimal System, observation skills, etc. (Allow children to browse the shelves as they work out which questions to ask.)

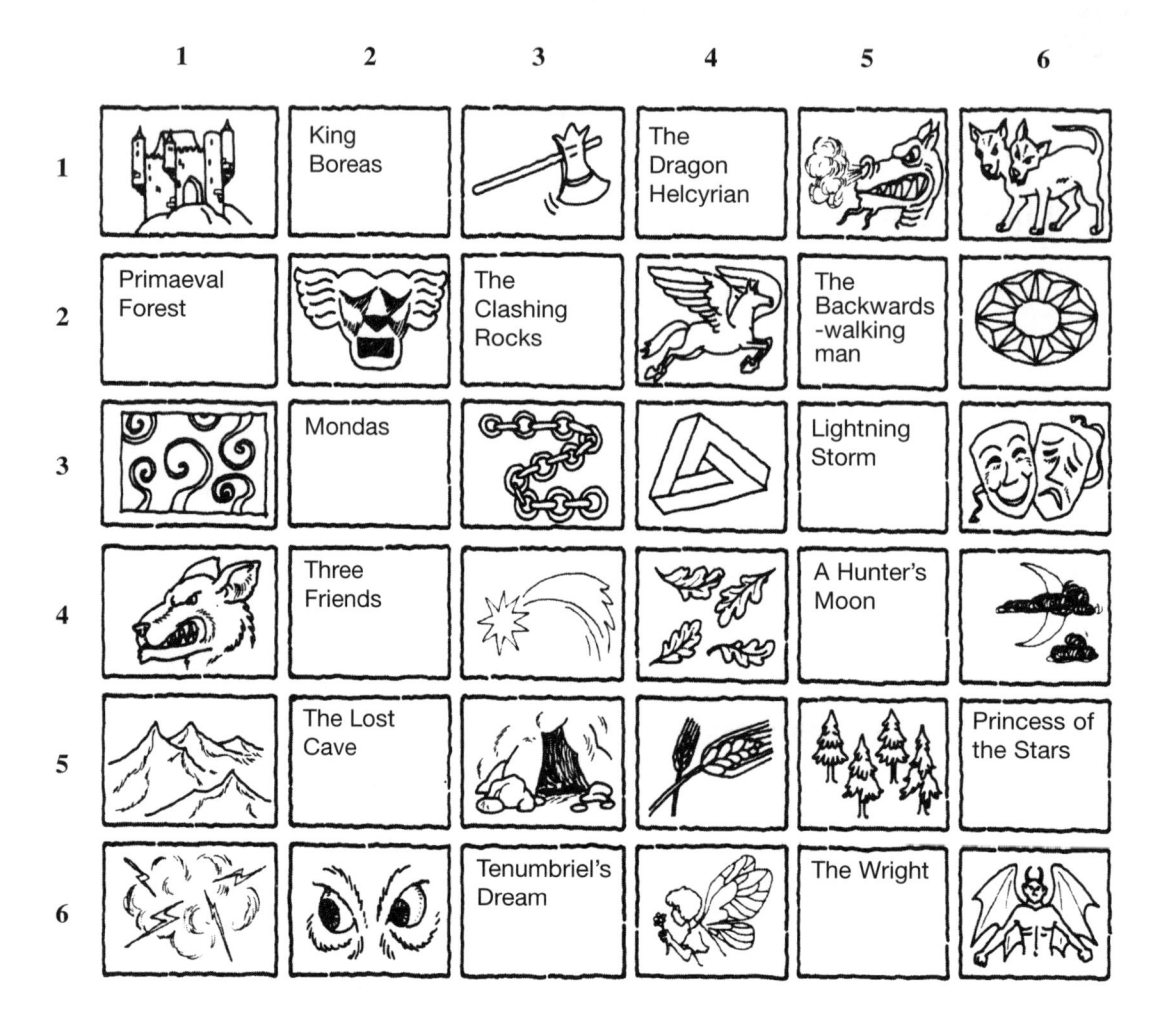

	1	2	3	4	5	6
1	[castle]	King Boreas	[axe]	The Dragon Helcyrian	[dragon breathing fire]	[wolves]
2	Primaeval Forest	[winged mask]	The Clashing Rocks	[pegasus]	The Backwards-walking man	[star/rosette]
3	[swirls]	Mondas	[chains]	[impossible triangle]	Lightning Storm	[theatre masks]
4	[wolf head]	Three Friends	[shooting star]	[leaves]	A Hunter's Moon	[moon and clouds]
5	[mountains]	The Lost Cave	[volcano]	[wheat]	[trees]	Princess of the Stars
6	[lightning]	[eyes]	Tenumbriel's Dream	[fairy]	The Wright	[demon]

Child 1:	Is it alive?
Steve:	Yes.
Child 1:	Is it evil?
Steve:	What do you mean by 'evil'?
Child 1:	Doing bad things.
Steve:	If I had chosen the mountains, and suppose there had been an avalanche in the mountains that killed some travellers, would that be a bad thing?
Child 1:	Yes.

Child 2:	Not if the avalanche squashed a load of bad guys.
Steve:	Let's suppose the travellers were good guys. Can we say the mountains are bad because the avalanche happened?
Child 1:	Well, no. It was an accident. It was a bad thing that happened, but the mountains weren't bad.
Steve:	Are there any other words we can use apart from 'bad' to describe what happened?
Child 2:	Can we get on with the game? … Does it have wings?
Steve:	No.
Child 1:	Does it have two legs?
Steve:	No.
Child 3:	Does it have six legs?
Steve:	What would it be if it had six legs?
Child 3:	An insect.
Steve:	There are no insects on the grid.
Child 1:	A monster then!
Child 2:	If it was 'The Three Friends', they'd have six legs if they were human.
Steve:	Well done, that's pretty smart. But it's not the three friends.
Child 3:	I'm stuck.
Steve:	Review what you've got. The thing I've chosen is alive, it doesn't have two legs or six legs…
Child 3:	Does it have four legs?
Steve:	No.
Child 1:	Does it have any legs at all?
Steve:	No.
Child 1:	Aha! It's alive but has no legs… Is it a plant?
Steve:	Well, to be precise, it's not 'a plant'.
Child 3:	Is it more than one plant?
Steve:	Yes.
Child 2:	Is it the leaves? (4/4).
Steve:	Is a leaf a plant?
Child 2:	Well, it's not an animal!
Steve:	If I showed you a cat's whisker, would that be an animal?
Child 2:	No. So it's not leaves because that's just part of a plant.
Steve:	That's right.
Child 1:	Is it the wheat? (4/5).
Steve:	What evidence is your question based on?
Child 1:	That the thing you've chosen is a plant.

◆ SECTION FOUR

Steve:	Apart from the leaves, which we've discounted, there are two other possibilities. [*The children look for them.*]
Child 2:	Is it trees?
Steve:	Wait a moment. I'm interested in you asking questions to narrow down possibilities, not just to eliminate items directly. We have three possibilities; wheat, trees and the primaeval forest…
Child 3:	I didn't notice that one.
Steve:	Because it isn't a picture?
Child 3:	Yes.
Steve:	OK, without guessing or naming one of those three things directly, ask a question that will get rid of one of the possibilities.
Child 1:	Is it taller than you are?
Steve:	Good. Yes.
Child 1:	So it's not the wheat.
Child 3:	Do many, many things make up what you've chosen?
Steve:	Yes.
Child 3:	In the picture of the trees there are only four trees…
Child 2:	So it must be the primaeval forest.
Steve:	Well done, you got that in fourteen questions. I wonder if you can get the next one in less…?

◆ Venn diagrams

We have come across a version of Venn diagrams in the 'Lensing' activity (p.61). One way of injecting some freshness into stories is to explore the areas where genres overlap.

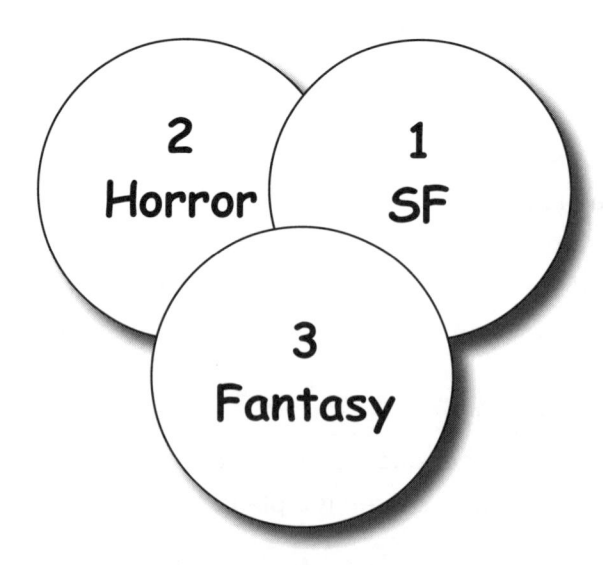

2 Horror

1 SF

3 Fantasy

STORYMAKER CATCH PACK – USING GENRE FICTION AS A RESOURCE FOR ACCELERATED LEARNING

Raise awareness of Venn diagrams by giving children a list of motifs. Ask them to decide in which area(s) the items should be placed. So:

- a spaceship would appear only in the SF circle where it does not overlap with other genres
- a castle would be placed where Fantasy and Horror overlap
- a cave would be situated where all three genres overlap.

And so on. You can extend the game by using characters, settings, snippets of dialogue or any other story element. See 'A melange of motifs' on p.164, which offers a checklist of items for you to use with this activity.

◆ Nameplay

Play is the essence of creative thinking. During children's early years the play they engage in helps them to make sense of the world: through play they rehearse their roles and responsibilities, testing the limits of what's possible and acceptable, sometimes going beyond those limits and discovering the consequences of their actions.

Towards the end of childhood and through into adulthood, play need not end. It may become formalised as the 'skills of play' evolve and become ever more sophisticated, usually within the domain of one or more of the natural intelligences (see Howard Gardner's multiple intelligence model). Creative writing is clearly linked to the development of linguistic intelligence – a love of and curiosity about language and the meanings it conveys. Implicit in this is the notion that 'the knower must be included in the known'. Language comes from the people for the people; it's plastic, it changes through usage over time. On an individual level, and especially within the context of genre fiction, words can be played with like clay, moulded into many forms to see what the end result will be like.

Nameplay is one aspect of this principle of experiment and adventure. Science Fiction and Fantasy are peppered with people- and place-names that help to define and texture the genres. Encourage children to take a playful approach when making up names. Here are a few games that might help...

- Take a **person's name** such as Brian. Subtract one letter at a time to see what happens: *Brin, Bran, Rian, Bria . . .*
  - Think about alternative spellings – *Bryan, Braean, Bryaan, Bryanne, Bryen.*
  - Check the origins of the name – Brian is a Celtic name of obscure origin, though it may have links with *hill* and *strength*. Perhaps that gives you an insight into what the character might be like.
  - Add letters as you use one of the techniques above – *Abrin, Brant, Riana, Brial ... Brylann, Bryannen, Ibryen.* Be aware of the *resonances* of these words. For me, Bryannen sounds Welsh, and Ibryen sounds Hebrew.

◆ SECTION FOUR

- Take a longer word that has several vowels and play with it in the same way. For example, the word 'unafraid' gives us:

Fragments	Reverse Fragments	Combin-	ations
Una	Arfan	Duna	Araf
Nafra	Anu	Danu	Urad
Frai	Diar	Finua	Aruda
Unaf	Iarf	Fria	Iana
Afrai	Arfa	Nauf	Daria

- Look in books of **myths and legends**; dictionaries and old collections of tales. You will probably find many names that have an authentic sound but which carry few or no associations in people's minds. A brief trawl through a few reference books produced: *Aodh, Assipattle, Bwbachod, Fuath, Killmoulis, Mooinjer, Tabhaisver, Yarthkins* (Briggs, see Bibliography); also *Audrien, Coraniads, Eladu, Gabhra, Locris, Mesroda, Rath Luachar, Tethra, Vran* (Dixon-Kennedy, see Bibliography). And *Ci-a-nos, Da-ne-da-do, Gan-nos-gwah, Ho-dar-da-se-do-gas, Qua-nos* (Kelsey, see Bibliography).

- Similarly, **dictionaries of place names** will yield up plenty of material for you to play with. One idea is to take objects, animals and phenomena from nature and link them randomly with the old roots or the modern equivalents of place names…

fox	breck (a brook)
moon	coomb (valley)
storm	grave (pit)
raven	holt (wood)
cloud	lea (forest)
hawk	mere (pool)
mouse	rick (ridge)
river	slade (slate)
autumn	scough (wood)
dawn	tor (rocky peak)

Even this small sample gives us *Foxslade, Moonlea, Stormrick, Ravenholt, Cloudscough, Hawkmere, Mousegrave, Rivertor, Autumnbreck, Dawncoomb*. Notice that this is by using each word in the left-hand column and each word in the right-hand column once only. Many more combinations are possible by reconfiguring the words in a grid template…

A BAGFUL OF STORY GAMES

	breck	coomb	grave	holt	lea	mere	rick	slade	scough	tor
autumn										
cloud										
dawn										
fox										
hawk										
moon										
mouse										
raven										
river										
storm										

Be aware that not all of the combinations will sound/look/feel right – which underlines the principle that you need to have lots of ideas to get some good ideas. Also highlighted is the notion that within the world of creative fiction, ideas are not so much 'right' or 'wrong', but more or less useful in the long run.

- **Prefixes and suffixes.** Our language is one vast wonderful hybrid of many other languages from around the world and through several millennia. Nameplay makes children more aware of where words come from and their layers of meaning. Make a list of prefixes and suffixes such as the one below. Have children add to the following lists, then mix-and-match (using root words as necessary) to invent new SF ideas and bits of technology. Allow alternative spellings and other manipulations so that the words look and 'feel' right as far as the children are concerned.

Prefix:	Suffix:	Root:
ante- (*before*)	-able, -ible (*capable of being*)	aqua (*water*)
bi-, bis- (*two, twice*)	-ain, -an (*one connected*)	audio (*I hear*)
circum- (*round*)	-ance, -ence (*state of*)	centum (*a hundred*)
com- (*together*)	-ant (*one who*)	creo (*create*)
contra- (*against*)	-el, -et, -ette (*little*)	fortis (*strong*)
cyber- (*steer*)	-er, -eer, -ier (*one who*)	manus (*hand*)
ex- (*out of*)	-ess (*female*)	octo- (*eight*)
fore- (*before*)	-fy (*to make*)	porto (*I carry*)
hyper- (*over, above, exceeding*)	-icle, sel (*little*)	primus (*first*)
inter- (*between*)	-less (*without*)	scribo (*write*)
post- (*after*)	-ling (*little*)	unus (*one*)
pre- (*before*)	-ment (*state of being*)	vanus (*empty*)
re- (*back*)	-oon, -on (*large*)	video (*I see*)
sub- (*under*)	-ory (*a place for*)	voco (*I call*)
trans- (*across*)	-ous (*full of*)	volvo (*I roll*)

◆ SECTION FOUR

Even from this small selection a little wordplay will give us: *aquarette* (a little water capsule), *scribatory* (a place where writing experiments are carried out), *cyberling* (a little steersperson), *octofy* (verb, to turn into eight of something, as in 'Steve, will you octofy that cake for me now please?'), *interport* (a halfway house where you can stop on a journey), *audioon* (a large sound; this may be like a cannon shot, loud and brief, or like distant thunder – softer, but creating an impression of huge size). [The section on prefixes and suffixes is reproduced from *ALPS StoryMaker* with the permission of the author.]

- **Kennings and compound words.** A kenning is a way of describing something by creating an impression of an action, of what the thing does, rather than just stating what it is. Often words are combined in strong and innovative ways in a kenning – perhaps two nouns, as in *fire-water* (whisky) or as a mix of adjectives and nouns, as in *Moon-watcher* (a character in Arthur C. Clarke's SF novel *2001: A Space Odyssey*).

    Kennings can themselves be compounded into no-nonsense action-descriptions of people, places or things, frequently with the use of alliteration and assonance. Consider the following…

> Tree tapper, grub grabber, writhing-maggot muncher, bright blood-red woodland dweller…
>
> Fresh grass-green-leaf hunter, spotted soarer, flying Fantasy flapping furiously; feathery featured, glisten-eyed small-speckled songster.
>
> What am I?
>
> [A woodpecker]

Anglo-Saxon stories and poems* are a rich source of descriptive phrases that give a new freshness and elegance to the things we see around us. Examples include:

- *war hedge*, the men in the second rank who held their shields over their heads as a protection
- *giant works*, impressive architecture (left by the Romans)
- *swan's way*, the sky
- *rooftrees*, the supporting beams of a dwelling
- *throng-noise*, the roaring of a crowd.

> * The strong and vibrant language of the Anglo Saxons is powerfully evoked in **Wordhoard** by Kevin Crossley-Holland and Jill Paton-Walsh, and in **The Earliest English Poems,** translated by Michael Alexander (see Bibliography).

The act of reframing the language in this way helps children to see with new eyes. The activity also develops confidence in the use of words, encourages creative connections and offers insights into word origins. Have children make up new terms like the examples below. Challenge another group to suggest what the terms refer to.

meltstone *wordhoard* *sky arrow*

firestick *datacoin*

imagebox *hourcircle* *imageportal*

For people's names, make a list in two columns as in the example below and mix and match to see what happens…

Day	hunter
Star	defender
Sea	dreamer
Moon	soarer
World	crawler
Road	flier
Sky	gatherer
Dawn	bearer
Night	wanderer
Time	warrior
Light	walker
Sword	rider

- For *'ordinary' names*, flip through a telephone directory or look along the non-fiction shelves in the library. Mix and match first and surnames. The results sound more natural than trying to make up a character's name. A few minutes' work gives us: Paul Goodwin, Carl Myles, Geena Kramer, Alan Dennett, Susan Gregory, Shakti Roet, Christina Wilson, Colin Moore, David Blum and Julia Thompson.

- *Flip-a-Name.* Another short and easy technique is to use coins and dice to choose a name. Flip heads – *yes*/flip tails – *no*.
  - Am I choosing a surname?
  - Does the name start with a vowel? (Review vowels.)
  - (*If yes*) Does the name start with A? (etc.)
  - (*If no*) Then it must start with a consonant? (Review consonants.)

◆ SECTION FOUR

- (*If yes*) Does it start with any of the first six? (Have children go through these)… And so on.
- Does the name have more than one syllable? (Review syllables.)

Very soon you will have the information you need to generate ideas… So, my character's first name begins with C and has two syllables…

◆ Alphabet roll

This game is introduced within the context of name creation, but it has other applications in storymaking.

When thinking of names for characters, roll the dice first to choose how many letters you'll select from the grid. Then roll the dice twice to choose each letter.

	1	2	3	4	5
1	A	B	C	D	E
2	F	G	H	I	J
3	K	L	M	N	O
4	P	Q	R	S	T
5	U	V	W	Y	X or Z

Example: First roll – 5. Subsequent rolls – N, T, F, U, B.

Now explore the following variations:

- Use as many of these letters as possible in one surname or first name – these will be the first letters of characters' names.
- Combinations of the letters give the initials of the characters.
- Roll the dice again to see where in a character's name a letter will fall; so for example, N will be the fourth letter of my character's surname.
- Dice-roll for a letter and match it with an item from the Fantasy grid that you've chosen by dice. So what are the links between each of the following pairs?

A BAGFUL OF STORY GAMES

O   C

X   S

◆ **Dragonslayer**

This activity explores names-as-functions in the Fantasy genre. Pick a word from each of the tables below and join them to create a new name. This can be the name of a character (Jack Firetreader, Diana Darkspinner), a character's purpose or type (Nightwatcher, Swordbreaker, Moonwhisperer), the name of an object with a hint of its purpose (Lightspinner, Stormbringer, Waverider) or a title – see 'Princess of the Stars' below. Trying many combinations will produce a few striking names, emphasising the principle that you need to have lots of ideas to have good ideas. A version of this activity appears on the CD resource.

moon	word	road	sky	dawn	night	time
light	sword	storm	lightning	hammer	jewel	dark
fire	silver	widow	king	crystal	sun	cavern
bow	forest	cloud	knife	day	rain	queen
dragon	axe	word	ice	star	gold	horse
eagle	wing	winter	chain	tree	tower	wave
bone	sand	rainbow	tide	shadow	mountain	wolf

surfer	rider	crawler	flier	gatherer	reaper	bearer
wanderer	warrior	carrier	walker	hoarder	bringer	holder
runner	killer	forger	hammerer	maker	weaver	traveller
springer	taker	writer	picker	spinner	slayer	hunter
digger	dancer	cleaver	breaker	howler	watcher	teller
sayer	healer	dreamer	buster	gardener	striker	burner
treader	whisperer	giver	teller	wielder	stalker	singer

STORYMAKER CATCH PACK – USING GENRE FICTION AS A RESOURCE FOR ACCELERATED LEARNING

◆ SECTION FOUR

Once children have created these combinations, ask them to describe the characters or objects that the names suggest.

◆ Princess of the stars

Pair items from the tables above to create the titles of Fantasy characters such as: *Dancer of the Night, Gatherer of Bones, Bringer of the Moon, Watcher of the Tide*.

Extend this activity by linking a name with a story ingredient (see p.44) to suggest a story idea.

Name/Title	Story ingredient	Suggested story
Gatherer of Bones	problem	The Gatherer of Bones is asked by the king of the land to retrieve the skeleton of a slain knight from the domain of the giant wolves.
The Queen of Forgers	challenge	The Queen of Forgers is commanded to find the true Mirror of the Future from among a thousand others that show only lies.
The Healer of Time	conflict	Against his deepest principles, the Healer of Time intends to alter the past to prevent the death of the woman he loves.
The Rider of the Eagle	mystery	The Rider of the Eagle must travel swiftly to the northern forests to find out why the Lawgiver has not arrived in the city.

Note: The name tables are reproduced in the photocopiable pages section of the CD resource.

◆ Stereotypes and character types

Children – and even adult writers – will often lift character traits and sometimes whole characters straight out of other stories and use them unthinkingly, without changing any details. This is how fictional stereotypes are born. Thus, the traditional fairy tale witch is ugly and bent, wears dark robes and a pointed hat and invariably sports a hairy wart on her nose. The fact remains that it's easy to use a stock character like this, something 'off the peg' that requires no creative thought. The shortcomings of relying on stereotypes are:

- the habit may transfer to real life
- one becomes desensitised to individuality and unique details

- the skill of reflective thinking can atrophy
- stereotype characters often go hand-in-hand with stock situations, formulaic plots and cliché language – in other words, low-quality writing.

The tendency to think stereotypically can be reversed in a number of ways:

- If a child presents you with a stereotype character in a story, roll a dice and ask him to incorporate that number of changes to make the character different. Encourage the writer to select differences for reasons that make sense within the story.
- Ask your class to notice one special detail in, say, six people; classmates, members of the family, passers-by on the street. (In this connection see 'Character pyramid' in *Imagine That*, p. 119.)
- Take a character from fiction and discuss various changes; make the voice higher, louder, faster; make the clothes more outrageous; make the character more/less evil, unpredictable, etc.
- Take a stereotype character and use his/her opposite characteristics.

Evil witch	Good witch
ugly	attractive
bent	straight
dark robes	bright fashionable clothes
lives alone in a dark old house	lives as part of a large friendly family in a modern city apartment

Note: Being sensitive to small details is an important skill having multiple applications. See, for instance, p.192, where 'vivid particularities' forms one of the four important areas for planning, reviewing and evaluating creative work.

◆ Character types

Character types, as opposed to stereotypes, grow from individual characters that are deliberately used across a number of stories, deepening and developing as they go. Such characters usually have special significance for the author. They may remind the author of someone (s)he knows, or form some aspect of the writer's personality, or represent the kind of person the writer wishes (s)he could be. Character types often have connections with ongoing themes that are relevant to the writer's own life.

◆ SECTION FOUR

Introduce the concept of character types to your groups by looking at a selection of stories by the same writer where they occur. For instance, in *Catch & Other Stories*, three clear character types can be identified:

- **1** the shy, quiet, very intelligent and rather withdrawn boy who often believes in strange/paranormal ideas and/or is out of the ordinary in some way
- **2** the more outgoing and confident companion (often the story's narrator) who acts as a protector to number 1 – it's a love–hate relationship
- **3** the tall, pretty, rather aloof girl who will often disdain number 2's attention and affection. She has hidden strengths or powers and is not always what she seems.

This is how the three types appear in the *Catch* tales:

	1) shy boy	2) confident boy	3) resourceful mysterious girl
She Bites	David Nimbley	Colin Williams	Eleanor Garou
Gurney	Scott Gurney	Ben Leech	
Catch		Phil Stevens	
Dragon's Egg	Austin Williams	Kevin	Hayley Masters
Brag	Ben Peterson	Steve	
Nanoman			Skat
House That R'Ork Built	Jeff Collis	Louis	
Forever Man	Simon Greaves/ Darren Phipps	Rob	
Burning	Brin		Karel

In my short stories and early novels particularly, my interest lay with character types 1 and 3 – the shy intelligent boy with unusual beliefs, and the resourceful girl. I sum them up below as Tony and Eleanor.

A character type can grow from any individual character or combination of characters' traits. The defining qualities are that the character type often has some importance to the writer personally, and grows and changes throughout the course of a number of stories.

◆ Design-a-monster

Fantastical creatures found in SF, Fantasy and Horror are frequently used 'off the peg' by young writers, and really amount to a kind of stereotyping. This is partly the fault of the genres themselves, where lower-quality books, movies, TV programmes, etc., are often derivative of their more innovative predecessors.

Character Types

Character types are thematic or generic characters that might appear in various guises throughout a range of stories. They differ from stereotypes in being used deliberately and mindfully.

Tony
- Tony is usually between 11 and 14.
- He is quite tall, dark haired and dresses 'quietly'.
- He keeps himself to himself. He has a few close friends but doesn't mix easily.
- He loves to learn and is an expert in some areas, usually science and the supernatural.

Eleanor
- Eleanor is usually a couple of years older than Tony.
- She is tall, fair and pretty but doesn't think she is.
- She is open and friendly, but has some deep secrets and fears.
- When she is tested to the limit, she finds strengths that even she didn't know about.

◆ SECTION FOUR

One way of countering this tendency is to encourage writers to design their Fantasy creatures a bit at a time, reflecting on the functional and dramatic purpose of each feature as they go. There could be an element of randomness in the choice through the use of coins and dice. Here is a suggested format.

Having decided on the genre…

Feature/question	Method of choosing	Consideration
How human is my creature?	Dice roll – where 1 is completely human and 6 is entirely nonhuman – 4/6. So this creature has some human features.	'Human' here means 'looking human'. The fact that my creature doesn't look very human doesn't mean he's 'inhuman' – i.e. a bad guy!
Is my creature male or female?	Coin – heads is male, tails is female. Flipped heads, so my creature is male.	So I wonder if these creatures live in families or packs, or if they are solitary wanderers?
How evil is my creature?	Decision. I want my character to be basically good, but with a quest or mission to complete which causes him to do some bad things.	My teacher asked if 'the ends can justify the means'. Is it right that my character should do bad things to carry out a mission that's good? I will need to think about this further.
Does my character have wings?	Coin – yes. I've decided they'll be like bat's wings rather than bird's wings because that's more dramatic!	Wings are a weakness as well as a strength. My character couldn't move easily through forests, narrow canyons, etc. And disguise would be difficult. Also, he could be vulnerable in the sky.
How strong is my character?	Dice roll – 2/6… I'm not happy with that. I wanted my character to be strong!	My teacher talked this through with me and we decided that the character's strength could change depending on the weather or the phases of the moon. Also, 'strong' doesn't just mean physically strong. My character could be very strong-minded and have strong feelings. That's more like it!

Notice how it's not vital for the writer to see or understand the character completely at this stage. The act of designing the character step by logical step moves steadily towards the 'big picture'. (However, some children might feel frustrated by this approach and want to be able to visualise the entire creature early on. In this case the technique called 'Add-a-bit' might be more appropriate – see p.97 and in the 'Writing Games' menu of the CD resource).

As the writer builds up a picture of her character she comes to understand more surely that successful creative writing is a matter of choice, decision and intentionality: giving the character big red horns, for instance, might look dramatic, and artistic licence might allow you to get away with it if the horns have no other logical purpose in the story. But there is also the issue of believability – especially in genre fiction, readers need to suspend disbelief anyway. Loading too many purely fantastical elements into the tale for no logical reason will diminish the power of the story and the reader's immersion within it.

As information about the character accumulates, suggest that the child reviews his creation from time to time. Encourage him to consolidate what he has discovered, perhaps by one of the following means:

- **Character pyramid** (see *ALPS StoryMaker* pp.174–175). Have the writer draw the pyramid template as shown and encourage her to fill in the sections with appropriate information. Emphasise that she will have to be selective and/or make the language work harder for her to compress the required ideas into the limited spaces. Note the inclusion of 'one unique detail', which is best added when the rest of the pyramid has been completed.

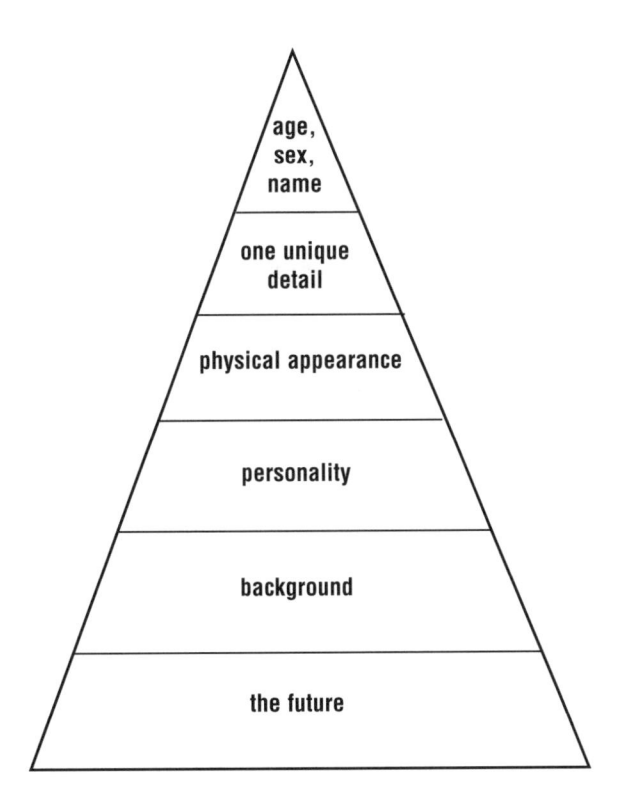

[Pyramid diagram with sections from top to bottom: age, sex, name / one unique detail / physical appearance / personality / background / the future]

- **Character pie**. This technique focuses more on the personality and 'inner world' of the character, and allows the writer to explore further once the character pyramid has been finished. 'Character pie' is itself a precursor to a more challenging and sophisticated technique I call 'The world inside'. Note that the character pie template shown overleaf can be adapted in any number of ways: you can divide the circle up into more or fewer sections and give them whatever headings you choose.

◆ SECTION FOUR

Loves   Hates

Fears   Dreams

If the image is photocopied to A3 size there's plenty of room in each section for 'stream-of-consciousness' writing, mind-mapping, etc.

Through the character pie template we learn that this person loves, say, the taste of pineapple, reading books, cuddling kittens, etc. Use an extension of the technique to put some more detail to these ideas…

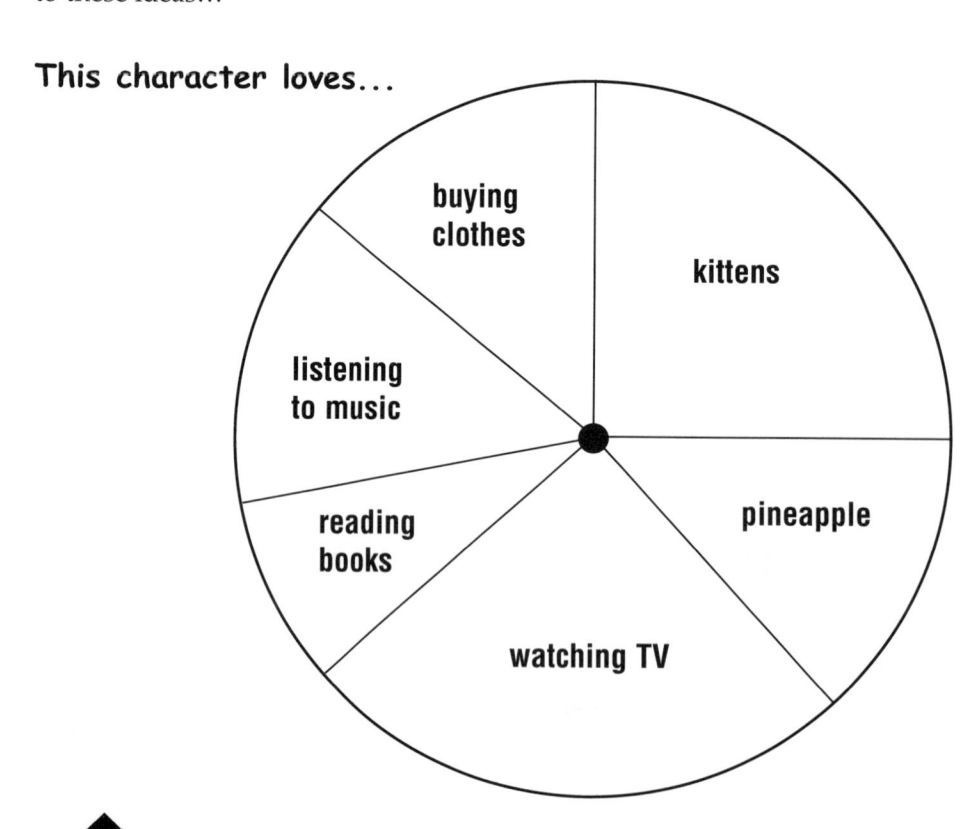

This character loves...

- buying clothes
- kittens
- listening to music
- pineapple
- reading books
- watching TV

STORYMAKER CATCH PACK – USING GENRE FICTION AS A RESOURCE FOR ACCELERATED LEARNING

Expressing the information graphically allows the child to make some fairly sophisticated judgements about comparisons and proportions without having to articulate these ideas first. After completing the task, she will be able to tell you things like 'This character loves watching TV a little bit more than cuddling kittens. And this character loves buying clothes about the same as she loves listening to music.' Such insightfulness leads to an understanding that the inner world has structure and connectedness, and that 'large areas of feeling' can be chunked down into smaller portions. The personalities of fictional characters can therefore be understood and described in at least as much detail as their external appearance. Furthermore, such inner explorations allow further insights into characters' motivations and reasoning. Beyond the world of the story, such understandings can be applied directly in children's lives as a way of developing their own emotional resourcefulness.

- **The world inside**. As an extension of 'Character pie', present your group with this visual or one similar (they can be created quickly by inserting items of clip art into a Word document, for example). Firstly ask the children just to notice what's inside the circle without any attempt to interpret. Then say 'Let's pretend these are thoughts going on inside the mind of a boy/girl. Why is (s)he thinking of these things – and *why is (s)he thinking of them in this way?*' Emphasise that there is no one right answer to that question, and that the character might have these things on his/her mind for any number of reasons.

◆ SECTION FOUR

Some of the responses I've had are:
- this person isn't very good at ICT. Computers make him feel small.
- this boy doesn't like school because kids there give him lots of lip.
- this boy has fallen in love with a girl in his class, but he's nervous about going to school in case she talks to him. He thinks the sun shines out of her eyes.
- this boy is frightened of going to school because he's being bullied. A bigger kid gave him a black eye once, a real shiner. He's a bright kid and his parents try to encourage him. They've told him that mighty oaks from little acorns grow. He does his best but he knows there are problems at home – he knows his mum and dad aren't happy.
- this person is working hard to get better at writing on the computer. He's trying to reach Level 4 in English. But he gets angry when the computer tries to correct his spelling – he can see his reflection in the screen.

Incidentally, this last idea raised an interesting point. I too had always seen this detail as a boy reaching for something beyond him –

– until a nine year old suggested he was waving to some buildings far away (and subsequently on an INSET day a member of staff imagined the child trapped between two sheets of plate glass!).

This is an effective activity for developing children's powers of interpretation. Implicit in the game is the notion that even something apparently clear and simple may be interpreted in different ways. The point can also be made that actually we can't see into other people's minds, although it's a common thing for people to 'mind-read' – to project their own thoughts and feelings onto somebody else.

Once children are familiar with the game of 'the world inside', the template can be used for reviewing their understanding of characters encountered in books, for planning fictional characters of their own, and also as a way of dealing with their own issues and problems (see *ALPS StoryMaker*, p. 178).

> **Tip:** By keeping copies of the 'circle characters' your group creates, you soon build up a useful resource bank for future storymaking.

◆ Add-a-bit

This activity helps children who currently find it difficult to make up characters, while encouraging them to 'think beyond the obvious'. In a more elaborated form, it also counterbalances the tendency to use stock characters in stories or to think in stereotypes.

The simplest version of the game is to take a descriptive detail from a character in a book – or a detail that you have just made up – and ask the child to add a bit.

Detail	Add a bit
This character – Sara – is a girl of twelve. She has long dark hair.	She wears it straight.

The easiest way to extend the activity is to encourage the child to 'add a bit more'…

Detail	Add a bit more
This character – Sara – is a girl of twelve. She has long dark hair.	• She wears it straight. • She washes it every other day. • Her favourite hair clip is made of silver. • Once she put in a red streak and her mum was very cross!

'Add-a-bit' combines the two useful educational tools of *scaffolding* and *chunking*. A 'scaffold' is a support structure put around something that can't stand up by itself. As it is strengthened and completed, however, the scaffolding can be removed. You can see that the Add-a-bit game as it stands is quite highly scaffolded.

'Chunking' means presenting and considering information at different levels or scales, or in more or less detail. The Add-a-bit game thus far is 'chunked down' so that the child is working with just a few small details. If you were looking at the character's entire lifespan and asking the child to add significant and major events to the time line, you would have 'chunked up' considerably.

You can use the details added by the child to develop a description and understanding of the character Sara in different directions…

◆ SECTION FOUR

Detail added	Add a bit more about Sara's relationship with her mum
(This character – Sara – is a girl of twelve. She has long dark hair). Once she put in a red streak and her mum was very cross!	• Sara's mum cuts her hair. • Sara's mum loves Sara's hair; she's proud of it. • Sara's mum wants Sara to get a good job. Sara thinks Mum pushes her a bit too hard to do well at school. • Sara loves her mum and helps her with the shopping on Friday.

Or…

Detail added	Add a bit more about the things that Sara values
Her favourite hair clip is made of silver.	• Sara's favourite favourite thing is a teddy bear called Clarence. • She also loves a photograph of her Grandma who died last year. • She does not take her little brother Richard for granted (though they quarrel sometimes!). • She really likes Indian food, but they can't afford it very often so it's a real treat.

Clearly, every detail that's added creates an opportunity to 'add a bit more' in your chosen direction of enquiry. Sara values her teddy bear – so what other possessions does she treasure? She values the photo of Grandma – what other fond memories does Sara have? She values her brother Richard – so what other relationships are precious in Sara's life? This particular focus raises a child's awareness that values are not just to do with possessions. Interesting, challenging and pertinent questions can arise from this:

• Do you think that Sara values her teddy bear more than her memories of Grandma?
• Can something that doesn't cost much to buy have great value?
• Can you value feelings?
• How do you know that you value something?

- How do you know *how much* you value something?
- Can two people value the same thing by different 'amounts'?
- What are some ways of measuring the value(s) of something?

> **Note:** Questions like these take us into the realms of philosophical enquiry. Philosophy for children (P4C) is a powerful tool for developing children's thinking and emotional resourcefulness. Stories and poems are often used as a platform for such enquiry, and although their use in this context is beyond the scope of **StoryMaker Catch Pack**, subsequent publications are intended to address the issue.

As I've suggested, 'Add-a-bit' can also be used with extant characters from books, including stereotypes. The CD resource for *Catch Pack* looks particularly at characters in the Horror genre with an emphasis on their traditional powers, strengths and weaknesses. Can I also encourage you to mix and match the activities in the *StoryMaker* books to form more effective strategies for thinking and learning? 'Add-a-bit' can also be used with, for instance, 'The world inside', 'Character pie', 'Character pyramid' and many others. Nor does it need to focus exclusively on characters. Use it also in connection with storylines; see 'Parallel story' on p.173 and in the CD resource as a way of extending 'Add-a-bit' into the area of plotting.

◆ How tall, how strong?

Younger children tend to perceive the world in terms of opposites and extremes – a person is tall or short, fat or thin, ugly or beautiful, etc. As we become more sophisticated thinkers we realise that the world is not black-or-white but exhibits infinite variety. In effect, in terms of perceptions, beliefs, attitudes, feelings, we *mediate between binary opposites* so that our mental maps-of-understanding reflect more closely the world's complexity.

You can develop and accelerate this process in children by playing the 'How tall, how strong?' game. Previously, perhaps using a coin to generate answers, your children might have asked: Is this character male? Is this character a good guy? Is this character tall? Using the template overleaf, children are encouraged to ask 'how much/how many?' questions.

You can use the template from scratch – as a first step in character design – or to develop a character whose basic details are known. Although values for the different qualities can be reached through discussion (the true basis of mediation), another approach is to use dice rolls to choose values at random.

◆ SECTION FOUR

How...						
	1	2	3	4	5	6
tall						
strong						
smart						
wealthy						
powerful						
attractive						
popular						
confident						
intelligent						
selfish						
cunning						
evil						

If you choose this way, use the following procedure:

- Explain first that the numbers 1–6 are not units of measurement but *degrees of comparison*. And so if you were to ask 'How tall is this person?' and roll 1, that would mean the character is very short compared to most other people; it doesn't mean that he is one foot tall! Once the roll is made (say it's 4/6) ask the children to articulate what that means.

- Now go on to find out how strong this person is – but ask, 'What do we mean by strong?' Children will of course talk about muscular strength, but they'll also quite likely talk about 'strong-minded' or having strong feelings. Draw out from the children what they mean by these ideas, and feed back to them. So we should maybe roll the dice three times: once to find out how physically strong this person is, then to find out how strong-minded, then to find out how strong this character's feelings can be…

- There is also an ideal opportunity here to explore interesting and relevant questions such as:
  - if someone is strong-minded, must they always have strong feelings too?
  - can someone who is physically very weak be very strong-minded?
  - can the opposite be true?
  - can you be strong-minded in some ways but not others?
  - what do you think 'weak-minded' means, then?

- how do you know if you are weak-minded?
- can you ever make yourself stronger-minded?

And so on. This game allows children to realise very powerfully that words have different meanings, depending on how they are used*.

> *When I was working with one group, a Year 5 girl called Ellie asked, 'How smart is this character?' and rolled a six. Nearby, Duane said, 'She must be a really intelligent person.' I pointed out that we already had 'intelligent' further down the list – so was there any difference between 'intelligent' and 'smart'? Ellie promptly replied, 'When you're intelligent you do well in your SATs. And when you're smart you do well in the rest of your life.'
>
> I told her that was a very smart reply.

- Continue down the list. You will probably end up with some interesting contradictions. (I think it was Somerset Maugham who said that 'human beings are bundles of contradictions'.) This allows you to explore the character in greater depth, and communicates the message that people are necessarily diverse and often inconsistent – and here I can quote Aldous Huxley, who asserted that 'the only completely consistent people are dead'.

- Invite the group to add more items to the list. Roll the dice and discuss what the result means.

- Play a game of 'What if?' with the group. Say 'Well, now that we know much more about this character, what if she found a wallet packed with money lying on the street one day?' Some children may begin by saying what *they* would do, in which case encourage them to put themselves into the character's shoes: how would the character act in a way that was congruent with what we have already learned about her? Focusing a child's attention in this way develops empathy and reinforces the diversity, complexity *and the reality* of a person's 'inner world'.

By making the practice of mediation habitual – by training the skill – growing learner-thinkers will develop the tendency to review and question their beliefs and interpretations more effectively. Reflection will be their default state rather than knee-jerk reflex opinions, generalisations and simplistic connections. Think back if you will to the section 'A note on creativity', p.13. Review your assessment of the statements offered and then reflect on how you come to hold those beliefs and opinions. With this in mind, it seems to me that the two most dangerous words in the language are 'They say. . .'

◆ SECTION FOUR

◆ Monster-maker

In finding our own voice as writers we rely heavily on the ideas and styles of others. My earliest stories were rehashes of plots from *Dr Who* and *Star Trek*. (Some would say I haven't changed!) Children's writing is often highly derivative, and I think that this is a necessary stage of development. However, we should encourage innovation wherever possible. Use the grid below to 'locate' common monsters in genre fiction, and to create some new ones.

Origin of Monster \ Nature of Monster	Person	Creative	Object	Place	Force
The monster comes from elsewhere.					
The monster comes from within.					
The monster is created by people.					

So according to these parameters, the Frankenstein monster is a person/creature that has been created by people. Edward Hyde is a monster that comes from within, but is essentially a person – the dark side of Dr Jekyll. A ghost (if you choose to call a ghost a monster) is a force that has come from within, being the disembodied spirit of a person.

- Now encourage children to explore the grid further. What would a monster from elsewhere that is an object be like? How would a monster that is a place created by people behave?*

> * One of the most frightening 'monsters' of this variety is Hill House – a place that was 'born bad' – and the setting for Shirley Jackson's excellent adult novel **The Haunting of Hill House**. The story was filmed in 1963 as **The Haunting**, directed by Robert Wise. It is infinitely superior, in my opinion, to the recent remake. Wise's film has a 12 rating, by the way – though I still can't sit through it by myself...

STORYMAKER CATCH PACK – USING GENRE FICTION AS A RESOURCE FOR ACCELERATED LEARNING

- Apply the grid to 'monsters' from Science Fiction and Fantasy. How well do they fit the pattern?

◆ Monster as metaphor

One of the ongoing issues in education is boys' motivation, especially in the area of literacy. One aim of *Catch Pack* is to make stories involving for children; to engage them in the active process of imagination as they read, write and tell stories from the three genres which form the emphasis of this book. But that is not the only justification for going into the realm of Horror fiction – I am not interested in using the elements of Horror stories as a way of sugaring the pill of writing. Kieran Egan in *Teaching as Storytelling* asserts that one of the deep values of Fantasy – and I suggest the same is true of Horror fiction – is that it acts as a kind of 'conceptual workshop': something more than simply casual entertainment, but a medium through which we make sense of the world and our experience. In this way all fiction acts as a template for the characters, situations, themes, motifs and outcomes we encounter in real life. Ironically, the mirror of fiction reflects profound truths about ourselves.

This process happens from early childhood. One of the key points of Egan's thesis is that even very young children must be engaging in complex processing in order to make sense of fairy tales. Higher-order thinking (though not yet the ability to fully articulate the outcomes) must be going on for these stories to mean anything. If a child appreciates Cinderella, for example, she must have wired up in her mind the general abstract concepts of hope and fear, love and hate, good and bad, jealousy, coincidence, and have in place the aesthetic sense of the 'rightness' of the story's resolution.

Take these conceptual tools forward some years and apply them to the Horror genre. Look at the great works of Horror fiction and we can appreciate the 'meaning-making' value of Frankenstein, Dracula and others. In understanding these tales we are using many of the same skills necessary to make sense of, say, history – a sense of causality and justice, an understanding of the struggle for freedom against violence, the power of knowledge over ignorance, and many more.

As teachers we don't necessarily need to make this explicit to our pupils. Because we recognise the connections we can build them in as part of the educational underpinning of what we do. As far as the boys are concerned, they are just talking about monsters.

- One way of raising awareness of the issues I've been discussing is to look at famous storybook monsters and begin to 'unpack' what they represent. Doing this also leads to a greater appreciation of why their stories are so powerful and have lingered in people's imaginations.

  - **Dracula** is immortal and powerful, is a shape-shifter; but he can be active only through the hours of darkness. His loneliness and longing for either life or death are immeasurable. During daylight he must rest on his own grave soil. He is physically incorruptible, but soulless and emotionally tainted. He is compelled to feed on blood, which represents the essence of human life. He lives, therefore, at second hand in a world of shadows. He is the ultimate parasite, pathetic and pitiable.

- **Frankenstein's monster** is the result of human curiosity and, perhaps, the outcome of Man's meddling beyond his capabilities. The creature is made up of parts, *but the whole is not more than the sum of those parts*. He does not even have a name which we attach to our own sense of self, identity and belonging in time and space. He is incomplete. What is missing? Does he have a soul? Is he innocent? He also represents the terrible consequences of his creator's actions – the creature destroys Victor Frankenstein's family. He is the product of ignorance and compulsion more than that of science, wisdom and the spirit of adventure.

- **The Mummy** is love that will not lie down! In movies the mummy is the priest-guard Kharis, protector of the Princess Ananka. Their stories are intertwined through great spans of time. The creature is hope and devotion, love and revenge shining brightly among death, decay and a long bygone age. There is a certain terrible nobility and heart-aching sense of romance in the mummy's reanimation. The creature also represents one culture's unshakable faith in the afterlife and its links with our actions now, in mortal form. Again we return to cause and effect, actions and consequences. The mummy represents such yearning and, perhaps, such awful regret at what might have been.

- Ask young writers to work in the same way with other 'classic' monsters: Wolfman, Phantom of the Opera, Jekyll & Hyde, The Invisible Man, the Zombie.

    - Encourage children to trawl through contemporary kids' Horror stories (*Goosebumps*, the work of R. L. Stine, etc.) and think about how the monsters might be more than just creatures sent to scare us (even if the authors think that's only what they are!).
    - Explore myths and legends to see how the monsters that appear in today's paperbacks and cartoons and movies often have their origins in ancient stories. Look through books of folklore* for 'new' monsters that can be used in Horror tales.

> * For example, **A Dictionary of Fairies** by Katherine Briggs. See Bibliography.
>
> You can often finds books of old legends and traditional tales in good second-hand bookshops. See the Links page on the CD resource for some links to follow.

- **Personify emotions**. Just as classic monsters symbolise feelings such as longing, regret, revenge, etc., so other emotions can be personified as new monsters. So, if Jealousy was a person, what would (s)he look like? How would (s)he behave? What would his/her motives be?
- **Look at fears**. The writer Stuart Voytilla (see Bibliography) suggests that the underlying fear in Fantasy, SF and Horror is powerlessness. Built on that are more local or personal fears – of darkness, being alone, creatures in great numbers, the

unknown. Look at why monsters frighten us and in what ways. You can keep this activity generalised; there's no need to ask individual children what scares them, but points that have personal relevance can be made. This activity follows the principle that raising awareness leads to greater understanding, which in turn gives us greater control. The activity reinforces the link between 'monsters' in a general sense, their motivations, the feelings connected to their deeds, and their symbolic value.

◆ Character grid

A 6×6 (or 5×5, etc.) grid is a basic, versatile visual organiser and a useful tool for storymaking. I tend to favour 6×6 because items can be chosen randomly through dice rolls, as we saw using the Fantasy grid on p.65.

A related activity allows writers to categorise characters they've read about, seen on TV or written about themselves, and in an almost endlessly variable way. In the example below, two parameters serve to guide children's thinking within the Fantasy, SF and Horror genres.

	More human →					Less human
Good	1	2	3	4	5	6
1	*					*
2						
3						
4						
5						
6	*					*
Evil						

Here, characters can be organised according to how human or non-human they are, and how good or evil they are. (This activity is like mediating between binary opposites with another dimension added.) When I run this game as a workshop, I mark out the extremes – 1/1 is totally human and thoroughly good… 6/1 is completely non-human but also thoroughly good… 1/6 is human but incredibly evil… 6/6 is utterly non-human and evil through and through. 1/1 and 1/6 especially represent the stereotype characters of the square-jawed hero and the despicable villain, while 6/6 is the stock monster whose job it is to terrorise its victims before being destroyed by the hero (1/1).

◆ SECTION FOUR

The value and power of the game lies in exploring some of the other character positions represented by the empty boxes. 3/4, for instance, would be a fascinating character: a creature that is only half-human (human in which particular ways, I wonder?) and capable of both good and evil acts (under what circumstances?). Immediately this perspective opens up a rich field of speculation. What does this character look like? What is it thinking and how does it see the world? (cf. 'The world inside', p.95). What would be the consequences if it were introduced as a character into a story that already exists? (see 'Parallel story', p.173).

You may want to use the grid for characters out of SF, Fantasy and Horror at the same time. However, if you looked at each genre separately, you would get more ideas from the group – What is 3/4 like as a Science Fiction character? What is it like as a Fantasy character? What is it like as a Horror character?

Here are some ideas for varying the use of the 6×6 grid:

- Change one or both parameters from time to time. So, for instance, you might replace more/less human with small–large. This encourages children to reconfigure the information they already have: some characters will be placed in different positions, some will no longer fit on the grid, while new characters are suddenly 'eligible' for inclusion.
- Use of the 6×6 template can apply in other subject domains. Allow children to review a topic on animals or dinosaurs, for example, by choosing parameters such as small–large, slow–fast, cold climate–hot climate, gentle–fierce.
- Use the template below to make the game less rigid. This organiser allows for more flexibility in positioning characters relative to each other.
- Use a similar template for thinking about landscapes. Use parameters such as flat–mountainous, cold climate–hot climate.
- Create character thumbnails on cards to fit on a 6×6 grid wall display. Thumbnails are small file cards on which are written some basic details about an invented character (see opposite).

Good and human	Good and non-human
Evil and human	Evil and non-human

◆ Thumbnails

In computer terms a 'thumbnail' is a small representation of something larger and more complex. Similarly, a 'thumbnail sketch' is a quick drawing or description that includes a few main features.

This idea can be used in storymaking. A character thumbnail, for example, fits neatly on a 127x76mm (5'x 3") record card and would contain interesting and useful pieces of information that a child has generated (or gleaned from somebody else's story). Suggest that there is at least one item of physical description, a personality trait, an event or experience from the past, and some indication of the character's plans for the future. I also encourage children to include at least one 'unique detail'. Because of the limited space on the card, a child will need to use discernment and judgement in selecting what she will write. A typical thumbnail might look like this:

> Don Jones – tall, dark-haired, 23 years old. He has a thin scar above his left eye. Don never had much of a chance in life. His father ran a used-car business in North London and was always on the fringes of the criminal underworld. Recently Don has come into some money through a Lottery win. He has big plans to travel the world and set up some kind of business – nothing illegal. But he has little confidence in himself and feels frightened to make a start.
>
> physical strength – 3/6, intelligence – 5/6, goodness 4/6

If you run this activity through a few times during the year – and it doesn't take long if characters have already been created using other storymaking games – you'll have a resource of almost 100 character cards that can be used in various ways:

- Play sequencing games. List the characters in alphabetical order of surname, or chronological order of age, or the order in which a child would like to meet these people.
- Select some cards at random and list any similarities between two or more characters.
- If your group makes a set of genre-character cards, fit as many as possible on to the 6×6 grid (see p.105).
- Have children work with thumbnails created by somebody else. Using discussion, coins, dice, etc., have the group elaborate on the thumbnail information.
- Draw out some cards at random and work out how these characters would fit together in a story.
- Collect some everyday items that might reasonably belong to a character described on a thumbnail. Explain how the character came by these things. Choose one object that is highly significant for that character and explain why.

◆ SECTION FOUR

Diamond ranking

Diamond Ranking is a technique for allowing some flexibility in sequencing items. Instead of a linear list of (in this case) character thumbnails ranked in order of how much you'd like to meet those individuals, use a template like this:

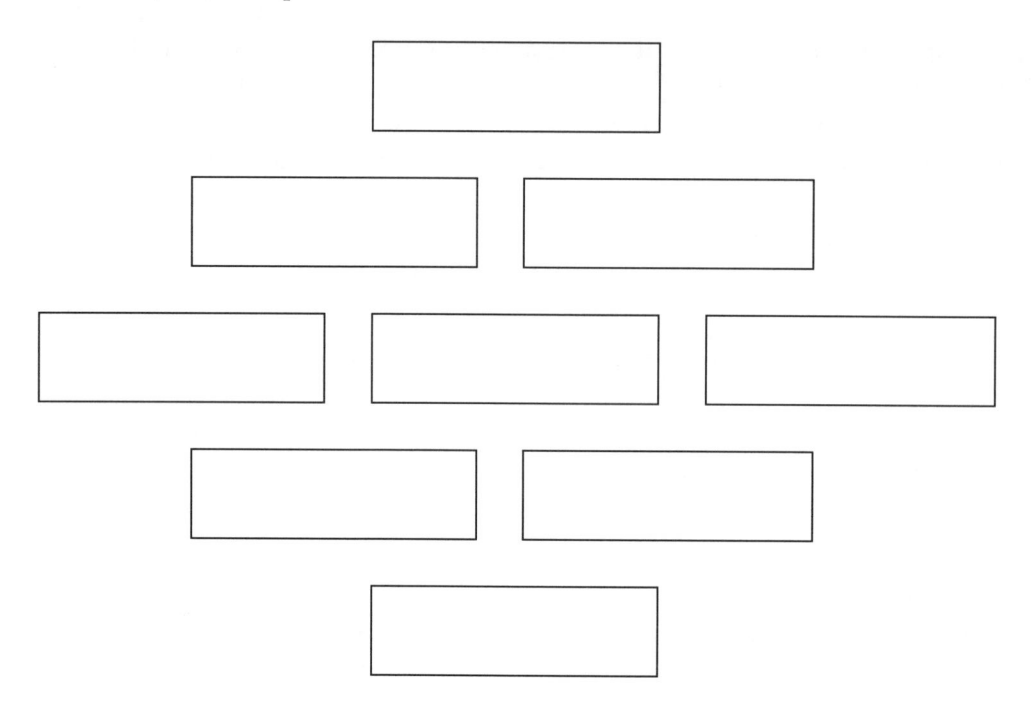

Follow up with discussion which compares (but does not judge) children's rankings. Ask individual children to explain the reasoning behind their choices.

Living graphs

Mel Rockett and Simon Percival in *Thinking for Learning* (see Bibliography) advocate living graphs as being one of the most productive types of thinking for learning strategies. A living graph makes information more accessible by personalising it, thus taking some of the threat out of analysing and interpreting data. As with many of the techniques to be found in the fields of Thinking for Learning, Accelerated Learning, etc., practising them first in the safe and engaging environment of storymaking gives children greater confidence and capability when those same techniques need to be applied in other domains.

In the example below, the subject is Don Jones from the thumbnail on page 107. The two parameters giving meaning and structure to the graph are 'time' and 'courage'. The graph plots a week in Don's life and how his levels of bravery versus cowardice vary during that period.

A BAGFUL OF STORY GAMES

Courage

Cowardice

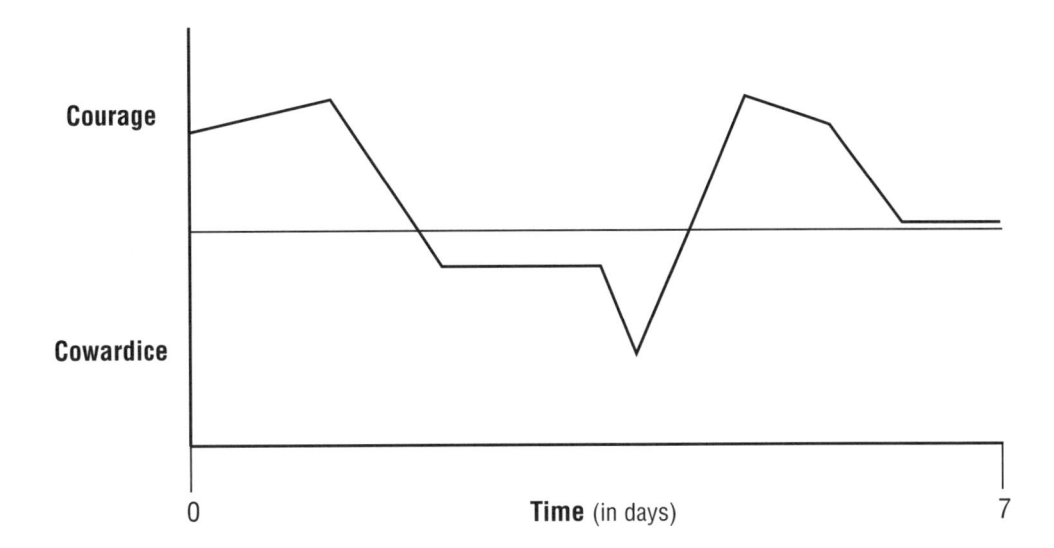

0   **Time** (in days)   7

- The most basic activity invites children to account for the peaks and troughs in the graph. In other words, what might have been happening in Don's life that could cause these reactions?
- Keep the graph line the same but change one or both parameters. So, instead of 'courage' have 'wealth' or 'stress levels'. A little ingenuity will supply you with plenty of ideas.
- Keep the graph the same but change the time span, so that instead of Don's courage varying over one week, make it one day or one hour. The children will need to reinterpret the data to fit the new parameter.
- Add a second graph line belonging to another character. Discuss the relationship between Don and, let's say, Sarah, and account for the differences in their 'bravery factor'.

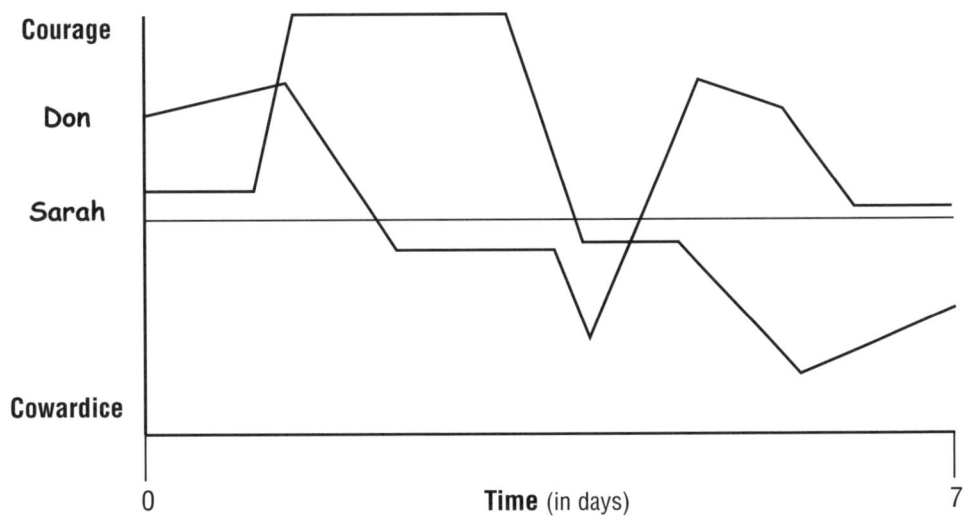

Courage

Don

Sarah

Cowardice

0   **Time** (in days)   7

◆ SECTION FOUR

- Add a second graph line relating to Don, based on another parameter. So, we keep the horizontal axis of time, but the vertical axis now represents , 'bravery' and, say, 'wealth'. Ask children to account for the relationship between the two lines, i.e. what happens to Don during the week that affects his level of courage and the fatness of his wallet!

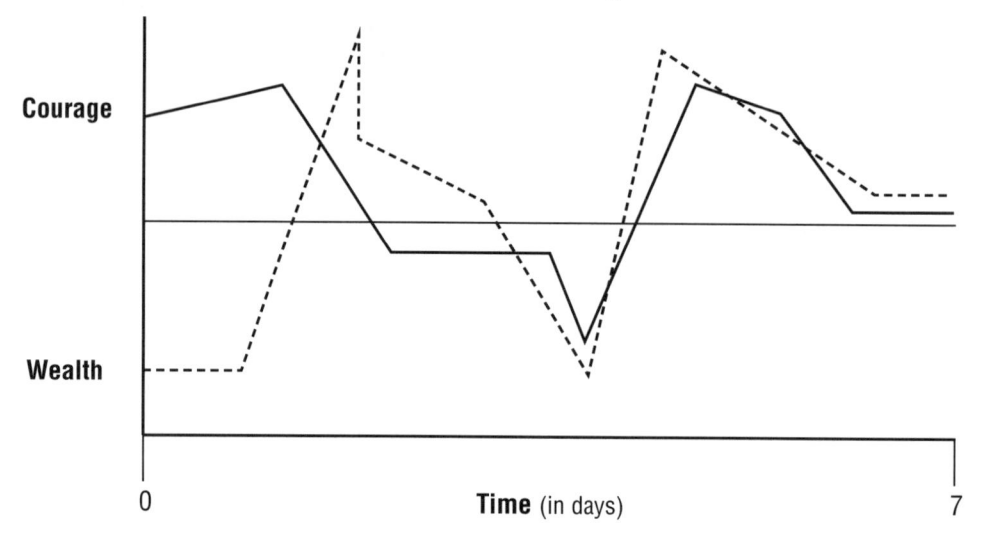

Courage

Wealth

0   **Time** (in days)   7

- Increase the sophistication of children's interpretation by adding a third, fourth line, etc., which traces different parameters in this part of Don's life.
- Ask children to construct living graphs based on stories they've read. For instance, set the task of plotting a living graph based on *Nanoman*. Have children work out the time-span of the story (see also see *ALPS StoryMaker,* p.132) with degrees of danger on a 1–6 scale, where 1 is minimal danger and 6 is mortal danger. A worked example is given below – although this is not intended to be 'the right answer'.

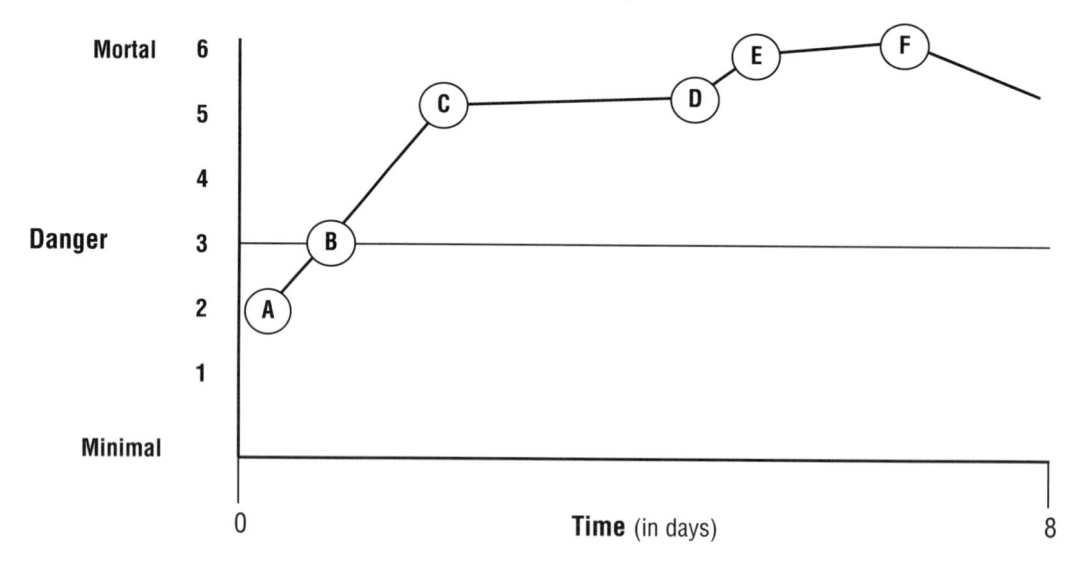

Mortal 6
         5   C   D   E   F
         4
Danger 3   B
         2 A
         1
Minimal
         0   **Time** (in days)   8

STORYMAKER CATCH PACK – USING GENRE FICTION AS A RESOURCE FOR ACCELERATED LEARNING

A Skat and her companions meet with 'John Doe' in the coffee shop.

B Skat and her friends move through the market quarter of the city, hiding from the Zone Kops.

C A patrol of Zone Kops passes by too closely for comfort.

D Skat's party reaches the recycle yard where they rendezvous with Hammer.

E Skat and her companions are ambushed by the General's troops and make their escape.

F The scarab vehicle in which Skat and her friends are travelling is shot down. The occupants escape…

Apart from practising the useful skill of manipulating data to create the living graph, through this visual representation children can have insights about the pacing of a story, in terms of both moving through time and increasing and decreasing the tension.

- Use the graph above with another group. Don't tell them the story it derives from; instead, ask them to suggest a storyline that fits the pattern
- The *Nanoman* graph is plot based. Have children superimpose another graph line plotting, say, Skat's level of fear through time, as these crises unfold.
- Use living graphs with story ingredients (see p. 175). Colour-coded templates are available on the CD resource. Here a circle represents *danger*, a star represents *conflict*, a triangle represents *mystery*. Have children plot a story by interpreting the available data, which is to say, judging the level or degree of danger, etc., what might have caused it (speculation), and how the different graph lines correlate.

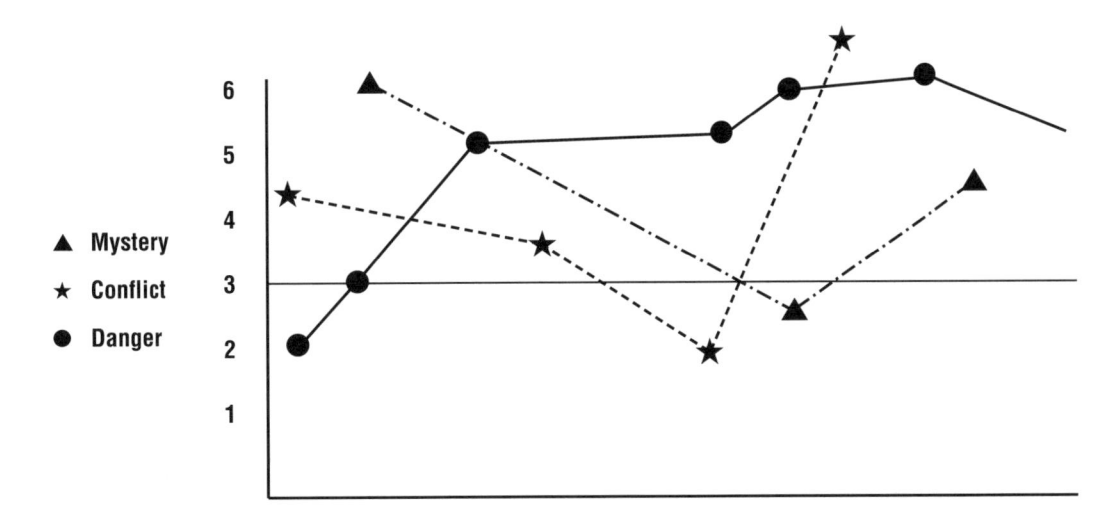

◆ SECTION FOUR

◆ Advanced thumbnails

Once children are familiar with character thumbnails you can run these more sophisticated versions of the game, which explore in greater depth the inner worlds of the characters. You can use basic thumbnails that have already been created as a starting point.

Version 1 – uses the template below. For more information about these ideas see *The Seven Habits of Highly Effective People* by Stephen R. Covey (see Bibliography). Clearly, children can use the organiser to think about themselves.

Basic description	(Picture)
Strengths	Weaknesses
Personal qualities (Assets/resources)	Negatively used
What allows me to do things in life? (Motivating principles)	What stops me from doing things in life? (Limiting beliefs)
Ideas that make me stronger (Empowering ideas)	Thoughts that make me weaker (Disabling self-talk)
The values I hold which help me (Positive paradigm)	Values I hold which hinder me (Negative paradigm)

- Guide children through first use of this thumbnail. Raise their awareness of what personal qualities are, and how they can be regarded as assets and resources (see also Gathering Treasures, p.125). Ask how these qualities might, however, be used in a negative way; a high level of verbal skill, for example, could be used to weave persuasive deceits; great physical beauty might be used to curry favour, etc.
- Raise awareness of the fact that ideas have power. (It has been said that ideas are the currency of the twenty-first century.) Explore what is meant by 'an idea'; wonder how ideas can be good or bad – are they good or bad in themselves, or are they made so by their application?

- Contrast an idea with a value. Explore the differences. 'Goodness begets goodness' is an idea. What values is it related to? Point out that networks of values form 'paradigms'. These are the perceptual boxes in which we live. Raise children's awareness of the expression living 'inside (or outside!) the box'. Discuss the notion of a mindset and make the point that 'set' can also mean set hard, like concrete. In terms of personal paradigms, a mindset is an unchallenged set of beliefs. How can a mindset be liberating and empowering? How can it be limiting? How can you break out of a limiting mindset?

Version 2 is based on the work of Robert Dilts (see Bibliography) who devised the neurological levels model of understanding and modifying patterns of behaviour. Put very simply, Dilts suggests that we can gain insights to how we behave – in terms of patterns of thoughts, feelings and physiology – by noticing how we express our understanding of the world through language. Limiting language will be related to one or more neurological levels. Challenging that language, and working at a more profound level, will help to change the behaviour in question. For useful elaboration of these ideas see, for example, Carol Harris's book *The Elements of NLP*.

For our purposes, and to introduce the notion of a hierarchical framework within which a person lives, apply the template below to our old friend Don Jones. Even using the minimal information on the thumbnail, we can see that Don's lack of confidence in himself to set up a business enterprise is based on limitations at the level of belief. If we were to devise a storyline around Don, we could fill in the neurological levels chart in parallel, each informing the other.

Level of	This means	How it applies to
environment	where and when we do things; opportunities and constraints	
behaviour	what we do; our actions and reactions	
capability	how well we do things; how we plan and use our skills and reasses our plans	
belief	why we do things; what moves us to act and what limits our actions	
identity	who we think we are; our sense of self; what defines us	
spirit	what we do things for; our sense of deeper purpose and place in the universe; an appreciation of something beyond and greater than ourselves	

◆ SECTION FOUR

◆ Context sentences and connective prompting

Context sentences actually have no context, the aim being to supply one. Because we are naturally curious, a context sentence always begs a number of questions…

> *Jones lay slumped on the sofa.*

What questions occur to you right now? You can make this activity more systematic by encouraging children to ask as many 'what' questions as possible, 'where' questions, 'why' questions, etc. – see 'Six Big Important Questions', p.70. Such a questioning process often throws up insights into Jones (in this case) and therefore ideas for stories that involve him.

Context sentence work can be combined with *connective prompting*. A connective prompt is a word that encourages a link between two or more statements/ideas.

The connective prompt *'because'* encourages logical links. Usually when I run this activity I set it up as a game. I explain that 'because' is like a link in a chain. And so –

> *Jones lay slumped on the sofa –* **because** *– he was tired.*

That counts as one link. The aim of the game could be to make as long a chain as possible, perhaps within a given time. Explain at the outset that 'because' has to link with an idea that follows on logically and sensibly, so ideas such as 'Jones lay slumped on the sofa because he was wearing purple slippers' or 'because he was a zombie and had just chainsawed twenty people' aren't acceptable.

This is part of a chain that a group of Year 5 children constructed recently:

> Jones lay slumped on the sofa – **because** – he was tired. He was tired – **because** – he'd been working hard – **because** – he wanted to earn more money – **because** – he wanted to buy a new car – **because** – he wanted to impress his new girlfriend – **because** – she liked boyfriends who had fancy new cars – **because** – as a little girl her family was poor and couldn't afford a new car – **because** – her father was lazy – **because** – no one had ever encouraged him…

This chain, of over twenty links in all, took a couple of minutes to create, but notice how much information we got out of it. We gained insights into Jones's work, his motivations, his social life – then the emphasis hopped effortlessly to Jones's girlfriend. We learned more of her attitude and background, and discovered something significant about her family, her father in particular. This swift gathering of information is one big advantage of the game.

A possible disadvantage is the unpredictable nature of the children's off-the-top-of-the-head responses. Sometimes (and sometimes kids do it deliberately!) the game 'sails close to the wind' and children come up with risqué ideas. One way of controlling this tendency is to use the three-card system: have a *green* card showing as long as answers are acceptable; hold up a *yellow* card if responses are close to the line, and when you reach for the *red* card the children know that the game will stop and that you are not pleased. These visual cues for behaviour are effective and usually you will not need the red card at all.

> **Tip:** Sometimes – as in SATs tests – children have to make up stories quickly. Encourage them to do some connective prompting during their, albeit brief, thinking time. They won't make up the best storyline in the world, but at least they'll have something to write about.

Connective prompting and the Six Big Important Questions

Once such a 'story chain' has been constructed, you can go back and explore it in more detail. Take one segment, ask some questions, and collect responses.

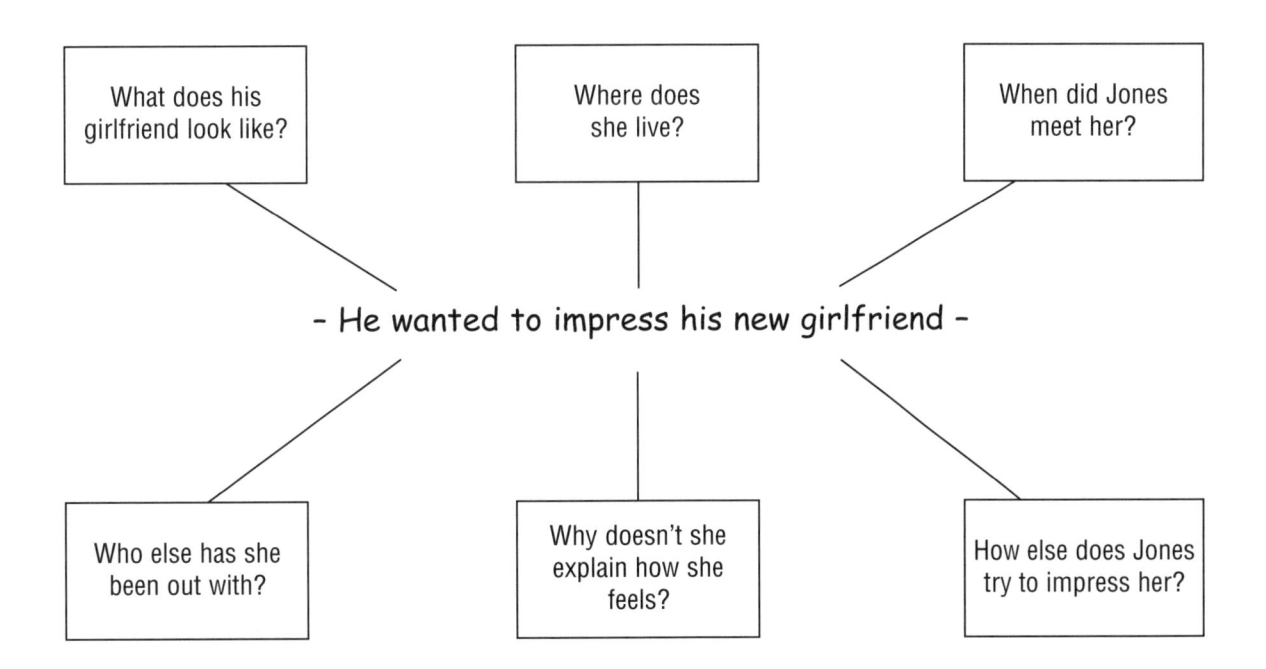

```
┌─────────────────┐      ┌─────────────┐      ┌─────────────────┐
│ What does his   │      │ Where does  │      │ When did Jones  │
│ girlfriend look │      │ she live?   │      │ meet her?       │
│ like?           │      │             │      │                 │
└────────┬────────┘      └──────┬──────┘      └────────┬────────┘
         \                      |                      /
          — He wanted to impress his new girlfriend —
         /                      |                      \
┌─────────────────┐      ┌─────────────┐      ┌─────────────────┐
│ Who else has    │      │ Why doesn't │      │ How else does   │
│ she been out    │      │ she explain │      │ Jones try to    │
│ with?           │      │ how she     │      │ impress her?    │
│                 │      │ feels?      │      │                 │
└─────────────────┘      └─────────────┘      └─────────────────┘
```

Connective prompting and lensing

(See 'Lensing' on p.61) You can revisit a context sentence and lens a story chain through different genres. So, using our example sentence you might say, 'Today we are going to make a Fantasy story using this sentence…' Now the children's perception of Jones and his situation is being filtered through the lens of 'Fantasy' and all its associations –

◆ SECTION FOUR

> Jones lay slumped on the sofa because he was worn out after creating a particularly complicated spell.

and SF –

> Jones lay slumped on the sofa because he was an android that had malfunctioned.

and Horror –

> Jones lay slumped on the sofa because he was a vampire and needed to rest during the day.

Other connective prompts

Other connective prompt words include:

- **after** simply takes you forward chronologically and the logical glue between statements does not need to be so strong. 'After Jones lay slumped on the sofa he put on his purple slippers…'
- **before** takes you back through time, of course. The particular value of this connective prompting game is that it helps to break the 'Beginning–Middle–End Syndrome'. Children are quite rightly taught that stories have a beginning, a middle and an end. But storymaking does not need to proceed in that order. Jones lying slumped on the sofa might be a scene from the middle of his tale, or the story's final image. 'Before' invites us to track back through Jones's journey to gain insights into motivation, and the causes of effects that become apparent later on.
- **while/meanwhile/as** tempt you to take more of an overview of Jones's world and move about it freely, letting your attention settle like a spotlight in various places. Practising this version of the technique decreases the tendency of the writer to stay with one character throughout the story. So…

> **While** Jones lay slumped on the sofa two burglars crept into a room upstairs and stole his portable TV – **while** that was going on the wife of one of the burglars burned his supper accidentally – **while** this was happening a lady who lived across the road from Jones saw two shadowy figures in his bedroom – **meanwhile** the burglar's wife saw smoke coming from the kitchen and rang the fire brigade – and **while** they were racing to the scene Jones's neighbour was calling the police…

A BAGFUL OF STORY GAMES

Mixing and matching prompts

These and other connective prompts do not need to be used in isolation. You might begin a story chain with 'after' and where appropriate switch to 'because', and then open out the action with 'meanwhile'. This kind of versatility will come with practice.

Connective prompting and parallel story chains

We learned above about Jones and his girlfriend. A more sophisticated version of the game creates two chains simultaneously, using one or more connective prompt words. The diagram below also indicates that specific links can be made between the chains.

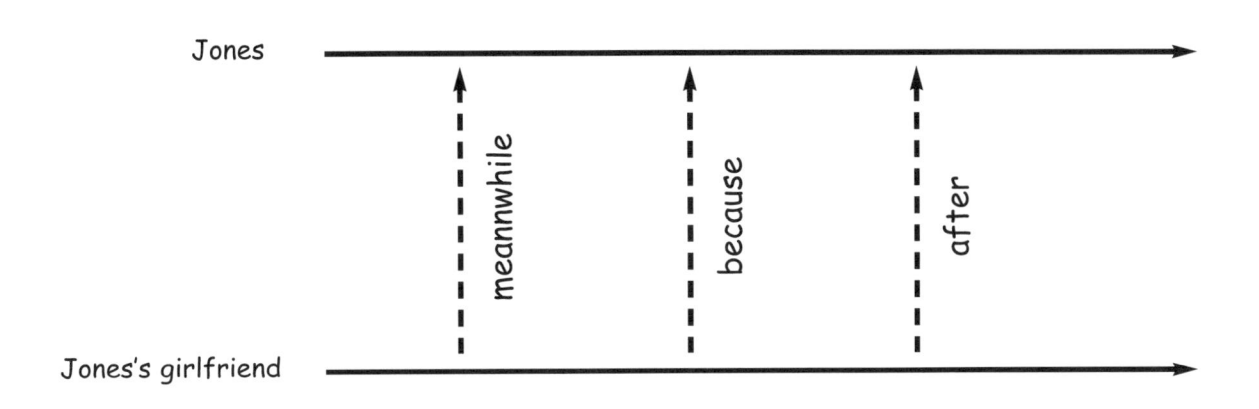

Diagram: Two parallel horizontal arrows labelled "Jones" (top) and "Jones's girlfriend" (bottom), connected by three vertical dashed lines labelled "meanwhile", "because", and "after".

Note: For connective prompting with regard to exploring feelings, see *ALPS StoryMaker*, p. 41.

◆ Fortune cookie phrases

The same tendency to contextualise that we found in context sentence work appears again with what I call 'fortune cookie phrases'– generalised statements such as you might find inside fortune cookies or in tabloid horoscopes – which tempt the imagination to fill in the details.

Imagine this phrase was related to the beginning of a story: 'Look for signals'. You might consider it on the basic level of a theme in the story. Or it might create a specific image: a guard looking out for some sign of danger or rescue, for example. Actually, choosing the level beforehand – theme, ingredient, motif, paragraph, sentence – primes you to see the phrase in that way.

The template overleaf (which is also reproduced on the CD resource as part of a writing game) can be used in a number of ways:

◆ SECTION FOUR

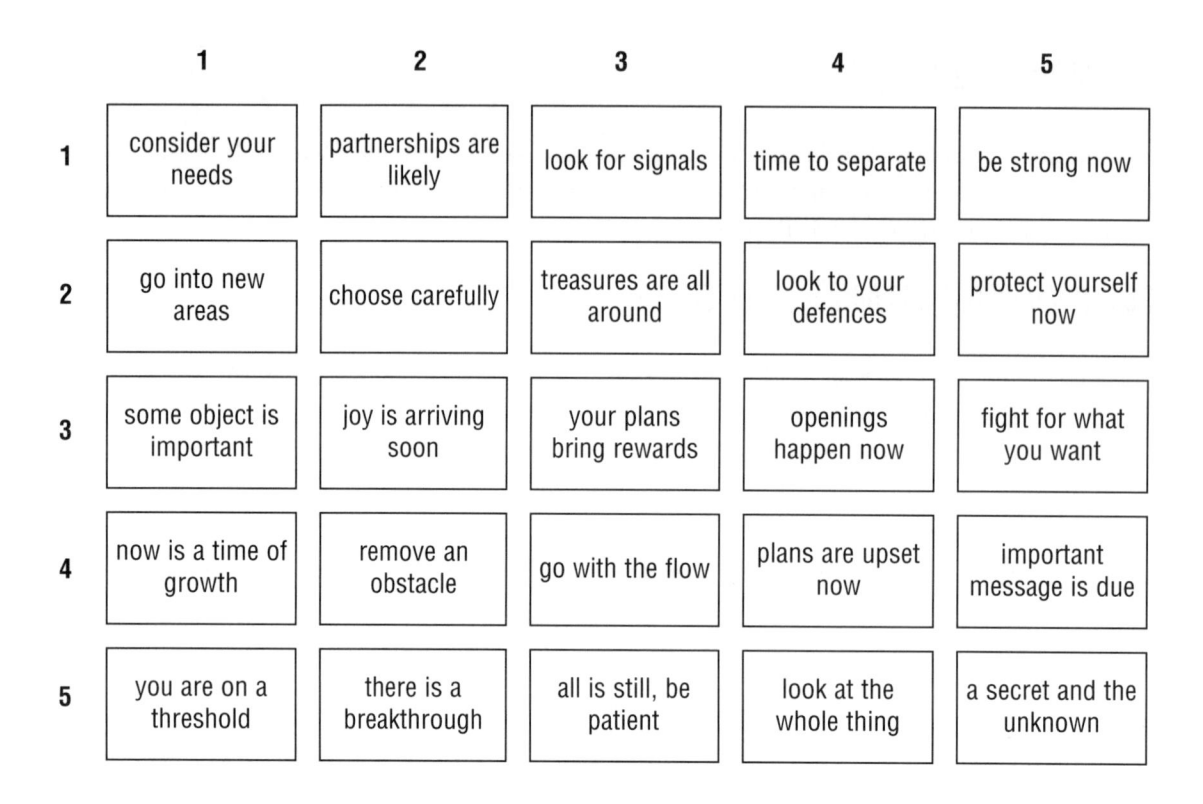

	1	2	3	4	5
1	consider your needs	partnerships are likely	look for signals	time to separate	be strong now
2	go into new areas	choose carefully	treasures are all around	look to your defences	protect yourself now
3	some object is important	joy is arriving soon	your plans bring rewards	openings happen now	fight for what you want
4	now is a time of growth	remove an obstacle	go with the flow	plans are upset now	important message is due
5	you are on a threshold	there is a breakthrough	all is still, be patient	look at the whole thing	a secret and the unknown

- Use dice rolls to choose two items at random. Combine them to create the opening scenario of your story.
- If a child gets stuck for ideas, ask her to choose a fortune cookie phrase and talk 'off the top of her head' (pole-bridging) about how it relates to the story so far. Even a brief session of 'muttering her understanding' in this way can put the storymaking back on track.
- Combine fortune cookie phrases with storylines. Give out templates like the example below, have children choose which genre they wish to work in, and ask them to fill in more details.

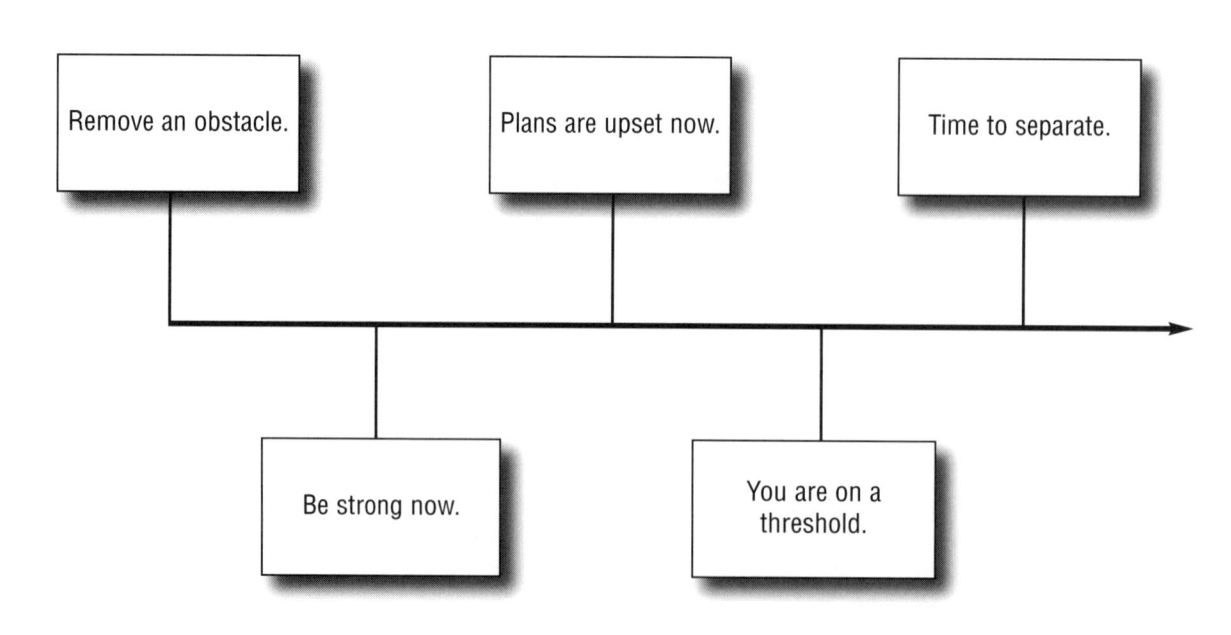

Remove an obstacle.

Plans are upset now.

Time to separate.

Be strong now.

You are on a threshold.

STORYMAKER CATCH PACK – USING GENRE FICTION AS A RESOURCE FOR ACCELERATED LEARNING

A BAGFUL OF STORY GAMES

- Combine fortune cookie phrases with story ingredients (see p.175). This can be done entirely randomly, completely through choice, or half-and-half. List some story ingredients and choose phrases to give them more focus. In these examples I used dice rolls. What ideas do they throw up in your mind as you read them?
    - danger – 5/3 fight for what you want
    - mystery – 4/4 plans are upset now
    - conflict – 4/5 look at the whole thing
    - secret – 2/4 remove an obstacle
    - treasure (something precious) – 1/3 some object is important.
- Use fortune cookie phrases to explore the 'inner world' of a character. Think about the phrases in a symbolic way. What might they represent in the character's life?

> Partnerships are likely
>
> Go with the flow
>
> You are on a threshold

- Combine fortune cookie phrases with a story map. Either supply a map with references already included, or ask children to choose phrases as they work through a dice journey. Choose your genre and explore the example below...

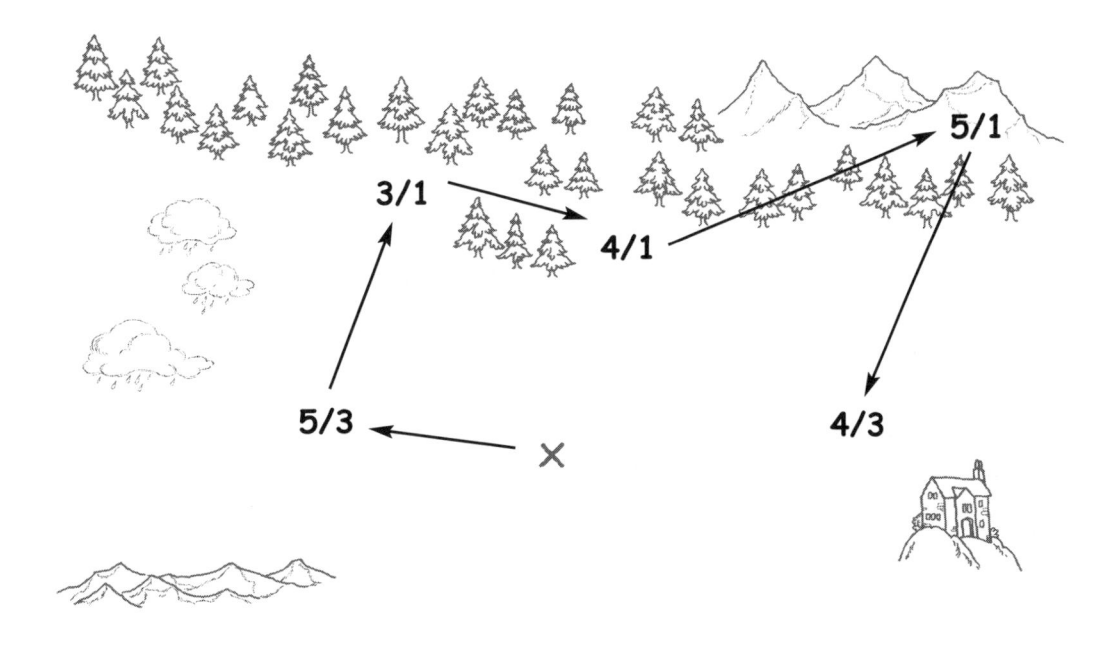

◆ SECTION FOUR

- Proverbs are a useful adjunct when working with fortune cookie phrases, being more particular examples of the general phrase. Either select a phrase and scan lists of proverbs to see which apply, or take a proverb and make it more general. Here are some to practise on.
  - A word to the wise is enough.
  - A calm comes before the storm.
  - All that glistens is not gold.
  - An old bird is not to be caught with chaff.
  - A little prevention is worth a lot of cure.
  - Catch the bear before you sell his skin.
  - Children are what you make them.
  - Catch not the shadow but lose the substance.
  - Do as I say, not as I do.
  - Don't put all of your eggs into one basket.
  - Every cloud has a silver lining.
  - Exchange is no robbery.
  - A faint heart never won a fair lady.
  - Fire is a good servant but a bad master.
  - Follow the river and you will find the sea.
  - Know which way the wind blows.
  - No use crying over spilt milk.
  - Kindle not a fire that you cannot put out.
  - Lend only what you can afford to lose.
  - Let sleeping dogs lie.
  - Liars should have good memories.
  - Many straws may bind an elephant.
  - Masters two will not do.

◆ Consequences

This is a variation of the old playground game.

- Prepare a template like the one opposite. Make copies and hand one to each member of the group. Each child chooses a theme, writes it down very briefly in the appropriate box, then folds the paper over so that the next section, 'Genre', is visible at the top.
- The papers are passed on. Another child chooses a genre (not necessarily SF, Fantasy or Horror), writes it down and folds the paper again so that 'Setting' is at the top. The papers are passed on and passed on until all the sections have been completed. Then unfold the papers to see the range of stories you've got.

- You can design different sections to suit your purposes. They might be much simpler such as: the hero/loves/hates/looks like/sounds like/dreams about/wears/he says/she says/consequences. Be clear at the outset how frivolous you want the game to be!
- Play the consequences game using the characters, settings, situations, motifs and dialogue from books already written. The game then becomes a good review activity.

Theme:
Genre:
Setting:
Hero:
Villain:
Other character:
Opening sentence:
Hero says:
Villain says:
Other character says:
Hero does:
Villain does:
Other character does:
Consequences...

◆ SECTION FOUR

◆ Odd-one-out

'Odd-one-out' used to be a standard 'exercise' (note the muscular vocabulary) in traditional English lessons. Which is the odd one out in the following list?

beech   elm   oak   apple   ash

If you are playing the game you are trying to work out the right answer. A child will know that the teacher has the right answer, and if she's struggling she'll be trying to guess what it is – a process that Edward de Bono has called 'reactive thinking'.

You can create a richer environment of language and ideas by playing the game in different ways:

- Look at each item in the list and decide on at least one factor for each that makes it the odd-one-out. For example…

  > - **beech** – because it's the only word that has a matching word that sounds the same but is spelt differently, and is the only item on the list to start with a consonant (review homophones, word contexts, consonants and vowels)
  > - **elm** – because it's the only item widely destroyed by disease in England (historical review of Dutch Elm disease)
  > - **oak** – because it's the largest and longest-lived item on the list and supports the greatest diversity of wildlife (review ecosystems)
  > - **apple** – because it's the only fruit in the list and is the only word there that has two syllables (review syllables)
  > - **ash** – because it's the only homonym in the list (review homonyms).

- Now play 'odd-one-*in*'. Find at least one similarity between all of the items.
- Play Odd-one-out using visual information. The items below are taken from the Fantasy grid on p.65. Why might any one of these be the odd-one-out? Now, what do they all have in common?

- Play 'progressive' odd-one-out. Add another item to the selection, another and another … and find at least one reason why each could be the odd-one-out.

A BAGFUL OF STORY GAMES

- Play odd-one-out using character or scenario thumbnails.

- Play the game using short stories.

- Use images and key words from different topic and subject areas.

◆ Personas

Carol Harris, in *The Elements of NLP*, reinforces the point that one powerful aspect of learning is mimicking, or modelling the behaviour of others. She refers to a technique that has come to be known as the 'Disney Strategy', based on the way that Walt Disney changed his behaviour to get different sorts of results. Three 'personas' that Disney used in creative problem solving were –

                    The Dreamer
                   ↗   ↖
        The Realist ─────────→ The Critic

When you go into Dreamer mode it's OK to daydream and let your mind wander and explore. You are allowed to have lots and lots of ideas, realising that out of that batch only a few will come up to the Realist's and Critic's high standards of usefulness. As the Dreamer it's fine just to scribble ideas down and not bother about neatness or punctuation or spelling. You don't even have to write in proper sentences.

◆ SECTION FOUR

As the Realist it's your job to turn the Dreamer's ideas into something that can exist in the real world. And so you put effort and commitment into composing the story (or whatever your project is) as a logical, readable and believable whole. You are still allowed to listen to the Dreamer who might whisper in your mind, because the Dreamer will still be coming up with good creative ideas, even as you write. But at this stage, the Realist has the final say and can decide when enough is enough.

We improve by noticing what we've done before and deciding how we can do better. And so the Critic's job is to evaluate with honesty and integrity the work of the Dreamer and Realist. The Critic is smart, however, and does not think about 'correcting mistakes' or making negative judgements. The Critic knows that 'good judgement comes from experience, and experience comes from bad judgement'. The Critic understands that whatever we do counts as steps along the road to doing it better. The Critic is delighted to notice ways of improving the next piece of work, and informs the Dreamer, whose next set of ideas will be even more powerful.

> **Tip:** One school that I visited made use of 'editor caps'. Children were not allowed to worry about neatness, spelling, punctuation, etc., unless they were wearing an editor cap. Naturally they were encouraged to be aware of these things during the dreaming and realisation phases of writing, but the caps were kept in the cupboard until it was time for the young writers to look back over what they had done.

The Dreamer, the Realist and the Critic are all good friends, part of the same team. Their primary roles correspond to the three main phases of storymaking: the thinking time, the writing time and the looking-back time. The worst thing a young writer can do is try to 'make it up as she goes along', because the different personas represent and require different mental, emotional and physiological states – our brains are doing different things in these different phases of creation.

Many of the character-making games you've seen invite children to get inside the mind and world of the character; to understand their persona through the skill of associating with the material. Encourage children to apply this skill to the writing process itself through the use of the Disney Strategy.

See also 'Characters as guides' in *ALPS StoryMaker*, p. 205.

> **Another tip:** Any lack of confidence can turn the Critic persona into a negative critic. Emphasise for children that the only valid criticism is that which allows you to progress in a positive way. See also the Section 5: Reviewing, Evaluating and Planning Creative Work.

◆ Gathering treasures

In the section on 'Story ingredients' (p.175) I make the point that a treasure is 'anything precious': words that are spoken, an act of kindness, bravery, honesty, etc.; a thought, a capability, an action (that might not be carried out for years). In other words, a treasure is equated with personal qualities, and the distinction is made emphatically between value and cost – a treasure in storymaking is not usually gold or jewels or money.

The notion of gathering treasures in this sense can be exploited within the realm of emotional resourcefulness and make use of motifs and characters generated by the children themselves or gleaned from books.

A basic activity takes an item that the children are already familiar with – let's say the castle from the 6×6 Fantasy grid (see p.65).

- Say 'What qualities does a castle have?' or 'What makes a castle a castle?' Responses I've had include:
    - strong
    - solid
    - dependable
    - stands proud
    - commands a good view
    - can decide what to let in and what to let out through the drawbridge.

- Prepare a laminated A4 picture of the castle (this and other icons can be found on the CD resource) and place it on the floor. Say, 'Now, if you stand on this picture you will know what it feels like to be that castle. And you might feel these feelings one at a time, or maybe all together as one brilliant powerful feeling. Now, who'd like to be the castle?'

- Pick a volunteer and have her step onto the picture. If she says 'I can't feel anything' say, 'Well pretend you can and tell me when you're noticing the feelings.' This little ploy works like a charm.

◆ SECTION FOUR

> By telling the children what will happen ahead of time you are engaging a phenomenon called **preprocessing** in their brain. In conscious anticipation of what's required of them, subconsciously they will be gathering up ideas, information, memories and all the resources they need to carry out the activity. Most children have experienced being proud, feeling strong, deciding 'what to let in and what to let out' – either directly or by seeing that behaviour in others. Even if children can't remember specific incidents or experiences embodying these qualities, through this technique they can, most importantly, gather those resources.

- As the child steps onto the picture, you may notice a change of posture and facial expression as she becomes the castle. You remind her that the castle is strong and proud, etc., or ask her to speak as the castle and tell you how she feels. (This is reminiscent of the use of the story stone, (p.68), and works by the same principles.)
- Tell her now that the feelings will grow and then perhaps begin to fade. As she notices them fading, she can step off the picture 'and bring those feelings with you as treasures that you can keep'. What you have accomplished with the child is bringing those emotional resources into her conscious awareness – into 'cognitive space'– where she can make more deliberate use of them.
- **Variations** of this game include:
    - making acrostic displays to remind children of the treasures they have gathered:

Castle

Centred

Admirable

Strong

Towering

Long-lived

Elegant

A BAGFUL OF STORY GAMES

- **stacking anchors** – using the 'Gathering treasures' game to select a quality from different images. Put the pictures together on the floor and say 'When you step on this stack of pictures you will have all of those feelings all together as one big wonderful feeling…'

- **ideas cascade**, a simple association game using one of the motifs. *Tip*: You will need lots of board space for this!

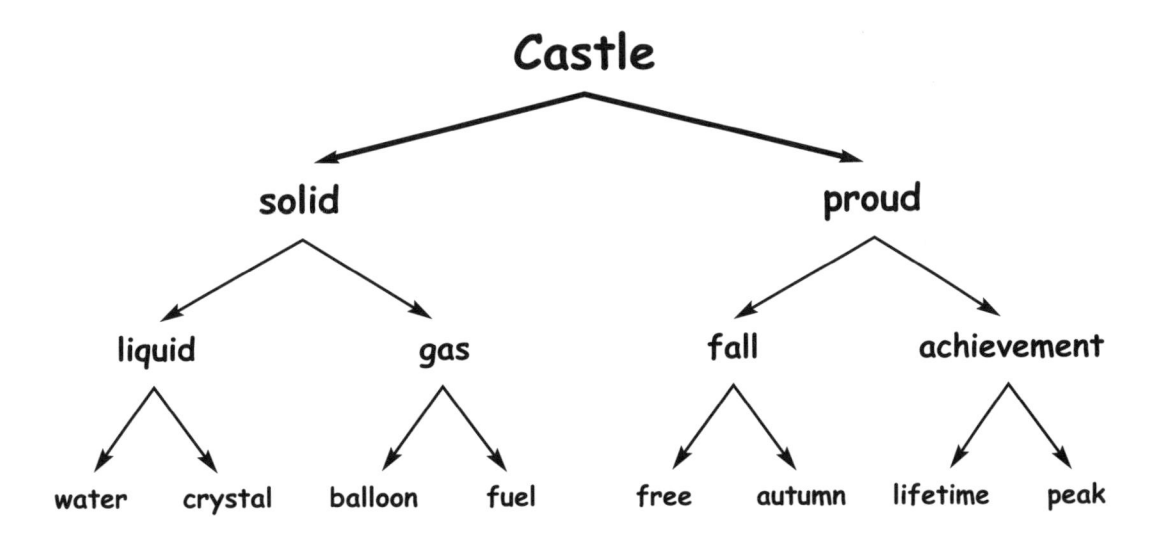

Castle

- solid
  - liquid
    - water
    - crystal
  - gas
    - balloon
    - fuel
- proud
  - fall
    - free
    - autumn
  - achievement
    - lifetime
    - peak

◆ SECTION FOUR

◆ Ideas wheel

The 'Ideas wheel' is a useful tool for consolidating many of the storymaking games you have already encountered and will meet later in the book. A basic ideas wheel looks like this:

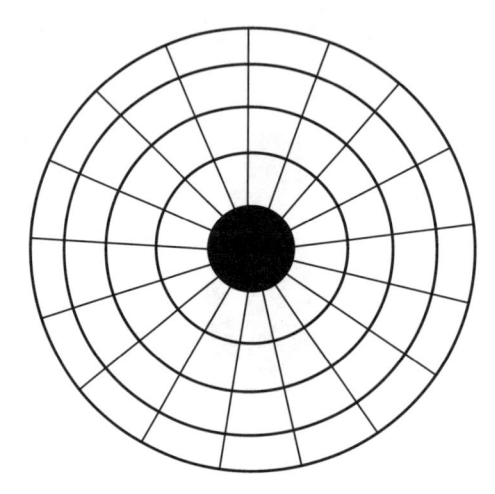

Key words and/or images are arranged around it and used for a variety of purposes. I have found that wheels which have an odd number of segments are more versatile.

A basic ideas wheel activity puts a circle of words around the outside, as shown opposite. Practise bisociations (see p.25) – creative linking – with the children by asking for connections between winds/cave, planets/wheat, seas/fire, etc. Notice that circling the wheel brings you back to rivers/winds, cave/planets – i.e. a different set of combinations, one of many sets. Remember that these creative linkings are also 'seed thoughts' (see below). So:

- The winds whisper and moan through the cave.
- Winds stream out of the cave from deep down in the earth.
- All the world's air streams out of the cave.
- The god of the four winds lives in the cave…

Nothing more need be done with these ideas at this point. They will settle into the fertile soil of children's imaginations and, over time, grow into something bigger.*

> * Intentionality is an important factor in cultivating seed thoughts most effectively. Encourage children to tell themselves that when they go back to these ideas in a few days' time, they expect and intend to know lots more about them. This stimulates subconscious preprocessing (see p.126) resulting in richer connectivity in the brain.

An extension of this basic idea is to put a motif or another keyword in the centre of the circle. Link two items on the circumference and 'bring them back to the centre'. So:

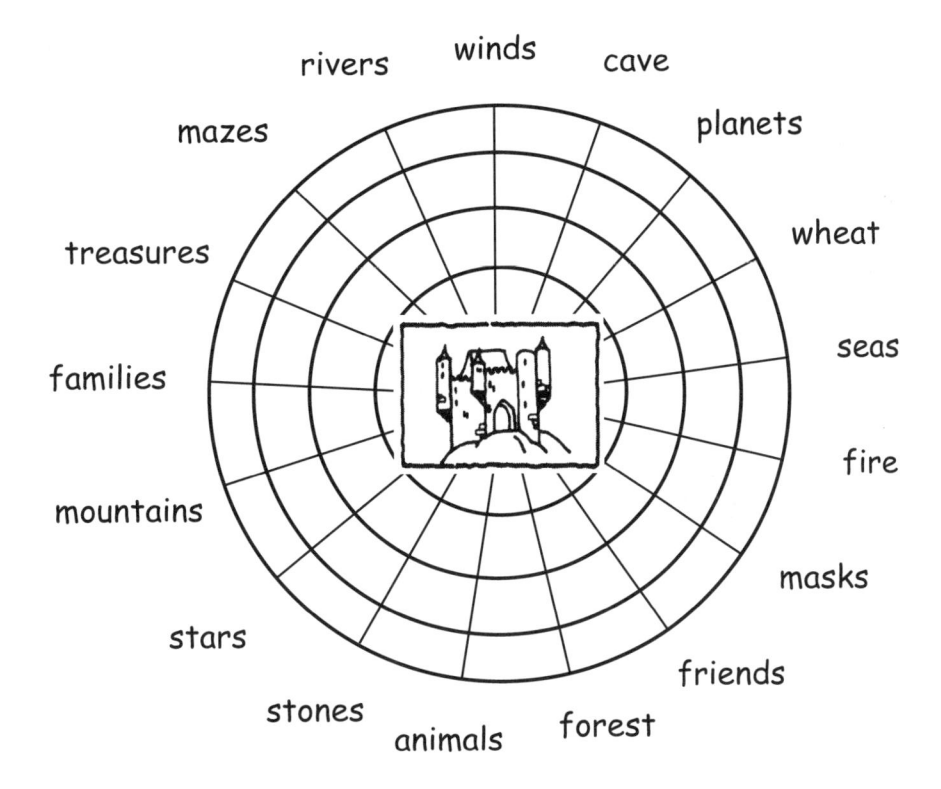

(ideas wheel with castle motif in centre; items around circumference: winds, cave, planets, wheat, seas, fire, masks, friends, forest, animals, stones, stars, mountains, families, treasures, mazes, rivers)

In this case, all links are brought back to the central point.

- **planets/wheat** – in the castle is an observatory where the King's astronomers watch the planets and stars to know when the wheat should be planted
- **seas/fire** – the castle is undercut by secret tunnels that take you down to the sea. If enemies attack and set fire to the castle, you can escape through these tunnels
- **masks/friends** – every year, to find out who his true allies are, the King holds a great masked ball. Every guest must wear a mask that he has fashioned himself which represents that person's true feelings. The wise King compares the expression on the mask with the eyes of the wearer, to see if they match

– and so on. Initially the children are likely to make unelaborated links between these items. Winds/cave – winds blow around the castle. There are caves near the castle, etc. But with practice, linkages will become more sophisticated and innovative.

Story darts

You can randomise the choice of items by laminating a copy of the ideas wheel, attaching it to the wall and having children toss sucker-tipped darts to select words or pictures. As the items

◆ SECTION FOUR

are selected in this way, the group has to incorporate them into an ongoing story – or, select six or so items and then consolidate them into a storyline.

- A variation of the game is to select, say, three items at random and find at least one linking factor. So: friends, mountains, fire – they all contain an 'i'. Increase the number of items per round as children become more proficient in the game.
- Or, select three or four items and play 'Odd-one-out' (see p.122). Find at least one reason why each item could be the odd one out.

◆ Story circles

> You can measure a circle by starting anywhere. (*Traditional saying*)

In the same way, you can begin storymaking by starting anywhere. 'Story circles', a close cousin of the ideas wheel, demonstrates this.

Stories in their completed form are basically linear, with modifications such as flashbacks and subplots. But writers don't usually create their stories in such a straightforward way. Here is a basic example of a story circle.

STORYMAKER CATCH PACK – USING GENRE FICTION AS A RESOURCE FOR ACCELERATED LEARNING

The images illustrate the plot of my story *Dinosaur Day* (see Bibliography). Read clockwise from the top, they depict the main plot of the story as it appears in the book:

> Tim and Tina Taylor sneak aboard their father's time machine and visit the age of the dinosaurs. There they meet an arrogant *T rex* who chews up trees to show off. While he is doing this, a splinter flicks up into his eye. *T rex*'s hands are too big and clumsy to draw the splinter, but Tina with her tiny delicate hands can do so without causing pain. And so the *T rex* learns a valuable lesson and makes two new friends into the bargain.

However, without revealing the plot to the children, pick a different starting point and ask one group to sweep clockwise to make a story. Ask another group to sweep anticlockwise from that point to make a story. Ask a third group to begin from another point, and so on… Groups can add pictures of their own if they wish. You may be surprised at the great range of stories produced.

Explicitly stating a theme keeps children's storymaking to the point: without consciously doing so, they will relate the pictures around the circumference to the central theme.

Note: These circles are reproduced on the CD resource.

- Give different groups the same story circle but with different themes, to create a range of stories.
- Place a picture in the centre of the circle and suggest that it must be incorporated at some point into the story.

◆ SECTION FOUR

- Place a small pack of motifs in the circle and encourage storymaking groups to talk through (pole-bridge) possible storylines, adding motifs as appropriate.
- Have children scribble notes inside the circle as they work out storylines.
- Overlap two story circles that share one image, so that the last part of one story becomes the opening of the next:

- Create different story circles that share a common theme:

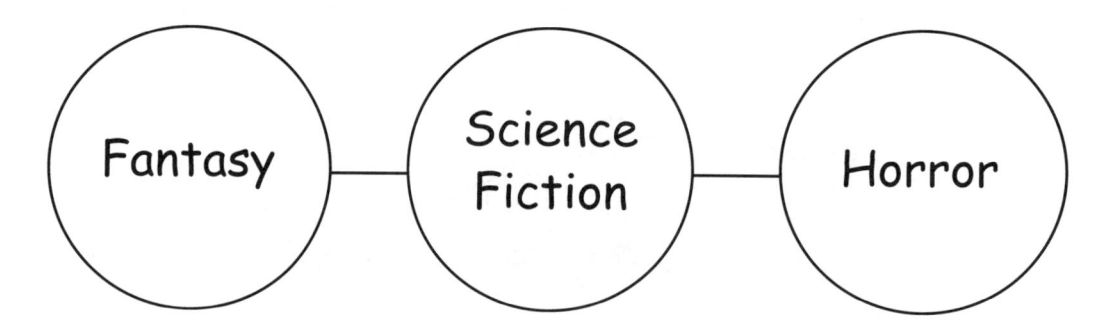

Fantasy — Science Fiction — Horror

It's never too late to learn

A story circle is also a good way of reviewing stories. Retell the story as a group and then have the children place keywords and pictures around a circle template.

◆ Start anywhere

Practised writers know that ideas can come at any time, from anywhere. Practised writers have confidence in the ability of their brains to make connections at a great rate, and to pop the results into cognitive space. Creative people of all kinds have heads that buzz with meaning and significance and possibilities. This is the default state of 'meaning-making' minds.

'Start anywhere' is a game that uses ordinary objects to forge creative links with characters, places and situations.

- Take an object, such as a pen. Ask about its qualities, its purposes, its usefulness. Abstract and broaden the children's responses…

> **Adam**: Well, it writes a lot!
> **Steve**: OK, its main job is to communicate in a certain way.
> **Syan**: But it can't write by itself. Someone needs to use it!
> **Steve**: Yes, a pen is always guided by someone else. It has no control of its own.
> **Ben**: The pen is mightier than the sword –
> **Steve**: In what ways, do you think?
> **Ben**: Um… Well, words can change people's minds.
> **Sanjeev**: Contracts and agreements can control your future.
> **Marie**: You sign your name to those. They're like promises.
> **Steve**: All of this is fine. Let's go back to the pen itself.
> **Dawn**: The ink runs out after a while.
> **Steve**: It has limited usefulness then –
> **Craig**: Especially if it's a disposable pen that you can't buy a refill for.
> **Adam**: Pens are thin. The plastic ones are brittle.
> **Syan**: If a pen leaks it makes a terrible mess!
> **Ben**: You feel lost without a pen sometimes.
> **Marie**: Pens can be a pound for ten, or you might pay hundreds of pounds for a really posh one.
> **Duane**: I chew my pen…

- Now review the abstracted details:
    - It's very useful in a certain way.
    - It needs to be guided and has no mind of its own.
    - The outcome of its work can be incredibly powerful – world-changing.
    - It usually has a limited lifespan of usefulness.
    - Physically pens can be brittle or extremely strong and durable.
    - They can command high prices.

- Now apply these details in another area. Say, 'If these qualities belonged to a person, what kind of character would he be? What would he look like? What sort of job or position would he have?' Practise the technique with a number of everyday objects, applying their qualities to people. Vary the game by translating qualities into situations. Take a tree, for example, and apply its qualities to a situation or scenario in a story:
    - It starts from a tiny seed that might have landed there accidentally.
    - At the beginning no one knows how it will turn out. It grows quickly, but needs the right conditions. It grows by itself, needing no help from anybody.
    - It becomes big and strong and powerful.
    - Lots of other creatures depend on it.
    - It has its season. There comes a time when it dies.
    - Powerful forces, like storms, can damage or destroy it.
    - It produces many copies of itself.

◆ SECTION FOUR

Of course this still sounds very abstract. To give it some focus, select an item of 'fortune cookie language' from the chart on p.118. (I chose 4/3 'Openings happen now'.) The addition of this theme might create insights as to how the list can translate into a storyline.

To put more detail in there, choose two items from the Fantasy grid on p.78. One item will represent in some way the beginning of the story, and the other item will represent the resolution. I chose the winged mask (2/2) and the chain (3/3).

> The winged mask arrives in the kingdom one day, no one knows how. It is an exquisitely carved antique of the hardest wood. But it clearly exists through powerful magics, for day by day its expression changes, and the rumour soon spreads that it is somehow reading the character of the people and their deepest thoughts, and even seems to be foretelling the possible future of the whole nation. The difficulty lies in interpreting its face, however, for apart from the obvious major changes of its mood, there seems to be a continual rearrangement of the very cells and grain of the wood itself, as though it is trying to communicate many complex messages. Its reputation and influence grow, and within a year the king commands it to be removed from public gaze and taken to the vaults far below his castle. There he employs a team of clerics and wise men to record the changes in the mask and to interpret their possible meanings. As the weeks and months go by, the impression grows clearer and more definite that a terrible conflict will engulf the kingdom. War, the mask appears to be telling them, war… So it comes to pass that the future and fate of the whole nation are chained to the existence of the mask. And no one ever suspects that right across the continent, other masks appeared just as mysteriously, and that in deep and hidden places kings and warriors and the wisest of the wise are paving the way for the legion of masks to take control…

This activity employs two very powerful principles:
- seeing in a new way
- moving motifs from one domain to another.

As we have already seen in the Introduction, one of the cornerstones of creativity is the drive to find practical solutions. Seeing a pen as a person might be the practical solution to the problem of generating a character for a story, but as children do this they are also developing the important skill of making meanings out of what they see around them and applying those meanings in new ways.

◆ Story maps revisited

I first mentioned story maps in *ALPS StoryMaker* (pp. 113–119), but I want to extend the idea here.

A story map is a way of allowing young writers to develop setting, character and plot by using a visual organiser to take them through the story. There are a number of ways to begin.

- **the minimalist approach**: use a whiteboard or a *large* sheet of paper if you're working on a tabletop. Mark on the cardinal points of the compass and a reference point.

- involve the children in a *group visualisation*. Having decided on the genre of the story and perhaps a theme, begin by saying 'Imagine we're looking to the North. What can we see, very far away…?' Sketch in some or all of the ideas – mountains, clouds, a pall of smoke, etc. – making sure that the ideas are sensible and consistent with one another and with the emergent story. Move on to the other compass points, then go around again to sketch in details from the middle distance and nearby. Have the children 'step in' to the picture (see 'Picture exploration' on p.55) and add any relevant details of colour, sound, texture, weather condition, etc.

◆ SECTION FOUR

- **the abstract art approach**: use pieces of abstract art to generate ideas to incorporate into your map. You can use this with the minimalist approach or indeed at any point in the story-mapping process. Show the group a piece of abstract artwork such as this:

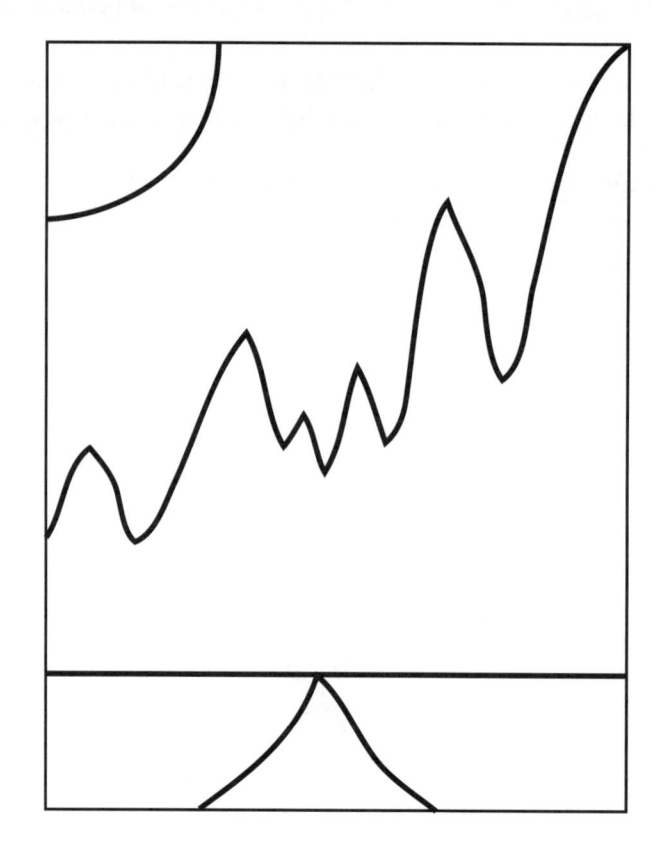

Say 'What could this be? What does this remind you of?' Ideas will come thick and fast. Select a few children beforehand to scribble them down. After a short while, turn the picture and this will stimulate new connections…

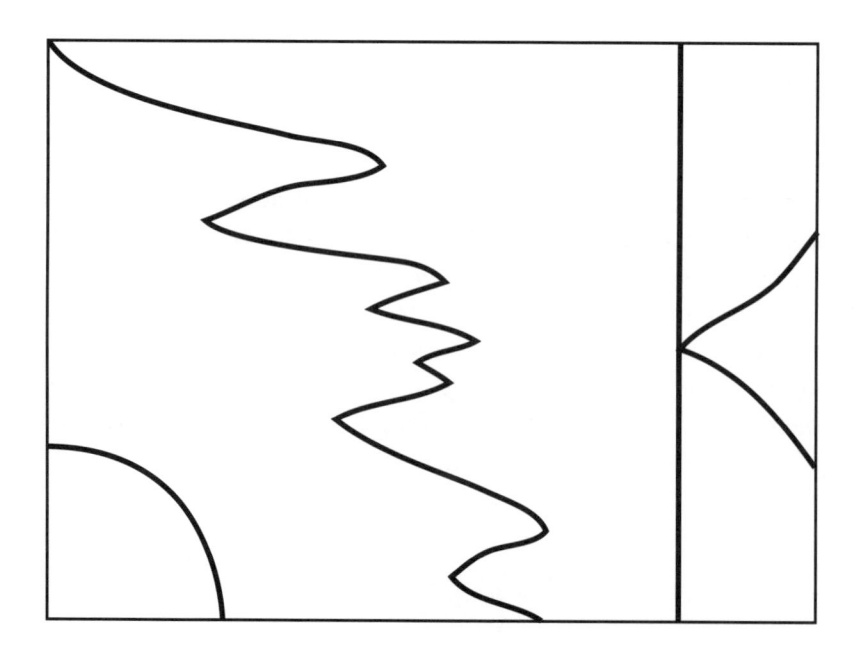

STORYMAKER CATCH PACK - USING GENRE FICTION AS A RESOURCE FOR ACCELERATED LEARNING

And again...

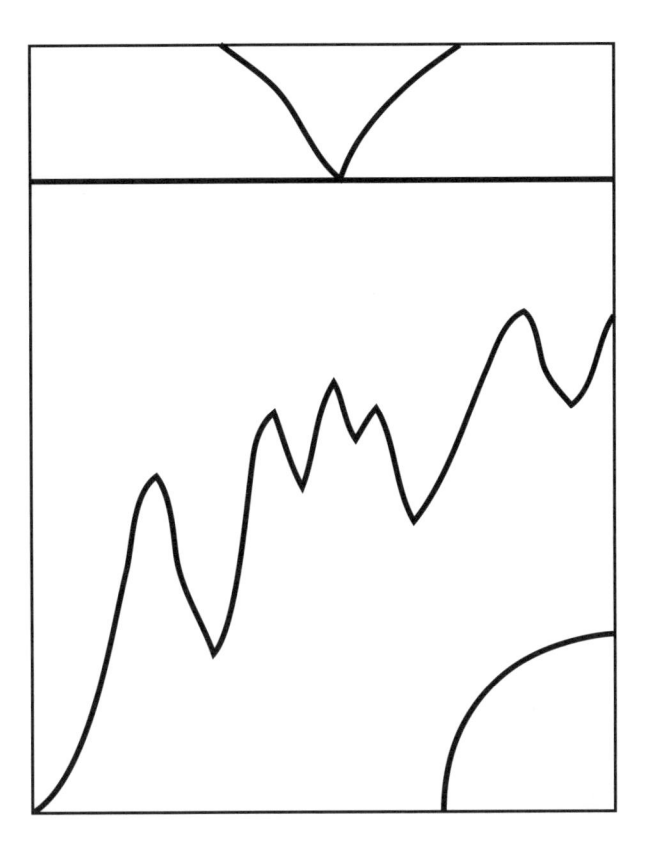

I usually say, 'Isn't it interesting how you can have even more ideas when you look at things in another way?'

Pieces of artwork like this can be prepared easily in a few seconds. By choosing your designs carefully you have more control over the ideas generated by the children: the design above normally brings up ideas like mountains, the sun, horizons, a road, caves, icicles, cracks in the ground, etc. – though one little boy was convinced he could also see part of a fried egg (check it out). One underlying benefit of this technique is that you are training the children to tolerate ambiguity (one of the elements of creative thinking) and to realise that there is not one right answer, but many possibilities that are more or less useful in the long run. For more information, see *Imagine That!*, pp.43–44.

- **the basic map approach**: you can provide your group with as little or as much information as you like. A map such as the one overleaf gives you more control over the basic features of the setting and can suggest aspects of the plot – the storm to the west might create problems for the characters, for instance.

◆ SECTION FOUR

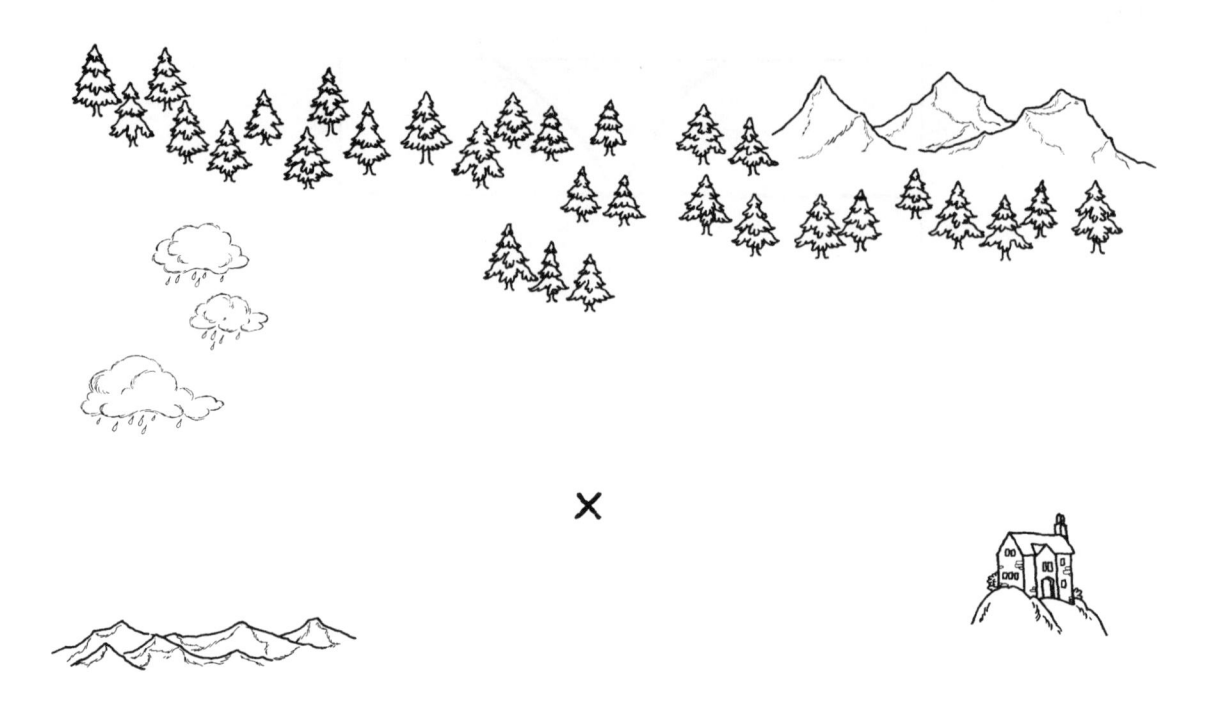

Always leave plenty of blank space for the children to draw more features and scribble notes when the time comes to get the story moving. A refinement of the basic map approach is to suggest things outside the frame of the picture…

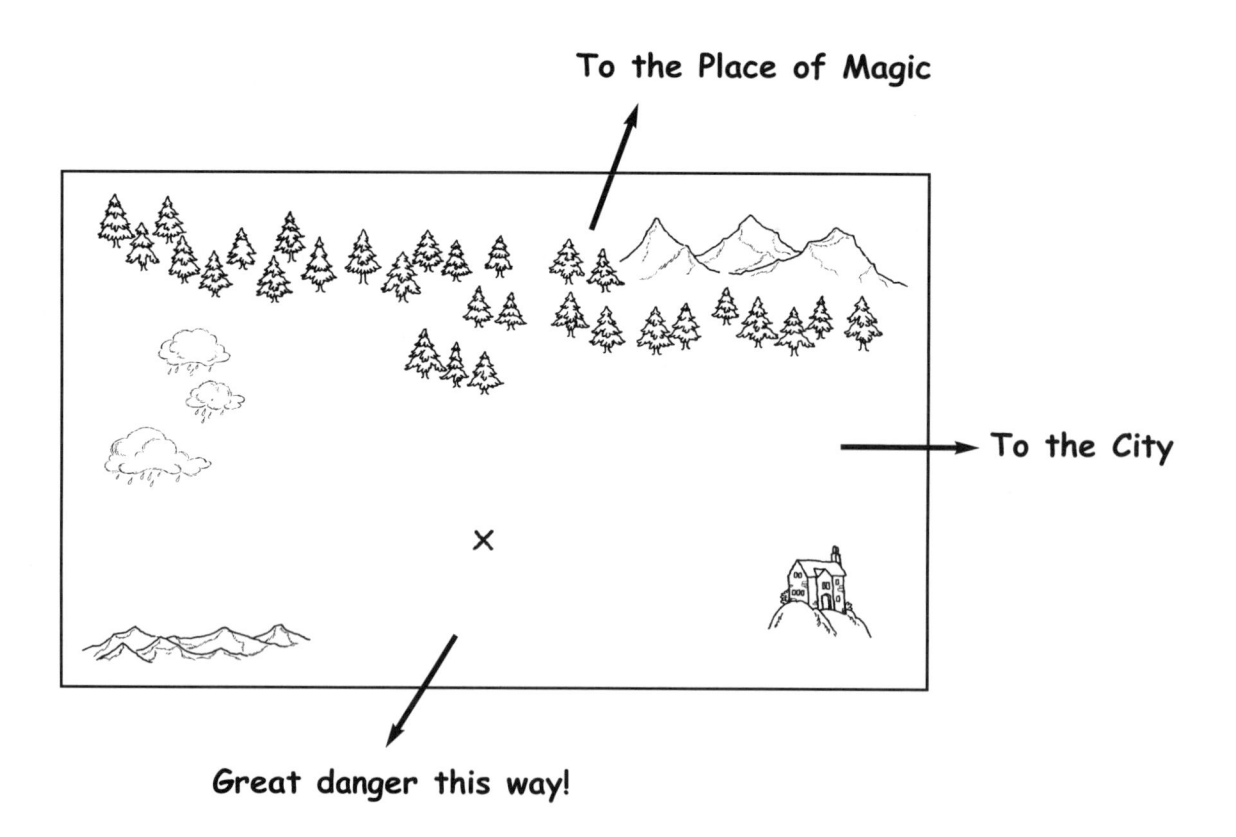

To the Place of Magic

To the City

Great danger this way!

STORYMAKER CATCH PACK – USING GENRE FICTION AS A RESOURCE FOR ACCELERATED LEARNING

A BAGFUL OF STORY GAMES

This technique stimulates preprocessing in the writers' minds: they will be gathering up ideas about the Place of Magic, the City and the Great Danger without even realising it at the time, though may well incorporate their thinking into the story later.

- **adding motifs**: you can help to enrich the story by adding a number of motifs. Suggest to the groups that they can incorporate some or all of these as they work through the tale.
- **story cards**: a similar idea is to cut out and laminate some motifs to make a card pack. As children work through a story, encourage them to select a card and brainstorm further ideas from there.
- **Story map** with motifs –

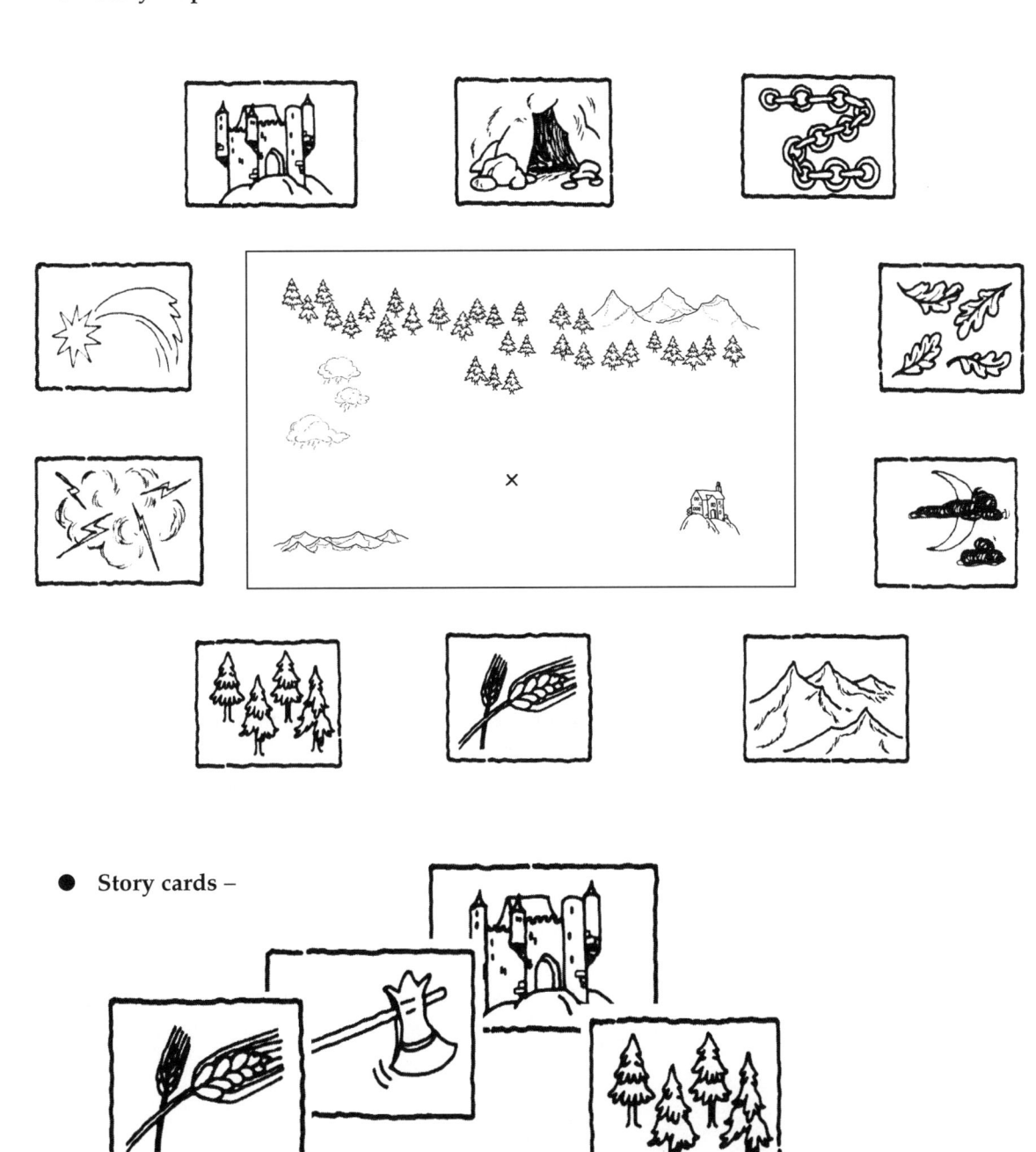

- **Story cards** –

STORYMAKER CATCH PACK – USING GENRE FICTION AS A RESOURCE FOR ACCELERATED LEARNING

◆ SECTION FOUR

- **adding story ingredients**: story ingredients (see p.175) are general components of most or all stories. I regard them as 'smaller' than themes but 'larger' than motifs, which are often genre-specific. Common ingredients are problems, secrets, conflicts, dangers, mysteries, treasures (i.e. something precious). Sprinkle your story map with a few of these to add some spice to the developing plot.

    Explain to the children that if their journey takes them to an 'ingredient spot' they must incorporate it into the story. (Also refer to pp.176–179 to see how ingredients can be incorporated into storylining techniques.)

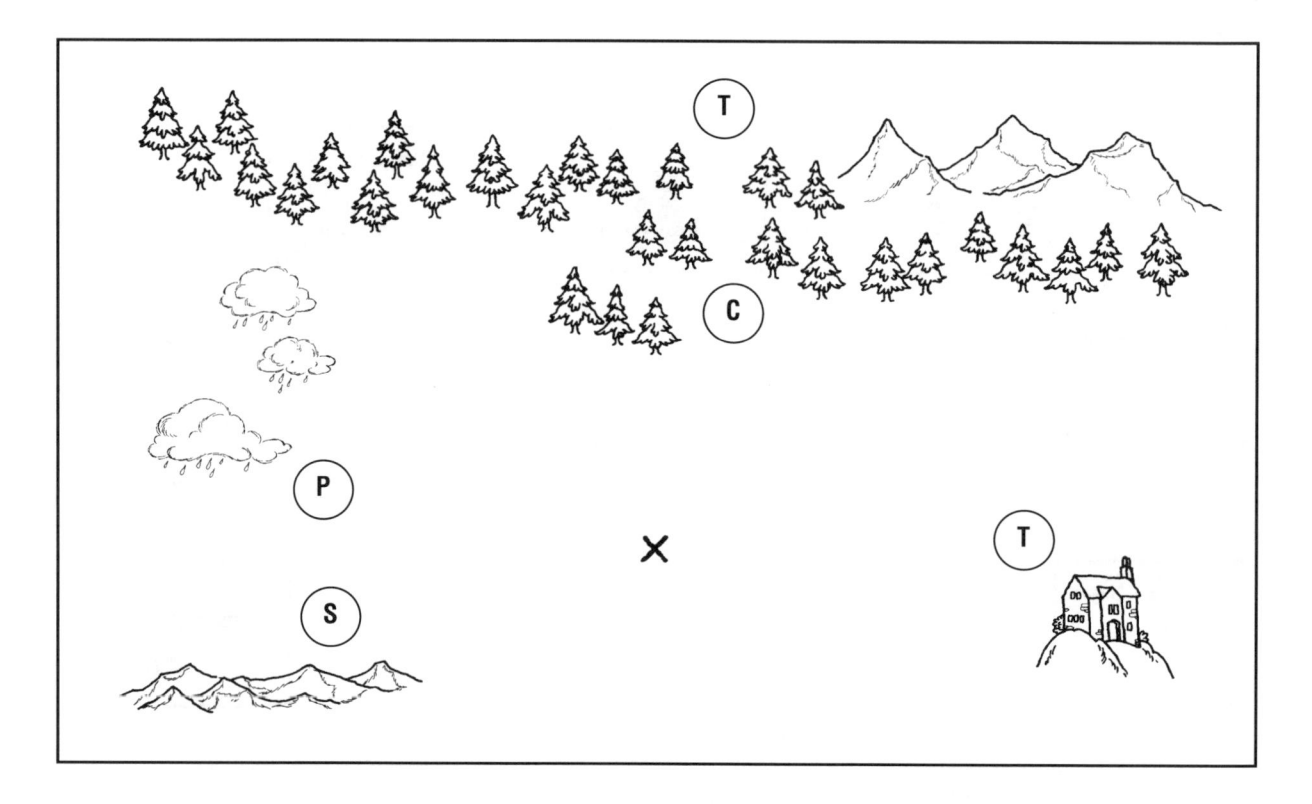

- **Mediations**: the technique that we've already used with characters (See 'How Tall, How Strong?' p.99) can also apply to settings, atmosphere (literal and dramatic) and ingredients. Children can discuss and negotiate how windy, how dark, etc., to fit in with what they already know about the story; or they can randomise the activity with dice rolls. Encourage the group to add to the list of adjectives.

A BAGFUL OF STORY GAMES

> **How...**
>
>   1   2   3   4   5   6
>
> cold
>
> windy
>
> dark
>
> stormy
>
> dangerous
>
> spooky
>
> populated
>
> passable
>
> forested
>
> isolated

Dice journey

All of this preparation allows a young writer to know more about the story than he is likely to include, which is the way that most professional writers work. The plot can now be 'activated' by running a dice journey. Children can work alone on this, although it does make for a lively group activity. I normally work in batches of six ideas when I do a dice journey, although you can use smaller batches to increase the pace of the game and/or according to the capabilities of the group.

This is how you do it:

- Once you have a story map prepared, place two or so characters at the reference point X (or the writer-as-character can visualise himself there). Say, 'OK, now what could happen – something really interesting and exciting to get the story off to a strong start…'

- Collect up to six responses. Note them. Roll the dice to select one option. *Make the point that none of the other ideas is wasted* – they can be used later in the story or in other stories.

- Now the characters will want to react to what has just happened. Invite ideas. Collect six and roll the dice to select. Proceed from here using this pattern – Now what?/six ideas/select – Now what?/six ideas/select…

◆ SECTION FOUR

> ## What's the problem?
>
> 1 We're being chased by wolves.
> 2 There's a sudden storm.
> 3 Night falls and we're lost.
> 4 One of us is injured.
> 5 There's a forest fire.
> 6 One of us is lost in a cave labyrinth.
>
> **Roll (say, 1) –**
>
> How can you solve it?
>
> ■ Run!
> ■ Split up and run.
> ■ Fight.
> ■ Start a fire to frighten them.
> ■ Set a trap.
> ■ Head for the caves in the mountains.

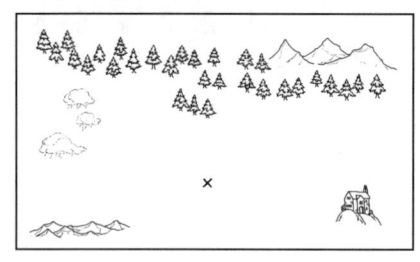

This version of 'Dice journey' generates a lot of detail and a good store of ideas. It also builds consistency into the plot, since each option will follow on logically from what has just happened.

- A simpler, faster version of the game uses a coin to choose between two options each time; so –

    - Look out, wolves! Shall we run (*heads*) or fight (*tails*)?

    - We run. Oh no – a river! What do we do? Swim (*heads*) or try to find a crossing point (*tails*)?

    - We swim. But halfway across one of us is washed away. Is it me (*heads*) or you (*tails*)?

    - Oh no – it's you! What do I do? Do I swim after you (*heads*) or reach the far bank and try to rescue you from there (*tails*)?

    - I swim after you. But the water is fast-flowing and we both get swept away. What happens now…?

And so on. This simplified 'coin journey' is immediate and involving and groups can get carried away (not in the river, you understand). The adventure can sprawl across several large sheets of paper. Encourage minimal note-making and subsequently have the children tell the entire story to you or another group and, as appropriate, revisit the tale to put more flesh on the bones of the plot.

◆ Jigsaw town

The fiction resource for *ALPS StoryMaker* is two books of short stories, the 'Double Dare Gang' adventures. The adventures take place in the town of Kenniston, which is loosely based on my hometown, though I have added bits so that all of the settings for the tales are conveniently assembled in one location.

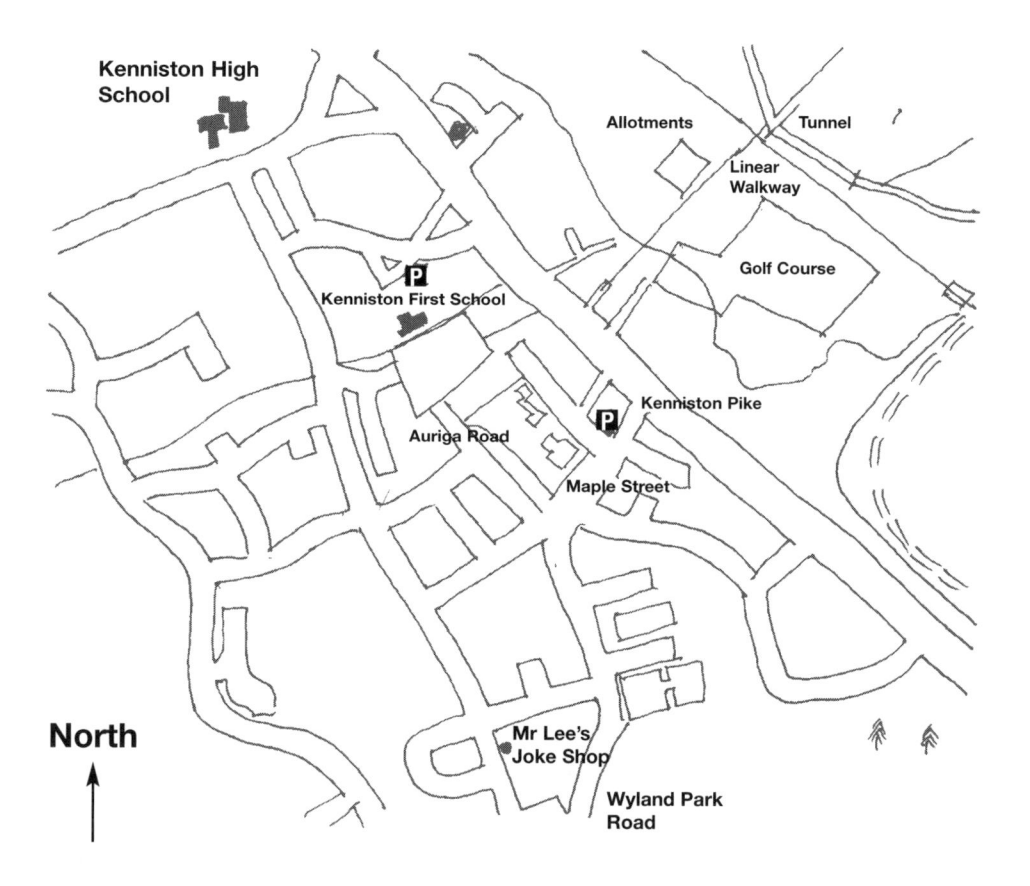

The layout of the map is completely made up, although some street names are real. A few items have been 'shipped in' from actual places elsewhere*. Such a 'jigsaw town' is fun to construct and gives the writer a Big Picture of a story's location, which helps with consistency during writing. An overview like this also makes it easier for the narrator to use time and space more flexibly: there is often the temptation to keep the narrative viewpoint fixed on one character as he moves around in 'real time'. However, with a map like this it's easier to leapfrog from place to place in 'Meanwhile, across town...', style. (See also 'Context sentences and connective prompting' on pp.114–117.)

> * Jigsaw towns crop up quite often in genre fiction, most famously perhaps in Horror writer Stephen King's 'Castle Rock'.

◆ SECTION FOUR

- Encourage children to create jigsaw towns if they want to use the same location for a number of tales, or if a single story features the complex interaction of places. This activity can be used as an adjunct to story mapping.

- Question children on small details of their locations. So – 'I see you've put Steve's house on the corner of Cross Street and Auriga Road. What kind of front door does he have? What colour is it? Tell me a bit more about the front garden…' As children notice their mental impressions they are 'exploring submodalities' – the subcategories of their sensory impressions. For more information see *ALPS StoryMaker,* p. 192, and references to NLP in the bibliography.

- Have children work in pairs to guide each other around their jigsaw towns in the form of extended visualisations. This activity develops concentration and clarity of thinking. It also generates many new details that writers can add to their maps. Make the activity more sophisticated by introducing characters; let them speak and interact. The 'guide' can make notes as the visualisation proceeds, while the 'visualiser' can scribble down impressions afterwards. (See also the section on visualisation in *ALPS StoryMaker.*)

◆ Story tray

A story tray brings a story map into the real world, as it were, and helps kinaesthetic learners especially to engage more meaningfully with the tale they are developing.

- A large rectangular tray works best for this activity, although a tabletop will do. Once a group has prepared a story map, send them out to fetch back objects that will represent the features of the map: stones, leaves, small gravel, sand, etc. Mirrors work well for lakes, blue ribbon can be used for streams – although you might want the children to come up with these ideas for themselves. Small plastic people can represent characters, while story ingredients may be coloured counters.

  When the tray has been set out as a 3D version of the map, ask the children if doing that has given them any further ideas for the story. Then suggest that objects on the tray could be moved, and how that would affect the plot, characters' actions, etc.

- Combine 'Story tray' with the 'Feelie bag' game. Prepare a large cloth bag (or cardboard box) filled with interesting small objects. The basic game is for a child to delve into the bag, select an object and describe it without being too specific and without naming it. Other children in the group attempt to guess the item.

- You can also use the items in the bag with a story tray. Have a child select an item from the bag and ask the group what that item could represent, and how it would change the narrative if it were included. If the item/idea seems useful, place it on the tray in its appropriate place.

- **Character tray.** The story tray activity can be modified to explore characters. In this case selected objects represent thoughts, feelings and issues going on within the character. Begin by placing a fairly thick layer of clean, dry sand in the tray. Point out that the sand can be shifted so that, for example, items can be partially or entirely covered: this represents thoughts or feelings that the character is not entirely admitting to herself. Discuss what kinds of objects could represent different feelings. There will be some obvious connections – green glass could represent clearly expressed (transparent) envy, a mirror might symbolise reflectiveness. But there are bound to be plenty of fresh ideas. Objects placed near the edge of the tray could be things that are apparent to other people, while items close to the centre are things that the characters know about, but are keeping to themselves.

  An interesting variation of the game is to prepare a detailed character description – or use a character from a book – and ask different groups to represent that person using a character tray. Then, discuss the different objects the groups have used to symbolise the different inner features of that person.

- **Story sticks.** Another way of 'getting physical' with stories is to make story sticks. Mailing tubes work well for this. There are a number of versions of the activity.

  - Using a story that has been written: cover the story stick in paper, or paint it a colour that represents the mood of the tale. Attach pictures, small items and key words to the tube so that the story is told from one end to the other. The story stick is a useful adjunct to story-telling. The child who is telling at the time will hold the stick, and pass it on at the appropriate time to the next child in the story-telling group.
  - Fill the tube with small items, motif cards, etc. Take these out one by one and brainstorm how they can be incorporated into a story that you are making.
  - Fill the tube with items that give insights into a character. Take them out one by one and 'pole-bridge' what you suddenly know about that person.
  - For long and/or involved stories, make a story stick for each chapter. Scramble the order of the sticks and have another group work out the logical order.
  - Swap story sticks between groups and have them work out and then elaborate on the narrative structure.

- **Story mobiles.** Prepare mobiles rather than story sticks. This activity combines visual, kinaesthetic and auditory elements (use tiny bells, wind-chime tubes, etc.).

◆ 'Story tree' revisited (again)

I have looked at story trees in detail elsewhere, and only come back to them now to refresh the memory (or in case you haven't got *ALPS StoryMaker!*), and to describe another activity using story ingredients – see pp.175–179.

Briefly, although a finished story is a linear structure, in the making of a story there are many points of decision, and multiple options at each point.

◆ SECTION FOUR

Run the story tree by starting with a scenario. Ask 'What can happen now?' I usually collect ideas in batches of three; any number greater than this is likely to generate an overly complicated tree very quickly. Then put each idea on the end of a branch. Focus on one option and say 'So now what?' Collect three ideas, repeat for each of the other two options and then proceed by the same pattern.

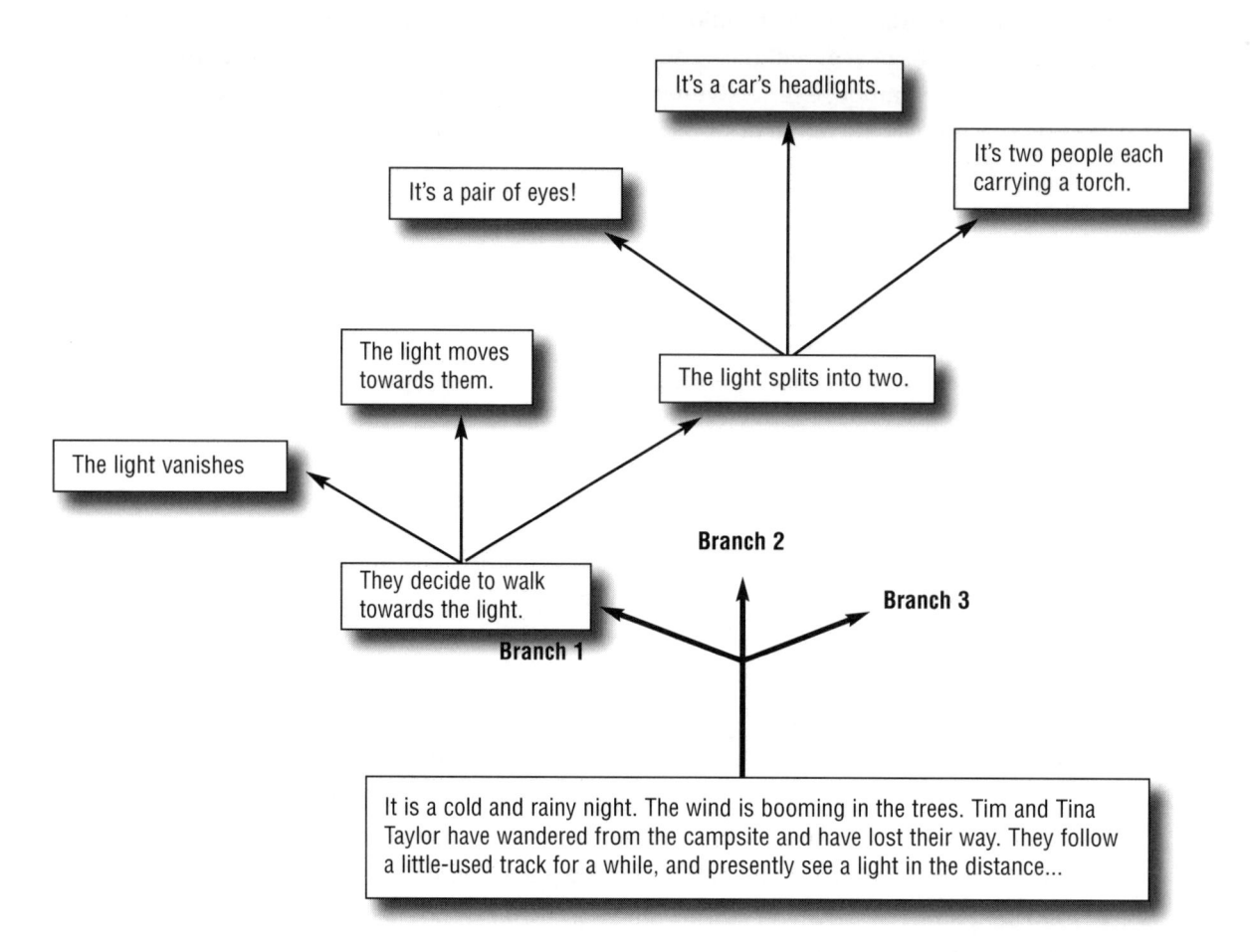

```
                              It's a car's headlights.
                                      ↑
                                      |                It's two people each
      It's a pair of eyes!            |                carrying a torch.
               ↖                      |               ↗
                                                
      The light moves
      towards them.          The light splits into two.
              ↑                       ↗
              |
  The light vanishes
       ↖
                    They decide to walk
                    towards the light.        Branch 2
                         Branch 1               ↑        Branch 3
                                    ←           |        ↗

            ┌─────────────────────────────────────────────────────┐
            │ It is a cold and rainy night. The wind is booming in │
            │ the trees. Tim and Tina Taylor have wandered from    │
            │ the campsite and have lost their way. They follow    │
            │ a little-used track for a while, and presently see   │
            │ a light in the distance...                           │
            └─────────────────────────────────────────────────────┘
```

Obviously you will need a large space to 'grow' a story tree. It's also worth noting that the same tree can be revisited many times, spending as little as a few minutes on each occasion making decisions and selecting options. Consider these ideas too:

● Make a story tree as a wall display, with the different options written/drawn on green paper leaves. A 'Dice journey' (p.141) provides another way of generating plot possibilities that can then be formalised as a tree structure.

● Combine this idea with 'Story sticks/Story mobiles' (p.145). Attach actual objects to the tree to give, literally, another dimension to the storymaking.

● Use the tree as a visual organiser for topic work. The arrangement of the branches gives graphic structure to the knowledge you impart. Invite the children to 'have a hand' in their own learning by attaching leaves to the topic tree, on which are written keywords, interesting facts and questions.

A BAGFUL OF STORY GAMES

Fossils

Carnivores   *Herbivores*

Sea & Air

Extinction

Evolution   *Climate*

DINOSAURS

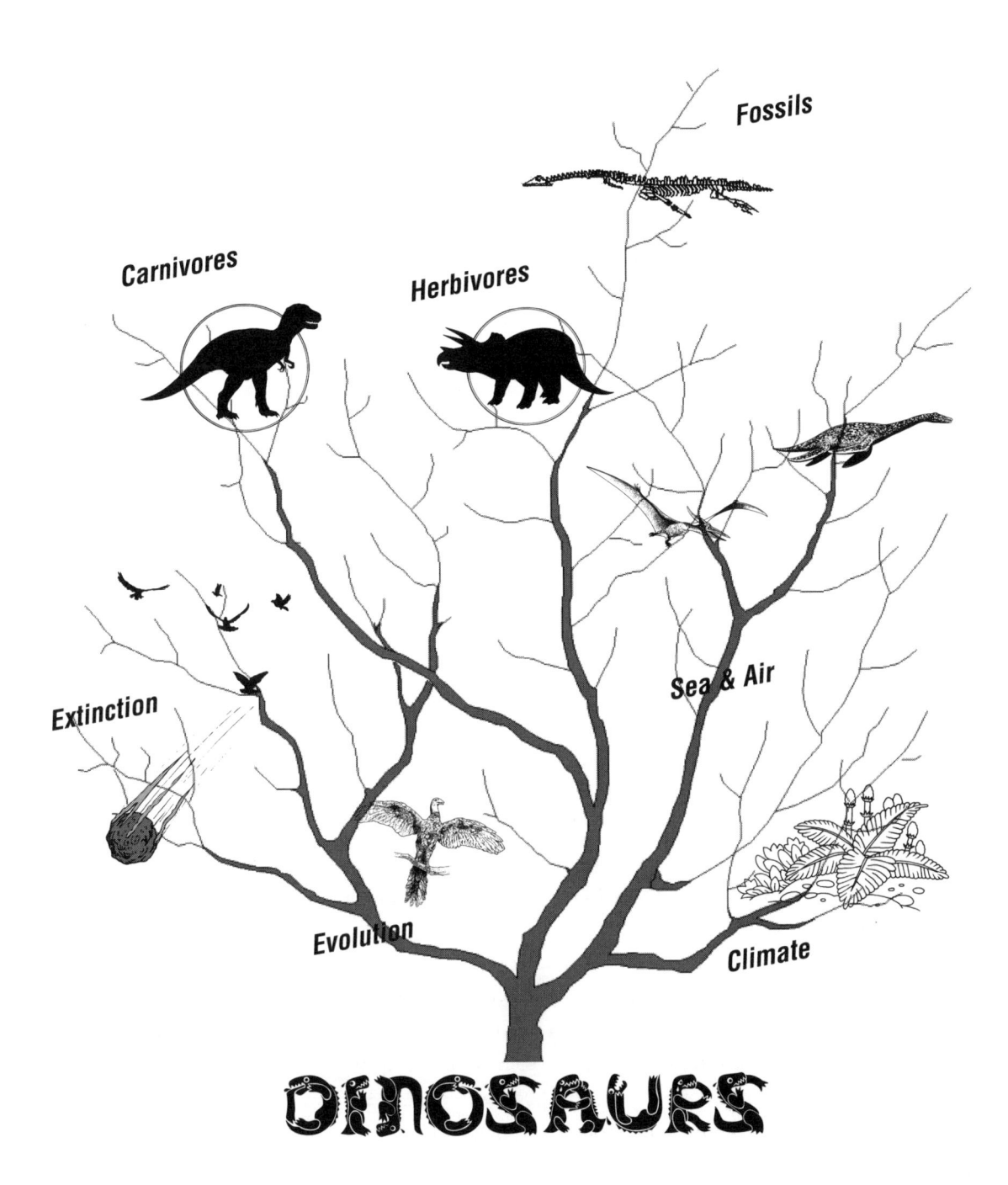

◆ Mystery mapping

This is essentially a problem-solving activity that can take a number of forms. Sequencing games constitute the simplest kind of mystery mapping – sequence 'Thumbnails', for instance (see p.107), in order of age, or alphabetical order of surname, or the order in which you'd like to meet these people. In this case you can include the more sophisticated element of having children explain their reasoning behind the choices they make. Or you might use a grid template to combine the two parameters, for example, climate (hot to cold) and ruggedness of landscape.

147

STORYMAKER CATCH PACK – USING GENRE FICTION AS A RESOURCE FOR ACCELERATED LEARNING

◆ SECTION FOUR

Climate →

Ruggedness ↓

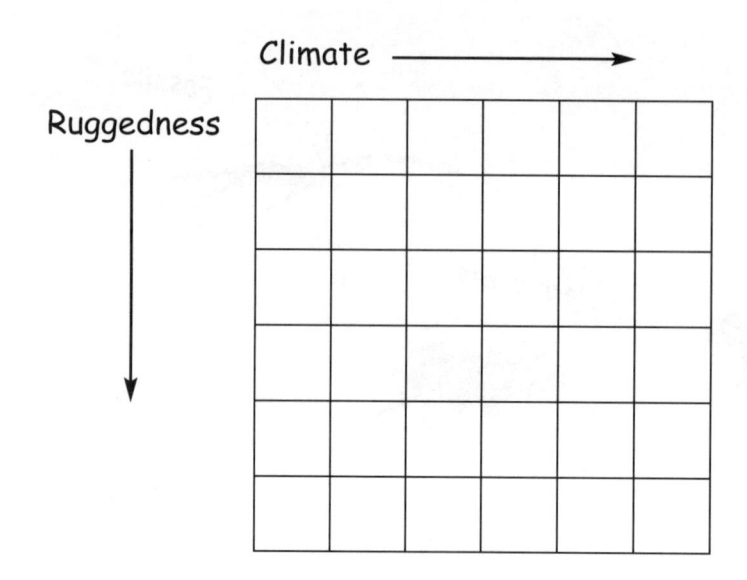

- Mystery mapping can also be done with texts. Take a story and literally cut it up into sections, then have children put the story back together again. The more sections there are, the more challenging the activity will be.
- A variation of this game requires more preparation. Cut a story into a relatively large number of sections. Also prepare some clues as to characters' motives, likely plot outcomes, etc. Hand out the sections that constitute the early part of the story, plus the relevant clues. Have children sequence the story up to that point and use the clues to discuss what the later sections might contain.
- Still using text: cut out sequences of dialogue and prepare thumbnails of the characters involved. Ask children to speculate on who says what, based on the thumbnail information.
- Cut out pieces of text that give clues about the genre of the story. Ask children to sequence the extracts according to how much information they provide.
- Have one group write a story based on a story map (see p.138). Cut up the map. Ask another group to read the story and reconstruct the map based on the textual information.
- **Comic cuts**: cut up comic book stories and ask children to reconstruct them.
- Delete the speech from the speech bubbles of comic book stories. Have children speculate on what speech the bubbles should contain based on the visual clues. (This is a good opportunity to raise children's awareness of the conventions of the medium. In the panels below, for example, notice the jagged nature of the speech bubble and the way that the string of Ss gets bigger. What information is being conveyed by these? What might the characters be saying?)

A BAGFUL OF STORY GAMES

From *Roy Kane – TV Detective* by Stephen Bowkett, A. & C. Black 1998.
Illustration by David Burroughs. Image used with the publisher's permission.

- **What's the problem?** My friend the writer Douglas Hill begins exploring every new idea with this question. For him the journey through a story might start with a line of dialogue, the fleeting glimpse of a person's face on the High Street, a colour, a sound – and he starts to develop it and make sense of it by asking 'What's the problem?' This is the engine that drives the story and (to mix metaphors) the glue that holds it together. Combine mystery mapping with 'what's-the-problem' thinking in these ways:

    - State the problem and encourage children to ask the Six Big Important Questions (see p.70) as a way of opening out the story. So –

◆ SECTION FOUR

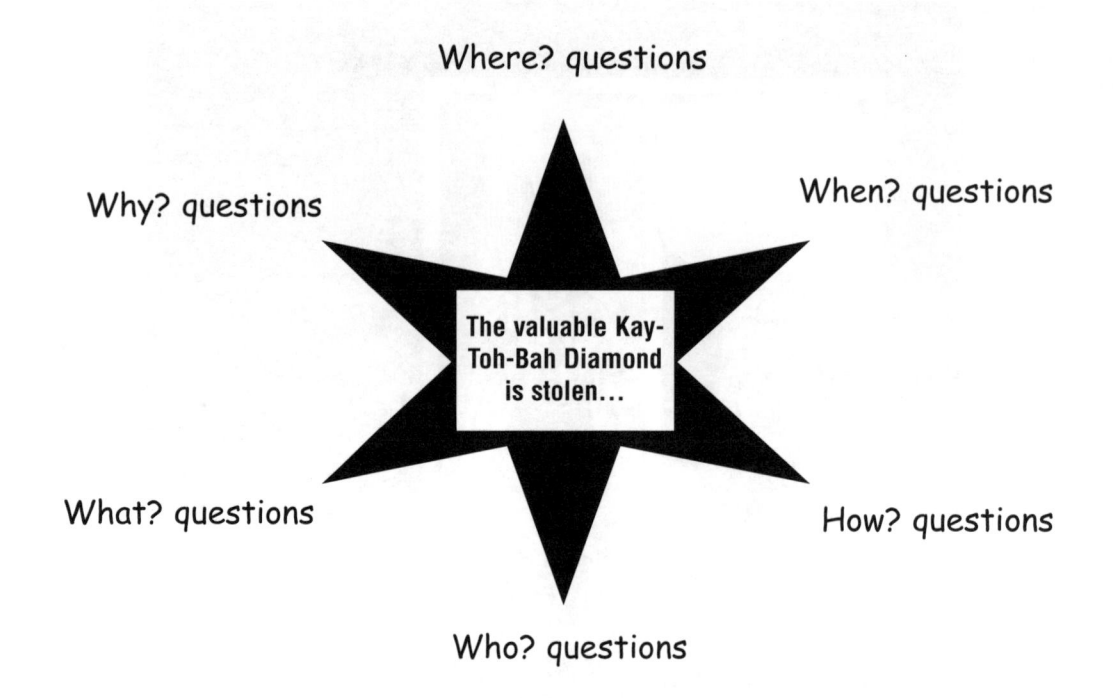

Star diagram with "The valuable Kay-Toh-Bah Diamond is stolen..." at centre, surrounded by points labelled:

- Where? questions
- When? questions
- How? questions
- Who? questions
- What? questions
- Why? questions

In other words, they are creating their own clues. If the central problem is based on a story that's already written, you can provide clues as the activity goes on to focus the children's questioning.

- You can work the game the other way round, offering clues on the points of the star and inviting children to define the problem. So:

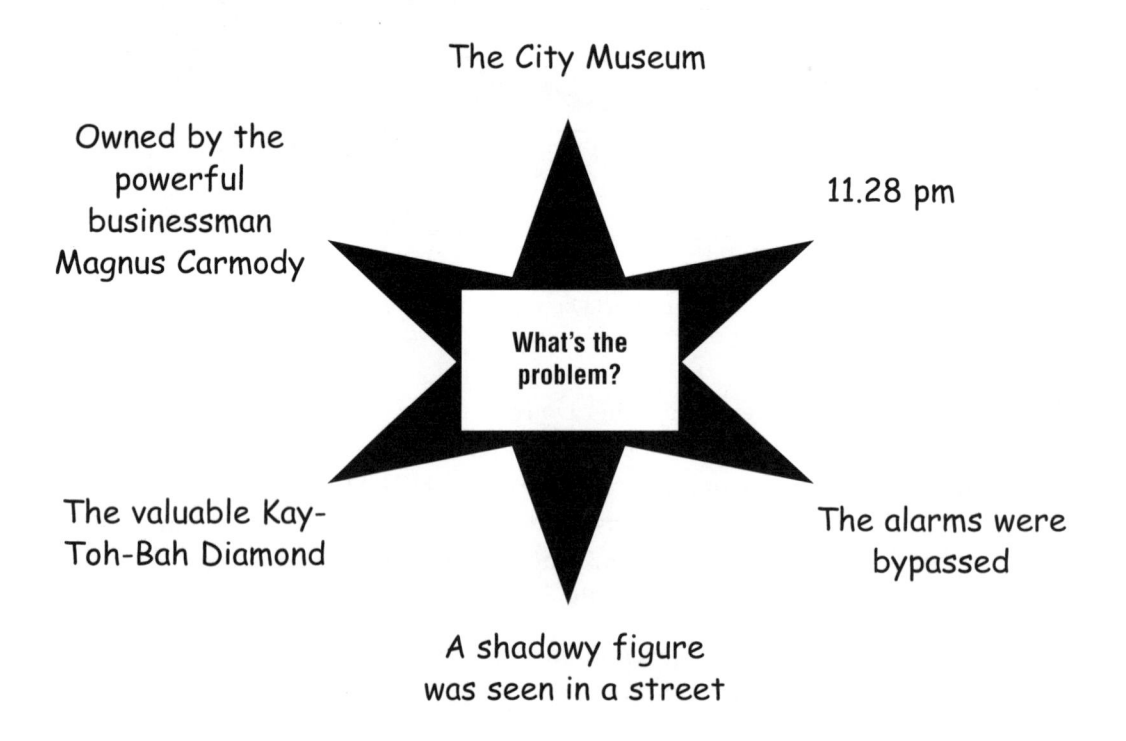

Star diagram with "What's the problem?" at centre, surrounded by points labelled:

- The City Museum
- 11.28 pm
- The alarms were bypassed
- A shadowy figure was seen in a street
- The valuable Kay-Toh-Bah Diamond
- Owned by the powerful businessman Magnus Carmody

150

STORYMAKER CATCH PACK – USING GENRE FICTION AS A RESOURCE FOR ACCELERATED LEARNING

A BAGFUL OF STORY GAMES

Here I've included one simple clue to match each kind of question. You can make the information you give as sophisticated as you like. Also, encourage children to use the Six Big Important Questions as a way of reaching a solution to the central problem. So, once they have consolidated the clues, they can continue with the exploration…

- **consolidation – what we know:** the valuable Kay-Toh-Bah Diamond was stolen from the City Museum at 11.28pm. Somehow the burglar alarms were bypassed. The diamond belongs to the powerful businessman Magnus Carmody. A shadowy figure was seen in the street close to the museum around the time of the theft.
- **speculation – what we don't know:**
  - Where were the security guards at the time?
  - When was the theft discovered?
  - How did the thief bypass the alarm system?
  - Who could the thief be?
  - What relationship, if any, exists between the thief and Magnus Carmody?
  - Why was that particular diamond stolen?
  - Why didn't the CCTV cameras give more information?

And so on. Get different groups to provide answers to these and other questions, swap ideas and discuss which would work most effectively in a story.

◆ Concept mapping

This follows on naturally from story-mapping. By the time young writers have created a few story maps and 'activated' them through a dice journey, they will most likely feel comfortable with the rather more stylised and abstract notion of concept mapping (which is itself a precursor to the well known educational tool of mind mapping – see Tony Buzan, *Use Your Head*).

A concept map is simply a visual organiser that lays out and connects elements of a greater whole. Its advantage is that the Big Picture becomes apparent at a glance, and that as you make the obvious or expected connections, other unanticipated links can leap to mind.

There are many ways of laying out a concept map: no Golden Rules seem to apply.*

> * This is also true of creativity as a whole. Somerset Maugham supposedly asserted that 'There are three Golden Rules to successful creative writing, and nobody knows what they are.'

When concept mapping a story, it seems natural to make the first links within the domains of people, places and 'things'. Taking the story *Nanoman* as an example, this is how those three clusters of elements might look:

◆ SECTION FOUR

This is simply a list of the *dramatis personae* with some indication of their function or motivation, and the obvious relationships between them:

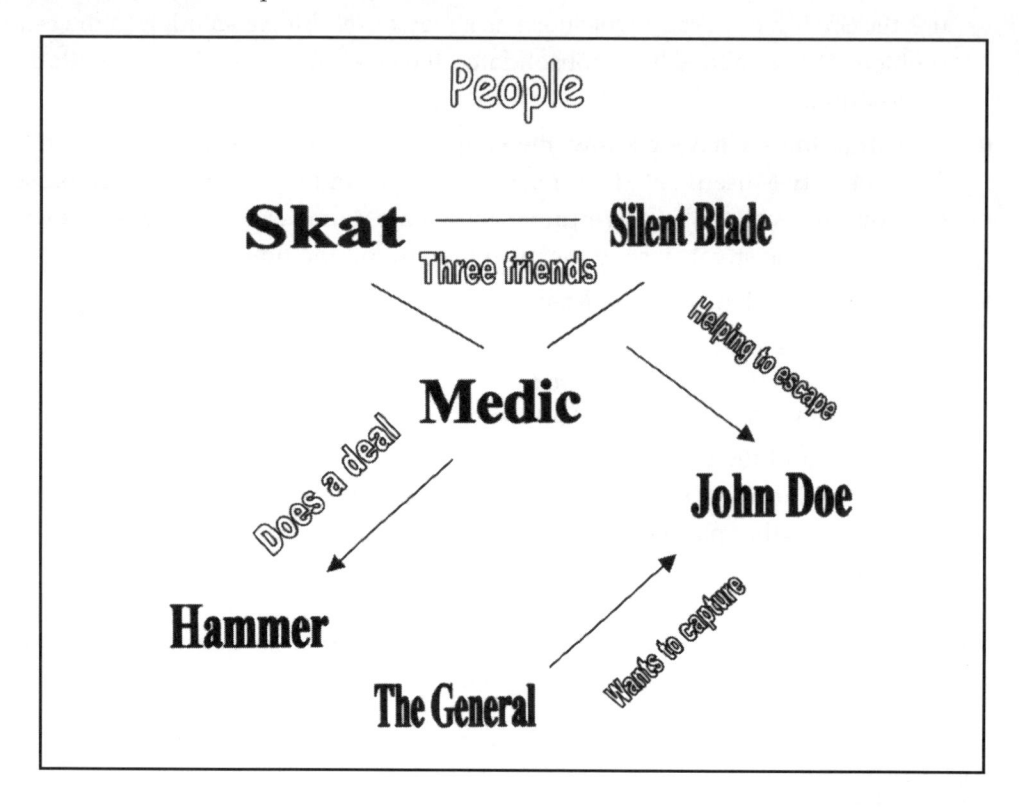

People

- **Skat** ── **Silent Blade** (Three friends)
- **Medic** (connected to Skat and Silent Blade)
- Medic — Does a deal → **Hammer**
- Silent Blade — Helping to escape → **John Doe**
- **The General** — Wants to capture → John Doe

Similarly, these are just the main locations, linked linearly as they appear in the story:

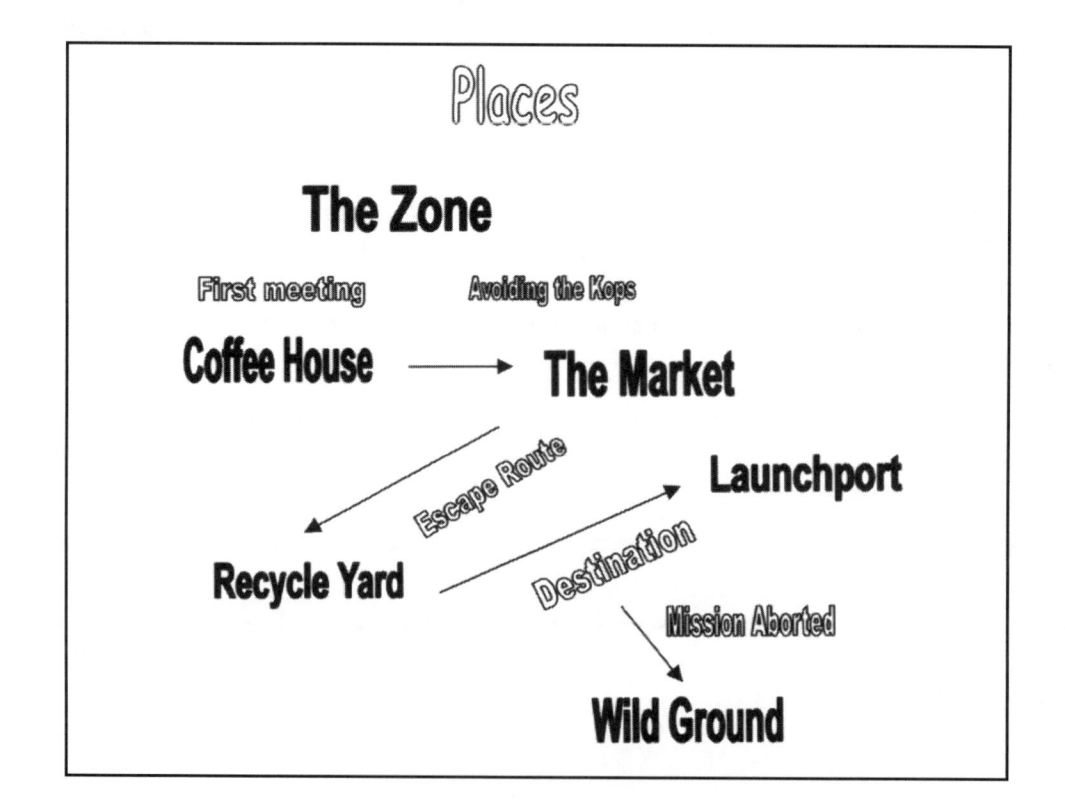

Places

- **The Zone**
- **Coffee House** (First meeting) → **The Market** (Avoiding the Kops)
- The Market → **Recycle Yard** (Escape Route)
- Recycle Yard → **Launchport** (Destination)
- Launchport → **Wild Ground** (Mission Aborted)

STORYMAKER CATCH PACK – USING GENRE FICTION AS A RESOURCE FOR ACCELERATED LEARNING

A BAGFUL OF STORY GAMES

These are the main objects, again connected in story sequence:

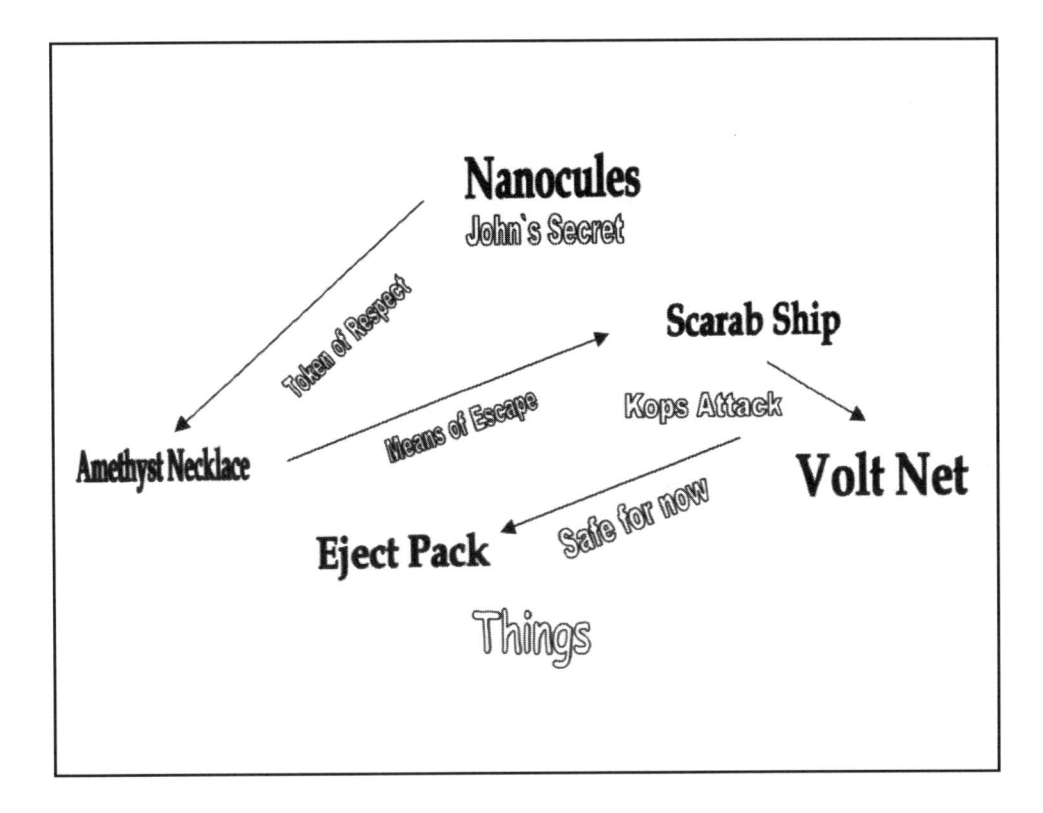

Nanocules — John's Secret
- Token of Respect → Amethyst Necklace
- → Scarab Ship
- Means of Escape
- Kops Attack → Volt Net
- Safe for now ← Eject Pack

Things

Create a more comprehensive overview by putting them together, apportioning an area of the larger map to each section. Then make some preliminary links between sections:

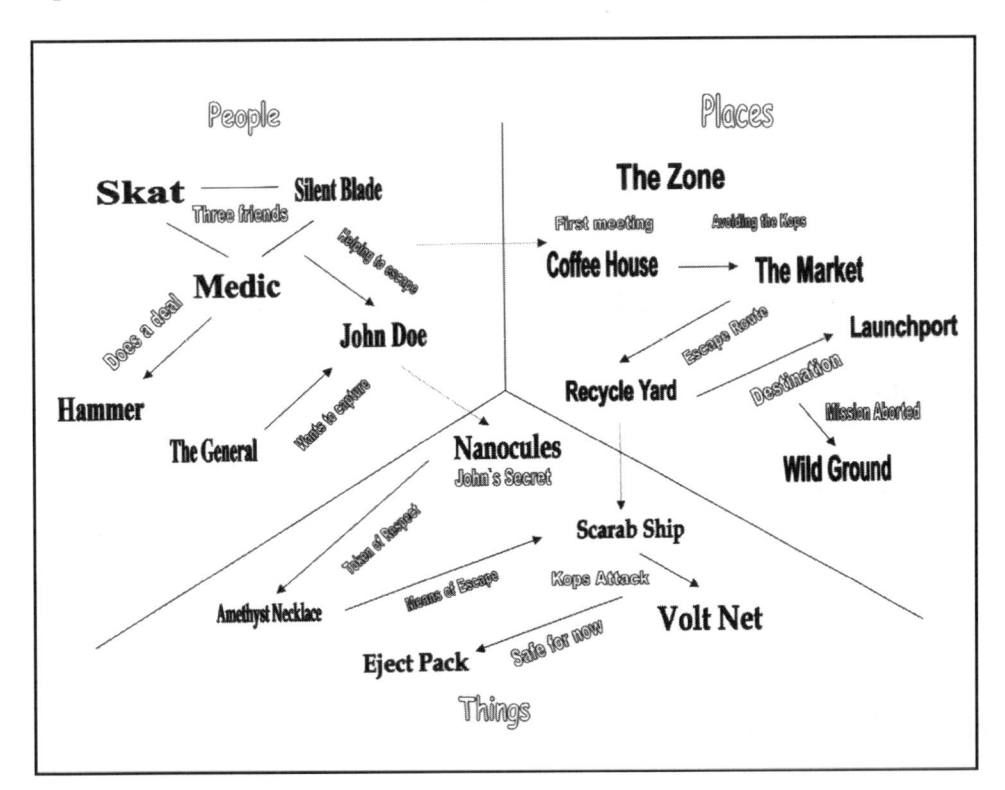

People
- Skat — Silent Blade (Three friends)
- Medic (Does a deal) — Hammer
- Helping to escape → John Doe
- The General — Wants to escape

Places
- The Zone
- Coffee House (First meeting) → The Market (Avoiding the Kops)
- Escape Route → Recycle Yard
- Launchport (Destination)
- Mission Aborted → Wild Ground

Things
- Nanocules — John's Secret
- Token of Respect → Amethyst Necklace
- Means of Escape → Scarab Ship
- Kops Attack → Volt Net
- Safe for now ← Eject Pack

153

STORYMAKER CATCH PACK - USING GENRE FICTION AS A RESOURCE FOR ACCELERATED LEARNING

◆ SECTION FOUR

Mel Rockett and Simon Percival in *Thinking for Learning* report the findings of using concept maps at a school in Northumberland. Claire Harbottle, one of the teachers at the Haydon Bridge High School, notes that concept mapping

- helped children to participate when they would not normally do so
- encouraged pupils to answer more questions as they verbalised their efforts
- proved popular as a group activity
- highlighted areas for development such as subject terminology and vocabulary associated with thinking skills.

You can use concept mapping to extend children's exploration of a story, while emphasising that good ideas arise out of making lots of connections. Encourage young writers to make links between people, places and things that do not actually appear in the story. What variations of the story and/or new stories do they suggest?

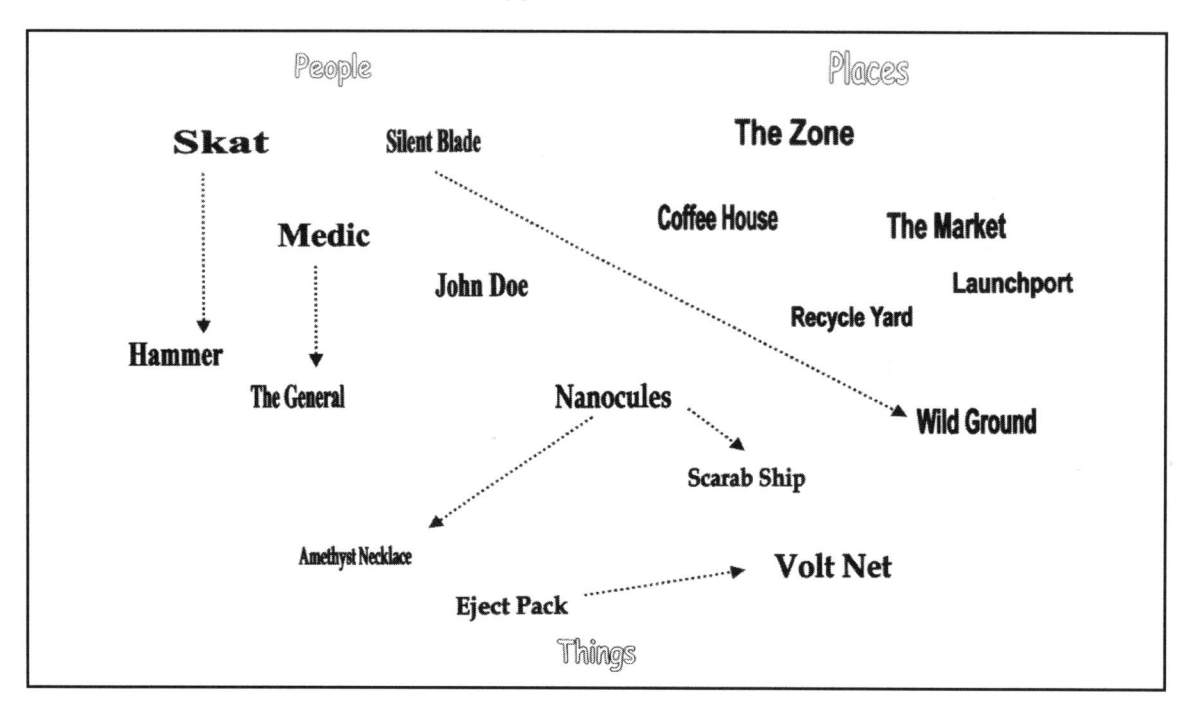

```
People                                    Places

   Skat        Silent Blade            The Zone

                                  Coffee House      The Market
       Medic                                              Launchport
                    John Doe            Recycle Yard
        ↓
  Hammer
              The General        Nanocules                   Wild Ground

                                      Scarab Ship

                       Amethyst Necklace      Volt Net
                                Eject Pack
                                    Things
```

Note: A full-sized version can be found on the CD resource.

◆ Other worlds

Modern Fantasy, Science Fiction and Horror continue the tradition of myth, legend and folk tale by taking the hero into other realms, both actual and psychological (although these are often intertwined). The main patterns are:

- the hero enters a fantastic world
- a being from a fantastic world enters the hero's 'ordinary' realm
- the hero already exists within a fantastic realm.

Variations of one or other of these patterns form the template for a huge number of genre tales.

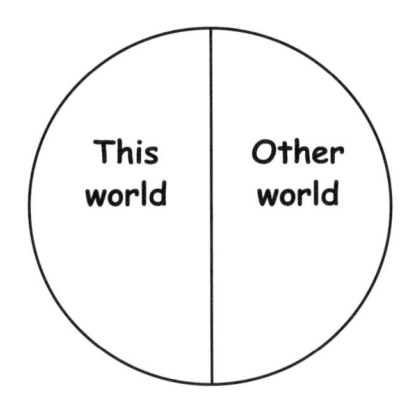

```
   This  | Other
  world  | world
```

Simply pointing this out to children can throw up plenty of ideas for stories, as they now have a basic 'mould', as it were, for characters, places and events to interact.

More detail and complexity can be added by superimposing 'the mythic journey' (see p.48) onto this template:

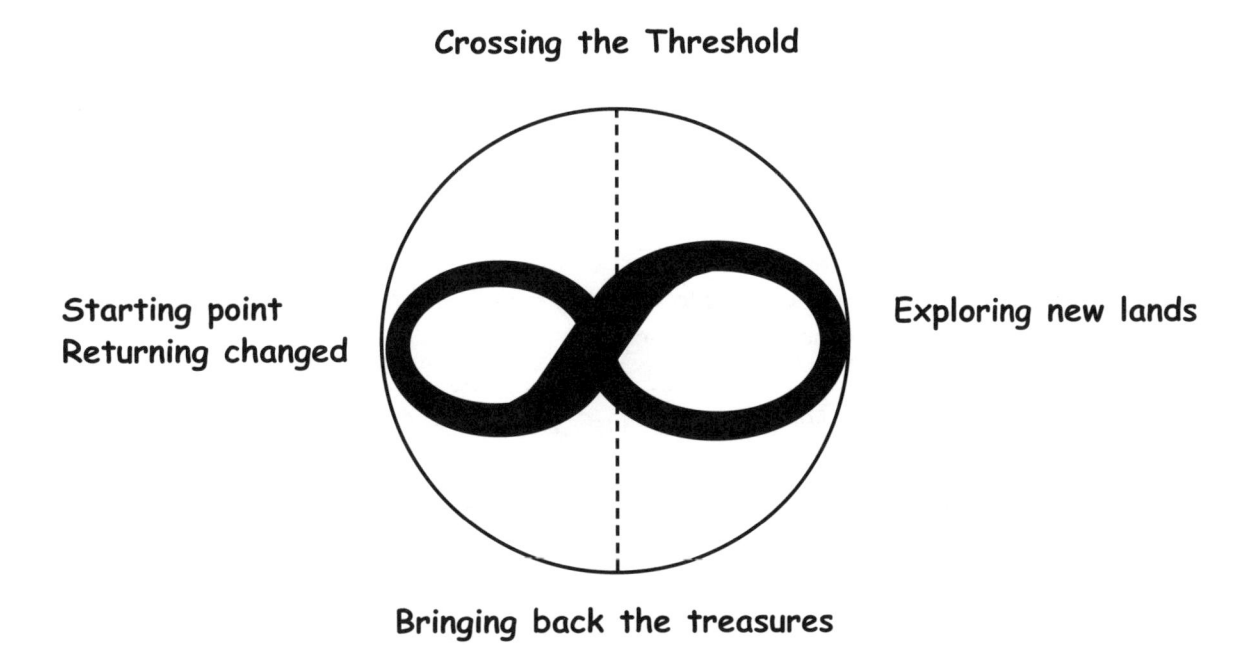

Crossing the Threshold

**Starting point
Returning changed**

Exploring new lands

Bringing back the treasures

So in this context Colin, the 'hero' of *She Bites*, explores the other world of Eleanor's supposed difference and, therefore, his paradigm of beliefs. He returns changed by the knowledge, but is destroyed by the 'villain' in a variation of the pattern above.

The three friends in *The Forever Man* cross the threshold of their known world and enter the other realm of Patchley Woods, a doorway to a labyrinth of domains. There they meet the mentor figure who is the Forever Man. One of the friends, Simon, takes on that role, we presume, while

◆ SECTION FOUR

Darren and Rob return to their own world with their perspective on life radically changed.

- Introduce children first to the 'this world/other world' template.
- Look at the main patterns of interaction between the hero figure(s) and the idea of these two realms.
- Superimpose the mythic journey on the two worlds template.
- Look at some familiar myths and legends to see how this model applies to traditional tales.
- Use *Catch & Other Stories* as examples of how this ancient pattern is just as relevant to the structure of Story now as it ever was.
- As appropriate, explore 'The deeper structure of stories', below, to put more layers of detail into the basic Other Worlds model.

◆ The deeper structure of stories

Stories are deeply rooted in human history because they are deeply rooted in the human mind. The template of Story – its themes, ingredients, motifs, its direction from past-to-future, its intra- and interconnectedness and symbolic or allegorical qualities – make narrative one of the most powerful ways we have of understanding the world and ourselves.

Increasingly I feel that developing the capacity to read and write (i.e. literacy) is a means to a much greater end. These activities are, as Elliot Eisner said, 'structure-seeking rather than rule-abiding'*. Kieran Egan, in *Teaching as Story Telling* (see Bibliography), summed up the point even more powerfully:

'The educational justification for learning to write has to be seen in the ecstatic power to create and express one's own world and one's own self.'

> * Elliot W. Eisner (1978): 'What do children learn when they paint?' **Art Education 31**, 3, pp.6–10.

Expressing one's own world and one's own self requires insight into those things as well as into their mode of expression. The whole purpose of taking stories apart is to be able to put them, and our own life-narratives, together in new and more meaningful ways.

Traditional stories** – folk and fairy tales – have much to teach us about expressing our world and ourselves. Some major components of such stories are found in the story wheel template opposite.

A BAGFUL OF STORY GAMES

> ** These have become sanitised and 'nicified' over the generations so that the power of parable has largely been lost. Nursery rhymes have turned into little sing-along frills in school days devoted to supposedly worthier pursuits. The symbolic power of these narratives seems to go largely unrecognised now, nor is any attempt made in schools to 'connect the learning' inherent in traditional tales with the more sophisticated — but no more significant — achievements of great works of literature.
>
> The 'hidden curriculum' of Fantasy, Science Fiction and Horror reconnects the deep teachings of fable, folk and fairy tales with the fundamental ongoing themes of human existence.

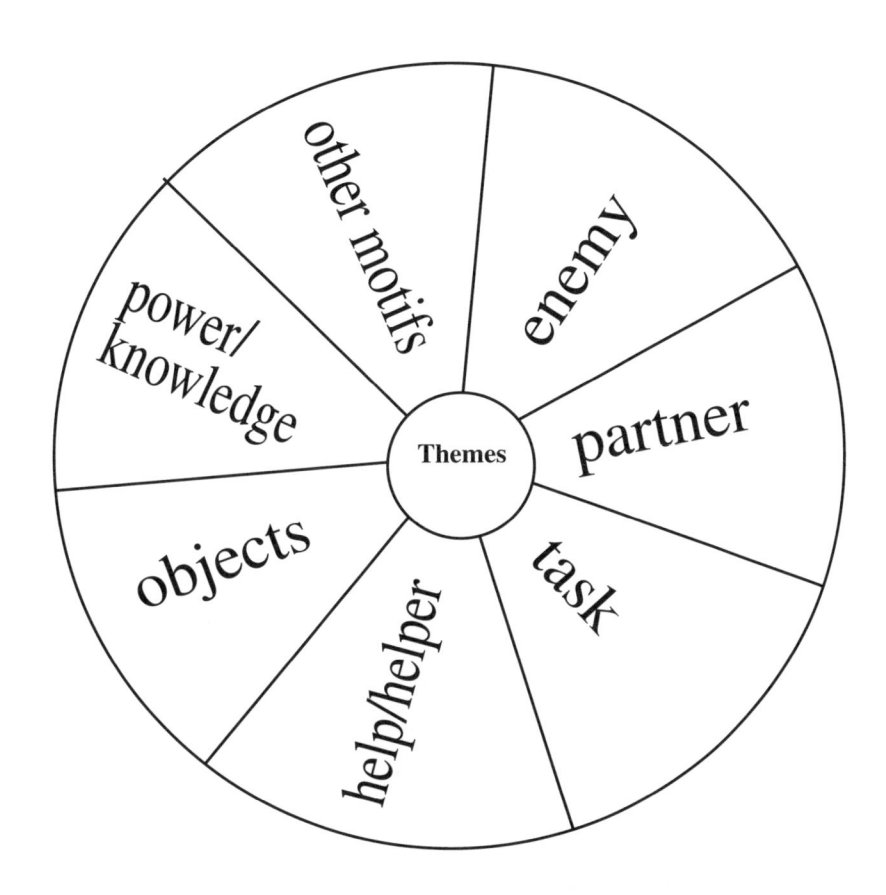

Themes wheel: enemy, partner, task, help/helper, objects, power/knowledge, other motifs

You will appreciate that this template can be used both for analysis and synthesis.

- Examine traditional nursery rhymes, folk tales and fairy tales. Notice that most of them contain most or all of the elements in the story wheel.
- Explore *how* these elements are used in specific stories. Can a partner also be an enemy? In what forms does a helper appear? What is the nature of the task that the main protagonist has to undertake? Who sets that task? What kinds of power or knowledge

◆ SECTION FOUR

help the protagonist carry out the task? What other major motifs (constituent features) appear in the story?

- Revisit 'Recipe for a story' (p.175) and amend or create recipes in light of what's been learned about narrative structure through the story wheel.
- Tease out the themes of traditional stories. If these are obscure, find a proverb or 'fortune cookie phrase' that can sit at the centre of the wheel.
- Look again at the notion of the 'learning journey' (p.48) and notice how many traditional tales follow this pattern: ∞.
- Examine some modern SF, Fantasy or Horror tales (the stories in *Catch* might be a good starting point) and separate out the elements indicated in the wheel.
- Superimpose the ideas wheel (p.128) on the story wheel (below) and brainstorm how the motifs of the outer circle can link with the elements of the story wheel. Turn the ideas wheel to a new configuration and repeat the brainstorming activity.

Story wheel and ideas wheel

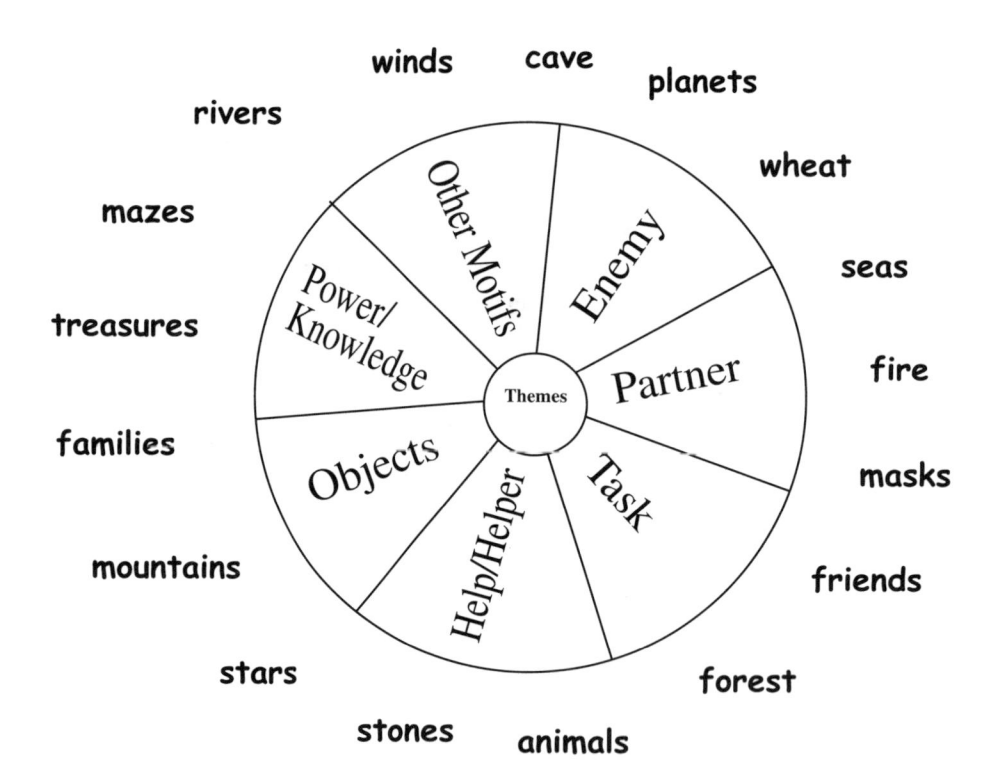

Outer ring (ideas wheel): winds, cave, planets, wheat, seas, fire, masks, friends, forest, animals, stones, stars, mountains, families, treasures, mazes, rivers

Inner wheel (story wheel) segments around Themes: Other Motifs, Enemy, Partner, Task, Help/Helper, Objects, Power/Knowledge

- Sample questions for brainstorming:
  - How can wheat be the enemy or aid the enemy?
  - What is the link between the hero or heroine's partner and masks?
  - What task involves the hero's friend(s) and how is this linked to the forest?
  - How might the stars offer help?

A BAGFUL OF STORY GAMES

- What object(s) might be found in the mountains? How could this be connected to families?
- What power could be discovered in a maze? In what sense can a maze represent knowledge?
- What other motifs that might be featured in the story can be brought by the winds?

You can generate another round of ideas by turning the story wheel within the ideas wheel to make new configurations. And the items around the outside of the ideas wheel can themselves be changed, giving you endless freedom to create new stories systematically within a structure.

Bringing it back to the centre

Sometimes stories can ramble (and essays wander off the point) because the central theme gets lost in the idea of the moment, and that idea can itself become fuzzy through the clutter of unnecessary detail. Reinforce the importance of the theme of the story by making simple links using the story + ideas wheel template.

We'll use some of the themes found in *Catch & Other Stories* to illustrate the point.

- **cave – enemy – transformation.** How could the enemy be transformed in or by the cave?
- **fire – partner – unexpected power.** What unexpected power does the hero's partner acquire (or lose!) through fire?
- **forest – task – appearances.** (What you see is what you get?) What task, undertaken in the forest, confuses the hero, partner or enemy through illusion?
- **stones – helper – destiny.** What significance do stones have for the hero's or enemy's helper in terms of his/her destiny?
- **mountains – objects – good and evil balanced.** What might be found in the mountains that balances the forces of good and evil within a person in the story, or within the story overall?
- **river – knowledge – the price to be paid.** What knowledge does the river bring that has to be paid for – and how?

Again, there's endless variety in this simple linking game. If themes seem a bit abstract, put a proverb at the centre of the circles and see what crops up.

- Look again at concept mapping (p.151). Take a traditional folk tale or modern genre story. Tease out the structural elements and create a concept map incorporating them. Here's an example taken from *Nanoman*.

◆ SECTION FOUR

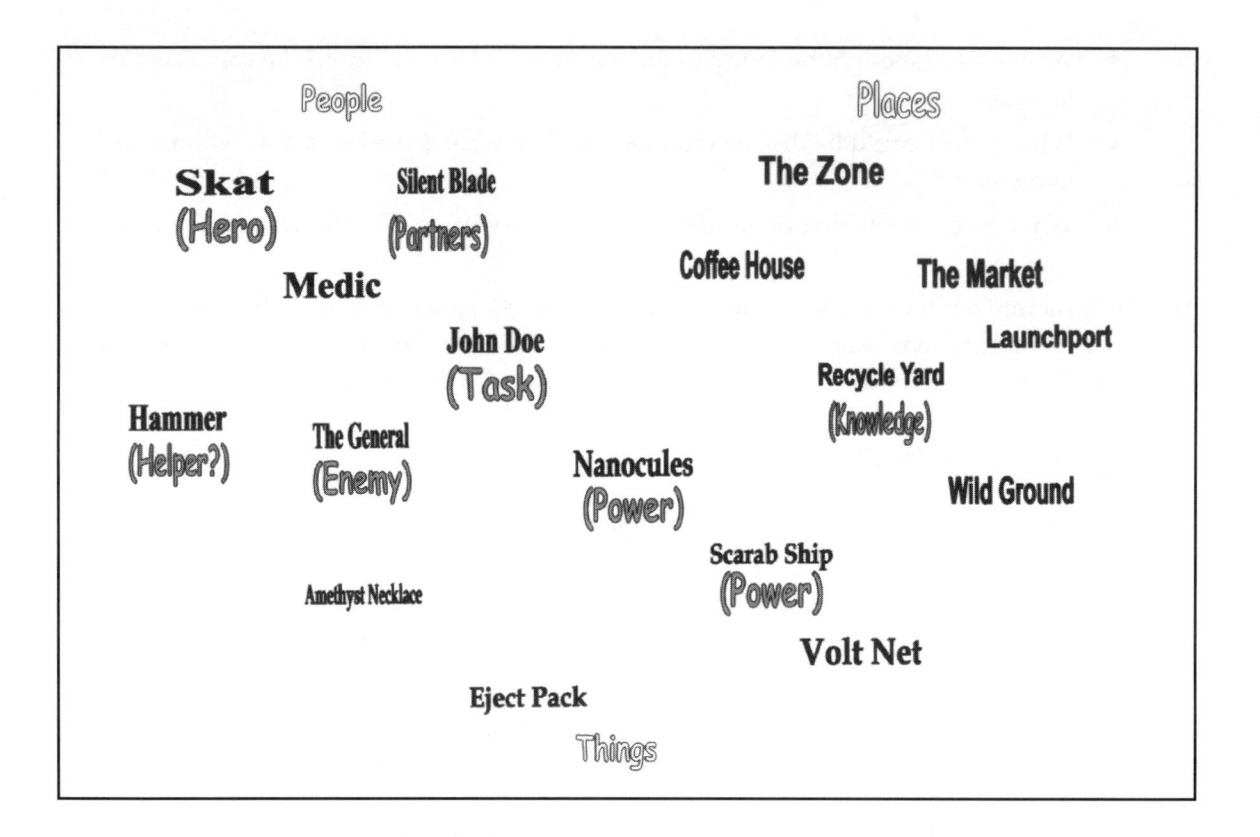

People   *Places*

Skat   Silent Blade   **The Zone**
(Hero)   **(Partners)**
                                    Coffee House   The Market
        Medic
                                                              Launchport
                  John Doe   Recycle Yard
                   (Task)   (Knowledge)
Hammer   The General
(Helper?)   (Enemy)   Nanocules   Wild Ground
                              (Power)
                                        Scarab Ship
              Amethyst Necklace   (Power)
                                                      Volt Net

                              Eject Pack
                                 Things

Story structure grid

Use the grid below for connecting the ideas we've been exploring to the 'obvious' structure of a story – which is that it must contain characters, settings, events and 'objects' (motifs).

	Person	Setting	Event	Motif
Name or type	Skat	The Zone	Escape	Nanocules
Function (what is it for?)	The hero battling against the odds. Acts as a way to find freedom.	Represents technology to the nth degree and social control.	To show that effort brings rewards/that decisiveness and courage make one strong.	A hope for the future/maybe the Grail – an impossible dream/maybe the two-edged sword of salvation or destruction.
Action (what does it do/what happens to it?)	She lives by her own resources and survives.	It has huge inertia – it resists (for now) attempts to rebel.	Although the mission is abandoned, the hero, friends and helpers stay ahead of the enemy.	They demonstrate their power and help to validate their creator's faith.

STORYMAKER CATCH PACK – USING GENRE FICTION AS A RESOURCE FOR ACCELERATED LEARNING

The usefulness of this grid is that it links the particular to the general within the framework of storymaking. In *Nanoman*, Skat is an individual but she is also an archetype (or at least a character type), the like of which can be found in many stories reaching back to the roots of folk- and fairy tales, and even beyond into myth and legend. Similarly with the Zone, the friends' attempt to escape, and the nanocules. These are contemporary elements of SF, and yet have their precursors in tales that stretch back hundreds and even thousands of years.

- Use the template to allow young writers to realise that all stories are linked in ancient and powerful ways; that the tradition of storymaking is the fundamental meaning-making activity in which we engage to make sense of our lives.

Variations on a theme

In reality, stories from around the world show much greater range and complexity than I've illustrated above: common roots give rise to a huge variety of fruits. Both the essential connectedness and the cultural diversity of stories are a cause for celebration. No man is an island, as John Donne said. We are all linked by storymaking.

Even a cursory glance at the finer structure of traditional tales can throw up plenty of ideas for new stories. Lens them through one or other of the genres and see what happens.

Here is a brief checklist of threads to be found in the tapestry of traditional tales. For a much more thorough exploration, see for example Propp's *Morphology of the Folk tale* (see Bibliography).

1. Moving away from familiar territory.
2. An instruction is given or implied.
3. A rule is broken.
4. A 'villain' appears.
5. There are consequences for breaking a rule.
6. The villain gains information about the hero or victim.
7. The villain attempts deceit.
8. The hero or victim is deceived.
9. The villain causes harm or injury which affects (directly or indirectly) the hero or victim.
10. Misfortune or lack appears.
11. The hero is approached with a request or command.
12. The hero or force for good decides on action.
13. The hero is tested.

◆ SECTION FOUR

14   A helper appears.

15   The hero acquires power.

16   The hero goes to a new place/to search for an object.

17   Hero and villain meet in direct conflict.

18   The hero is 'marked'.

19   The villain escapes.

20   The villain is defeated.

21   The situation is resolved.

22   The hero returns.

23   The hero is pursued.

24   The hero is rescued from pursuit.

25   The hero goes unrecognised.

26   A false hero appears.

27   The false hero makes deceitful claims.

28   A difficult task is proposed.

29   The task is undertaken.

30   The task succeeds/fails.

31   The hero is recognised.

32   The false hero is exposed.

33   The hero is given a new appearance.

34   The villain escapes.

35   The villain is punished.

36   The hero is rewarded.

Even just skimming through myths, legends and folk tales will allow you to see the rich mix of elements that go into their making. For our purposes an examination of these ideas allows us to make more sense and develop a greater appreciation of stories, and gives us plenty of grist to our own storymaking mill. Although the elements above are 'traditional', that doesn't mean we can't play with them. Any of the elements can be spun in different ways, and mixed-and-matched to see what the combination produces. Use a 6×6 number grid to try out the game. Roll a dice two or more times to select at random a number of elements. What variations on traditional stories appear?

A BAGFUL OF STORY GAMES

∞	1	2	3	4	5	6
1	1	2	3	4	5	6
2	7	8	9	10	11	12
3	13	14	15	16	17	18
4	19	20	21	22	23	24
5	25	26	27	28	29	30
6	31	32	33	34	35	36

Here are a few I prepared earlier…

a) 4/4 (element 22) – the hero returns… 5/2 (element 11) – the hero is approached with a request or command… 3/3 (element 15) – the hero acquires power.

My first idea is for an SF story:

> The hero is a member of an interplanetary exploration team that discovers some unusual artifacts on a now uninhabited world. News stories abound as to what these mysterious objects are and what they might do. During one of the many social events following the crew's return, the hero is approached by an influential businessman who offers him great wealth and power in return for the chance to examine the artifacts. So, not only can the hero live comfortably from now on, but he can also realise his dreams of further exploring the alien world that has captivated him.

b) 6/3 (element 18) – the hero is 'marked'… 4/1 (element 4) – a villain appears… 2/6 (element 32) – a false hero is exposed.

This could become a Horror/thriller tale:

◆ SECTION FOUR

> A young archaeologist accompanies his mentor on a dig in New Mexico to investigate an ambiguous discovery of some pre-Columbian dwellings and artifacts. During the work the young archaeologist is tainted by fumes that escape from a jar accidentally dropped by one of the workers. The fumes confer on him the power of precognition and other subtler senses, like being able to intuit the location of buried objects, etc. The mentor becomes intensely jealous of his young colleague's rapidly growing reputation and attempts to discredit him by implicating him in the theft of valuable antiquities from the museum attached to their university. The young archaeologist must now use his abilities to clear his name and expose the trickery of his rival.

c) 1/1 (element 1) – moving away from familiar territory… 1/5 (element 25) – the hero goes unrecognized… 6/2 (element 12) – the hero decides on action.

This could be a Fantasy story:

> The young hero-adventurer goes away to seek his fortune in new lands. Upon his return two years later he finds that nobody knows him; indeed, the whole character of the people has changed. Now they are subdued, compliant and lacking the humour and vigour he remembered so well. Most disturbingly, his true love seems to have forgotten him too – she, like the whole population, appears to be only half alive. Clearly something sinister has happened in the hero's absence, and he determines to find out what it is and put matters right.

Bear in mind that these are first impressions, initial ideas that can grow into more solid and polished storylines – or else I could choose to discard them. I might treat them as 'seed thoughts' and come back to them later, or work on them more systematically, using other storymaker games.

◆ A melange of motifs

As I have mentioned elsewhere, in my mind a motif is a constituent feature of a story that can be used and interpreted literally, symbolically or both. A motif might be a character, an object, a setting or its components, a sequence of action, a piece of dialogue – in fact, any aspect of the story that helps to define and describe the genre of that tale. Also, to my way of thinking, a motif differs from a theme (which is far broader), an ingredient (which is a non-specific constituent of a story), and an element – to use Vladimir Propp's terminology – which is a story constituent that has a direct bearing on the narrative dynamic structure of the tale.

And so let's suppose I'm writing a Fantasy story based on 'There is always a price to pay' (*theme*). At one point a villain appears in a puff of smoke (*an element made up of two motifs, the villain and the nature of the appearance*). However, the villain trips over (*motif*), and the hero (*motif*) takes advantage of this by scooping up a handful of mud and hurling it in the villain's face (*attempt at slapstick humour – ingredient*).

I am very aware of a statement once made by the philosopher Alfred North Whitehead, that taxonomy is the death of science – and also of creative writing, I might add. But I feel that it's useful to go this far in teasing out some of the threads that make up a story, because they allow us to weave a tale or spin a yarn more deliberately. In this regard, I remain mindful of the advice of the haiku poet Matsuo Basho – 'Learn the rules well and then forget them.'

What follows is little more than a checklist of some of the motifs I have found useful in writing SF, Fantasy and Horror stories. Although they are roughly grouped I tend just to let my eyes skim over them lightly, not looking for any particular order or specific application. As I do this, quietly and unhurriedly, I notice the impressions drifting across my mind's eye. Very often this is all I need to kick-start the storymaking process; once the ideas are flowing, I can work on them systematically through one or a combination of the techniques found elsewhere in this book and in *ALPS StoryMaker*.

adventurer	guide	wise one	prince(ss)
ruler	witch/wizard	guardian	wanderer
hero(ine)	beast	enchanter	maiden
lover	keeper	captor	liberator
learner	mentor	companion	trial
quest	mirror	blade	barrier
road	gift	theft	descending
ascending	earth	air	fire
water	metal	wood	stone
higher/lower	coincidence	circle	repetition
pattern	order/chaos	disguise	mountain
pool	shore	threshold	woods
darkness/light	morass	tower	labyrinth
bridge	crossway	house	city
door/gateway	key	hut/hovel	palace
uncharted way	high seas	life/death	sleep

◆ SECTION FOUR

wish	bond	mother	father
siblings	great/less	trickster	maker
giant	creature	bird	fish
serpent	tree	plant	seed
shoe	crown	mantle	ball
talisman	mark	touchstone	colour
bowl	weapon	wand	crystal
word	dance	alphabet	number
moon	stars	sun	phases
time	edge	axis	centre
rim	tangent	transformation	betrayal
abandonment	salvation	body	blood
flesh	egg	essence	pact
promise	faith	doubt	mind
dream	feeling	game	goal
journey	destination	puzzle	growth
healing	help	opposites	action
stillness	identity	imagination	inner/outer
ladder	hierarchy	retrospection	memory
forgetfulness	mirror	origin	ritual
split	wholeness	theft	union
unknown	wheel	web	age

Note: Important references for working with these motifs further are Tom Chetwynd's *Dictionary of Symbols** and Nancy Mellon's book *The Art of Storytelling* – see Bibliography.

> * Chetwynd asserts that 'Inner visions seek expression, while outer facts seek meaning.' This seems to me to be a wonderful justification for storymaking!

◆ The idea as hero

Science Fiction especially, and Fantasy and Horror to some extent, stand out from other genres in featuring what has been called 'the idea as hero'. Obviously some fiction is plot led; other stories focus more on characters and relationships; sometimes setting, atmosphere and mood are paramount. In the case of SF, all of these things can be subservient to a central notion that helps to *define and describe the genre, and without which the story could not exist.*

One example is Ray Bradbury's classic tale *A Sound of Thunder*. In this story a big-game hunter goes back to the Cretaceous Age to track down a *T rex*. He must follow a specially prepared metal pathway and on no account stray from it. However, in the heat of the kill he stumbles off the path and crushes a single butterfly. Upon returning to the present, he finds that civilisation has changed dramatically.

Now we can recognise the theme of the story as 'small beginnings have great consequences'. This is a theme I use myself – see p.45. But the form that the theme takes is idea-as-hero – the story cannot exist without it. This was the essence of Science Fiction for the writer Bob Shaw. Similarly, the central notion of the TV series *Doctor Who* is that the Doctor can explore time and space in his vehicle the *TARDIS**. Without that idea-as-hero there would be no story to tell. The notion of a go-anywhere vehicle could be translated into another, linked, genre; its Fantasy equivalent might be a genie**; in Horror the genie might become a demon with the power to project a character to another place and time. But the central concept remains unchanged.

> * 'Time And Relative Dimensions In Space', for the uninitiated. When I talk to children about my love of Dr Who, I point out that the TARDIS is much bigger on the inside than the outside, a bit like their brains.

> ** One useful distinction between Science Fiction and Fantasy is that SF makes the possible seem probable, and Fantasy makes the impossible seem possible.

Speaking in a purist sense, therefore, much of what is termed Science Fiction isn't so. The excellent *Star Wars* saga has been described, cruelly but not inaccurately, as 'cowboys and Indians in space'. Luke Skywalker becomes the hero-in-white, Darth Vader is the black-cloaked villain, the Imperial Troops translate into faceless Indian braves, Princess Leia is only another damsel-in-distress (albeit a highly capable one), the spaceships might just as well be horses or, if set in the modern day, fast cars.

- Discuss other definitions of SF, Fantasy and Horror.
- Unpack genre tales to see if the idea-as-hero applies.
- Use these notions with other storymaking games to create new tales.

◆ SECTION FOUR

Idea-as-hero and Catch & Other Stories

- *She Bites* – a boy is fearful that a girl he likes might not be what she seems. This idea could take many forms in lots of different genres. So: ✗

- *Gurney* – a boy can physically transform his flesh so that he can be anyone he chooses, but struggles just to be himself. Here we have themes to do with transformation and loss of identity, but the story couldn't happen without Scott Gurney's amazing ability. ✓

- *Catch* – A friendship develops between an old man and a boy as they fish literally in the ocean of time. Although 'the ocean of time' is normally used metaphorically, in this story its literal presence allows the story to exist. ✓

- *Dragon's Egg* – a boy's loyalty is torn between hanging around with his friends and not wishing to miss the hatching of, in this case, a dragon's egg. Here the egg simply represents a special event that might never recur. ✗

- *Brag* – a boy's skill is pitted against that of a sinister stranger. Implicit in the contest is the threat that the loser will pay heavily. This could just as well be a gunfight in a stereotypical one-saloon town in the American mid west of the 1850s. ✗

- *Nanoman* – a group of streetwise kids risk their lives to smuggle a top scientist and his breakthrough discovery away from danger. The conclusion of the tale sees the transference of John Doe's persona into the girl Skat, in the form of billions of nanomachines. The particular technological nature of John Doe's power lies at the heart of the story, which could not exist without it. ✓

- *The House that R'Ork Built* – some powerful invaders camouflage themselves to conceal their presence, trapping two boys who pose a threat to their secrecy. The transformation of the house towards the end of the tale is simply R'Ork the invader revealing himself. ✗

- *The Forever Man* – A group of three friends help the keeper of the portals between dimensions to prevent entities from straying out of their proper domain. At first glance this might be taken as a 'defence of borders' type tale, although here the domains referred to also represent accepted realities, so it's not just a case of strangers coming to town. ✓

- *Burning* – In the future, children with special powers are raised in isolation to be used in military conflict between warring states. The use of time as a force that Brin can control is not essential to the tale: he might just as well have a bomb in his hands. ✗

Feel free to disagree with these conclusions. You might find persuasive arguments to the contrary.

A BAGFUL OF STORY GAMES

◆ Storylines

Stories by and large are linear structures, and we can exploit that idea to help young writers to plot systematically. One of the most basic facts that children are taught about stories is that they have a beginning, a middle and an end…*

> * Except in one school I visited, where the whole class knew that a story is composed of 'Orientation, Complication and Resolution'. I said, 'Wow, those are long words. What do they mean?' None of the children could remember. I said to the teacher, 'Wow, those are long words. What do they mean?' She coloured up and pointed to a folder. 'Um… Well, I read it here.' I call this naming-of-parts teaching.

This template gives the Big Picture of a story's structure in a simple but effective way.

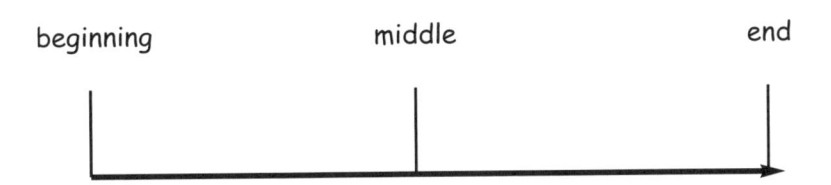

beginning — middle — end

There is also plenty of potential here for adding refinements…

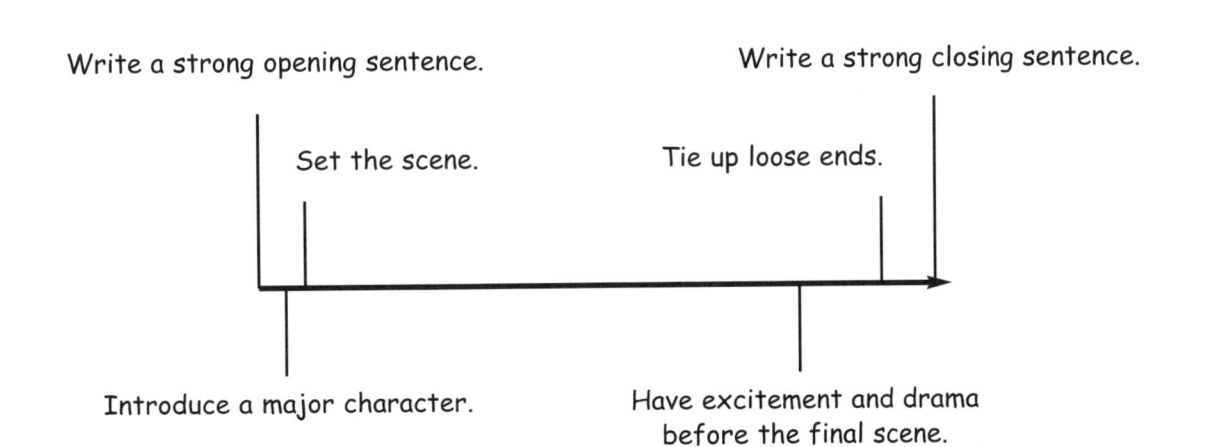

Write a strong opening sentence.   Write a strong closing sentence.

Set the scene.   Tie up loose ends.

Introduce a major character.   Have excitement and drama before the final scene.

◆ SECTION FOUR

The same visual organiser can be used for the analysis of stories. Below is a simple breakdown of the story *Brag*.

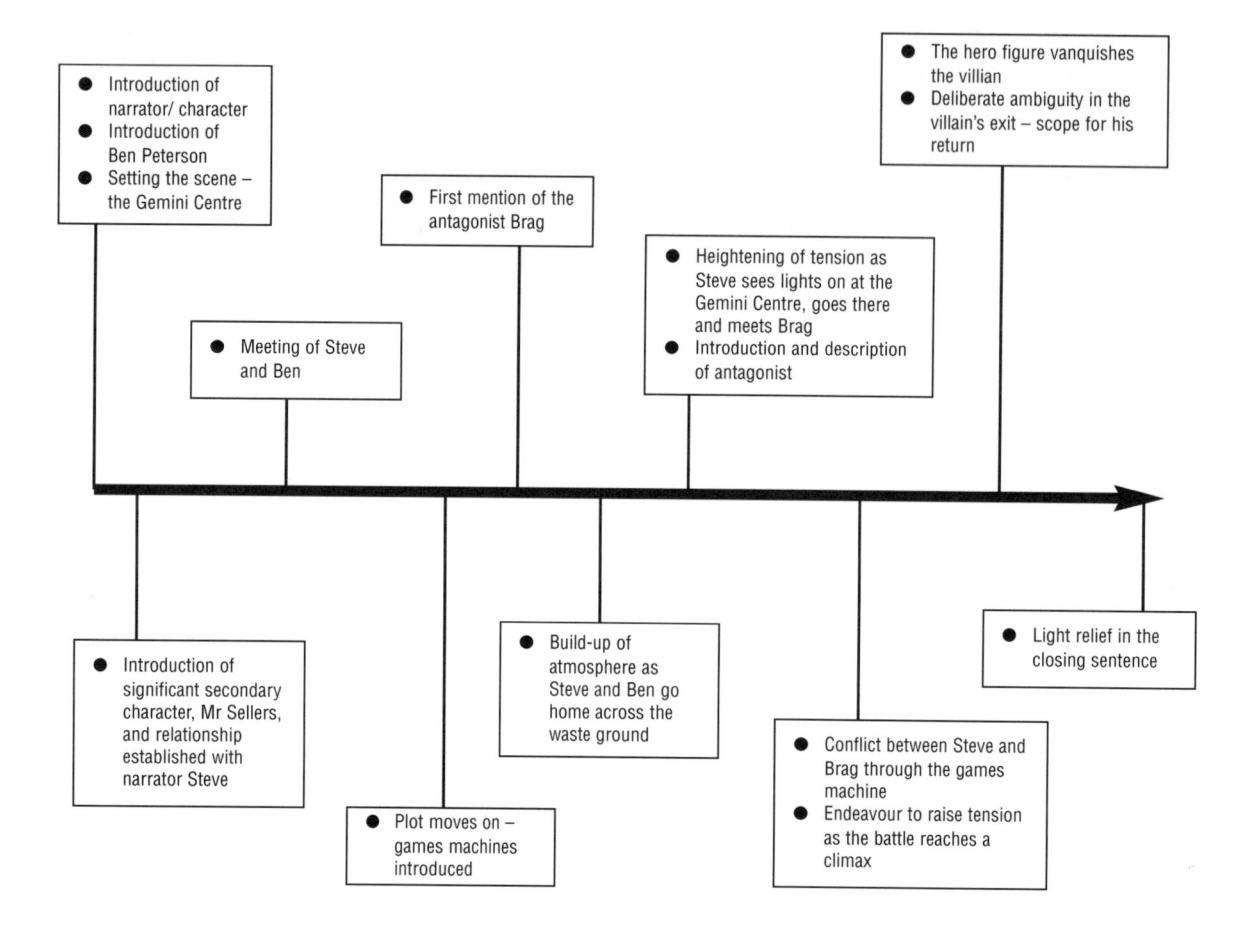

Above the line (left to right):
- Introduction of narrator/character
- Introduction of Ben Peterson
- Setting the scene – the Gemini Centre

- First mention of the antagonist Brag

- Heightening of tension as Steve sees lights on at the Gemini Centre, goes there and meets Brag
- Introduction and description of antagonist

- The hero figure vanquishes the villian
- Deliberate ambiguity in the villain's exit – scope for his return

Below the line (left to right):
- Meeting of Steve and Ben

- Introduction of significant secondary character, Mr Sellers, and relationship established with narrator Steve

- Plot moves on – games machines introduced

- Build-up of atmosphere as Steve and Ben go home across the waste ground

- Conflict between Steve and Brag through the games machine
- Endeavour to raise tension as the battle reaches a climax

- Light relief in the closing sentence

Because this is a short story, all of the major elements can be included on one storyline. When studying or planning novels, create a separate storyline for each chapter, and then incorporate the most important aspects of each chapter into an overall visual…

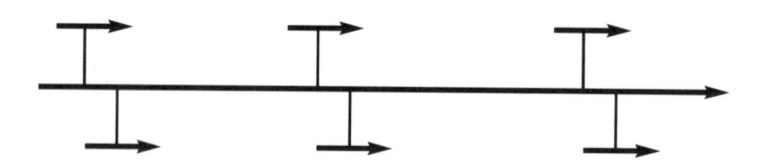

- Use storylines with story ingredients (see p.175). If you draw the storyline on a large sheet of paper and work at a table, write examples of ingredients on cards. As ideas for the actual story emerge, move the ingredients cards around to generate variations of the story and/or ideas for new stories. This version of the activity introduces a kinaesthetic element.

A BAGFUL OF STORY GAMES

Strong opening sentence — **Danger** — **Climax**

Set the scene — **Conflict**

Pose a problem — **Secret** — **Resolution**

Introduce a character — **Mystery**

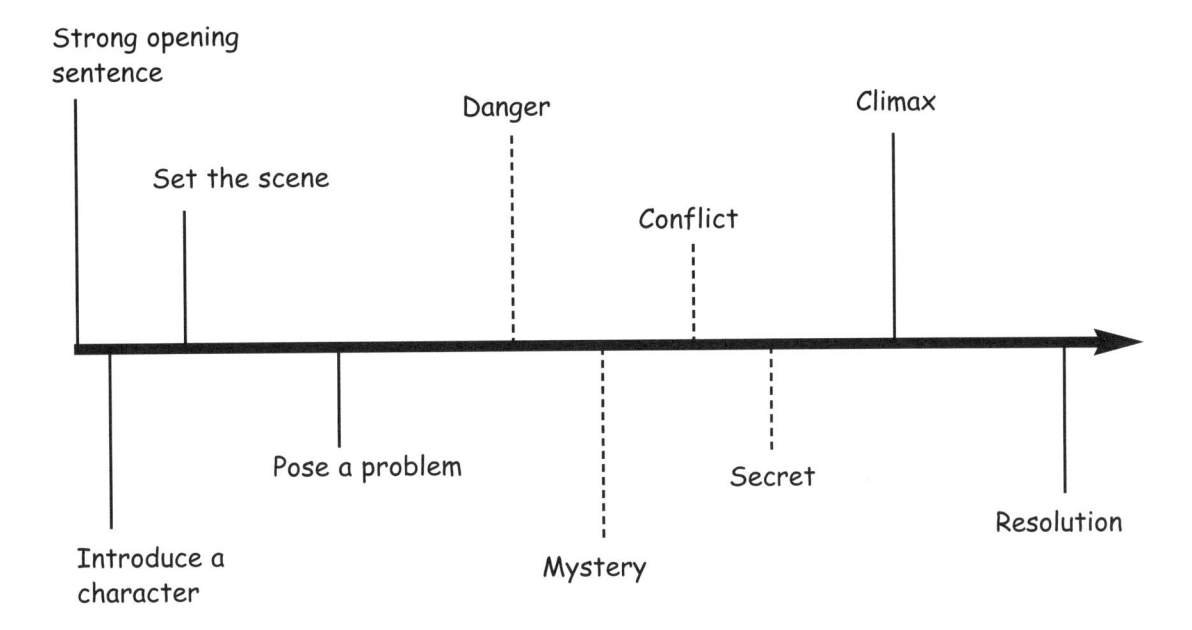

- Put more detail into the activity by using motif cards. In the example that follows, the opening sentence and scene-setting can *make reference* to the castle – the story does not have to open in the castle. Similarly, the introduction of the first character and the initial problem in the story will have something to do with the dragon – the character and problem do not need to *be* the dragon. Bear in mind also that these motifs can be considered as metaphors. The castle could represent strength and a commanding presence, for example, while the dragon could represent uncontrolled rage. In this case both motifs might refer to an enraged character whose fury is a problem for himself or others. Knowing that gives us insights into the kind of situation that might prompt that character's reaction.

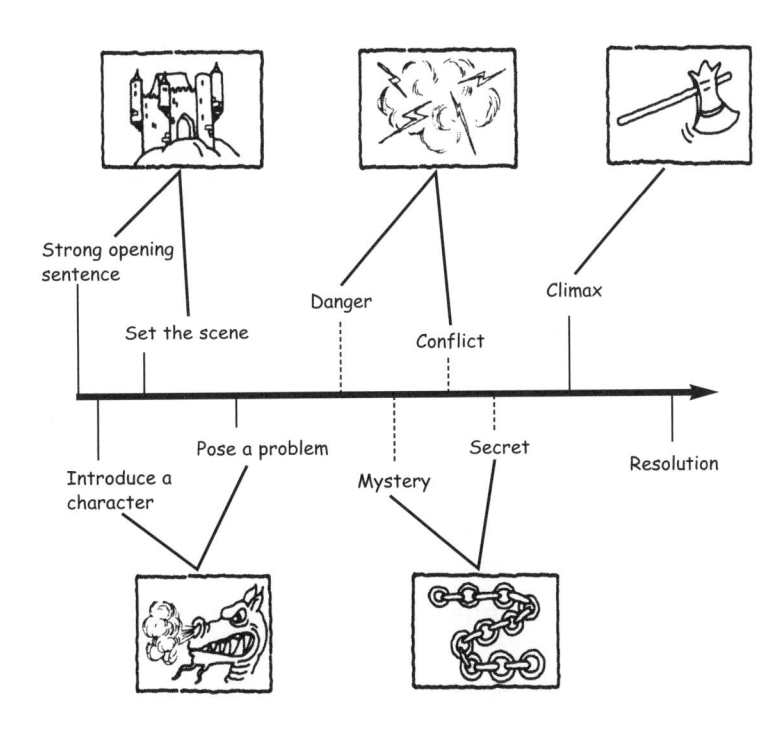

STORYMAKER CATCH PACK – USING GENRE FICTION AS A RESOURCE FOR ACCELERATED LEARNING

◆ SECTION FOUR

- **Sub-plotting**. This is a refinement of the basic linear story, where subsidiary incidents – involving the main or secondary characters – highlight and give insights to the main plot incidents. The idea of sub-plotting can be introduced using storylines – and see also 'Context sentences and connective prompting' on p.p.114–117. Again we'll use the example of *Brag* to illustrate the point.

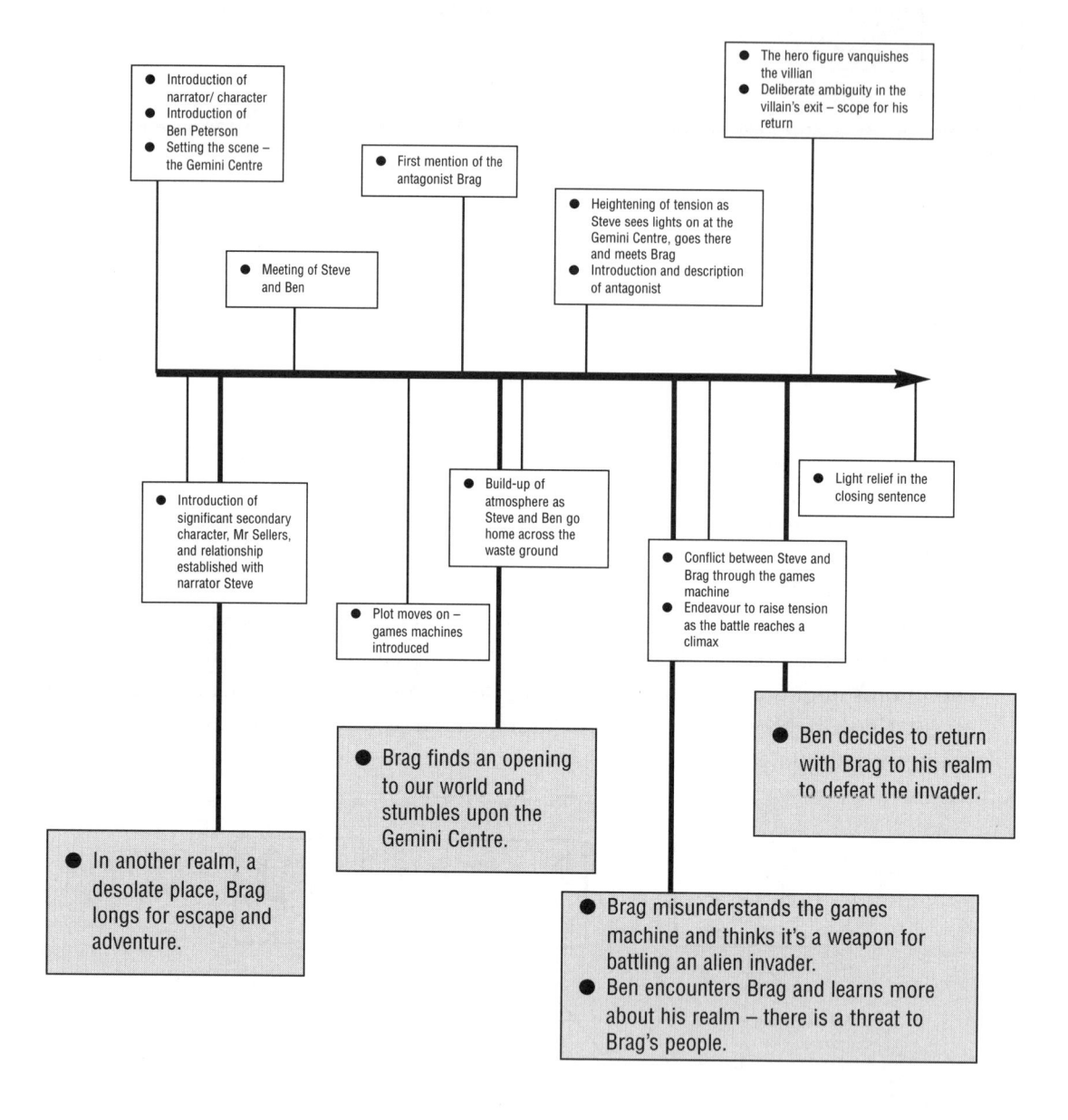

Above the timeline (main plot):

- Introduction of narrator/ character
- Introduction of Ben Peterson
- Setting the scene – the Gemini Centre
- Meeting of Steve and Ben
- First mention of the antagonist Brag
- Heightening of tension as Steve sees lights on at the Gemini Centre, goes there and meets Brag
- Introduction and description of antagonist
- The hero figure vanquishes the villain
- Deliberate ambiguity in the villain's exit – scope for his return
- Light relief in the closing sentence

Below the timeline (sub-plot):

- Introduction of significant secondary character, Mr Sellers, and relationship established with narrator Steve
- Plot moves on – games machines introduced
- Build-up of atmosphere as Steve and Ben go home across the waste ground
- Conflict between Steve and Brag through the games machine
- Endeavour to raise tension as the battle reaches a climax
- Ben decides to return with Brag to his realm to defeat the invader.

- In another realm, a desolate place, Brag longs for escape and adventure.
- Brag finds an opening to our world and stumbles upon the Gemini Centre.
- Brag misunderstands the games machine and thinks it's a weapon for battling an alien invader.
- Ben encounters Brag and learns more about his realm – there is a threat to Brag's people.

Sub-plots can enrich a story and take the idea into new areas (in Ben's case, literally so!). Encourage children to come up with a range of possible sub-plots – have lots of ideas in order to choose the best ideas.

- Mr Sellers secretly belongs to the Intergalactic Police and is recruiting new space fighter pilots by seeing who does well on the games machines.
- The games machines actually *are* weapons, and when Steve plays them the battle is really occurring somewhere in space.

- Unknown (at first, anyway) to Steve, the contest with Brag is a test to see which of them is smarter, faster and more determined. Should Steve lose, Brag's race will invade our world. Ben finds out about this and faces the dilemma of whether or not to tell Steve: if Steve finds out it's for real, it could shatter his confidence.
- Brag has actually escaped from the house in Patchley Woods as featured in *The Forever Man*. The characters from that story join with Steve and Ben to recapture Brag…
  - Ben decides to explore the rooms of the house. He becomes lost and the other characters have to find him.
  - Brag does not wish to be recaptured. He starts a fire in the house in an attempt to destroy the portal.
  - Brag does not wish to be recaptured. He opens more portals in the house to create confusion and fear.

Storylines and the deeper structure of stories

Construct storylines by adding elements from the selection on pp.161–162 and add others of your own that come to mind. Examine some traditional fairy tales with your group and see if they conform to a common pattern (the fairy tales, not your group).

Parallel story

Combine analysis and synthesis by creating parts of or an entire parallel story. Begin with a short story that has a relatively simple structure (one of the *Catch* stories would be suitable) and make changes along these lines:

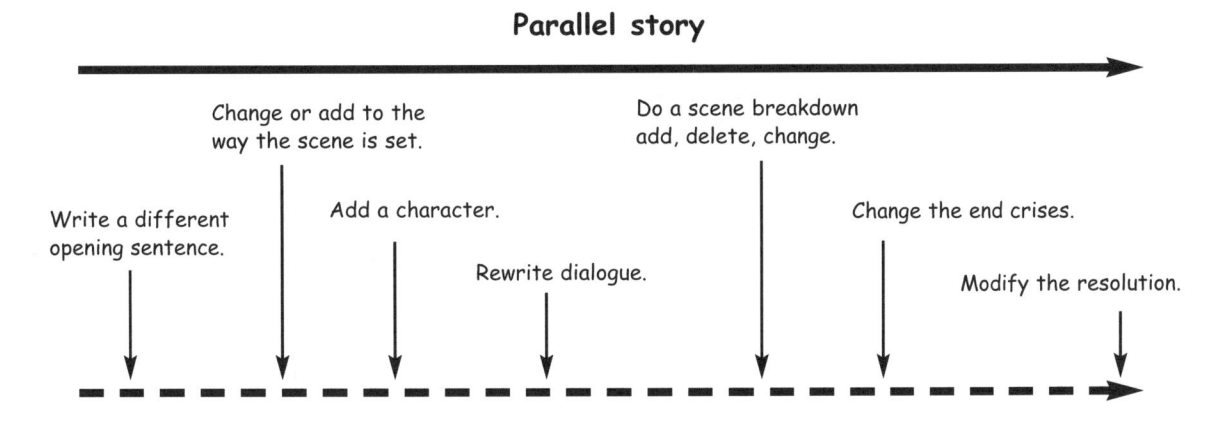

Parallel story

- Write a different opening sentence.
- Change or add to the way the scene is set.
- Add a character.
- Rewrite dialogue.
- Do a scene breakdown add, delete, change.
- Change the end crises.
- Modify the resolution.

Of course you can make as many or as few changes as you like to an already existing story: it's probably best to start with small details before making major structural changes – don't knock down a wall before you know how the house has been built.

> **Tip:** If you decide to use a story from **Catch & Other Stories**, copy the text from the CD resource and paste it into a Word document. Make your changes using a different colour of text. You might also consider annotating the changes – create a table with two cells: import the story into the right-hand cell and write your notations in the left-hand cell.

◆ SECTION FOUR

- Add insight to the process of parallel storymaking by using the visual organiser below to allow children to appreciate at a glance whether they are making many alterations or deep structural changes to a story. You can revisit the activity many times, working your way down from the top.

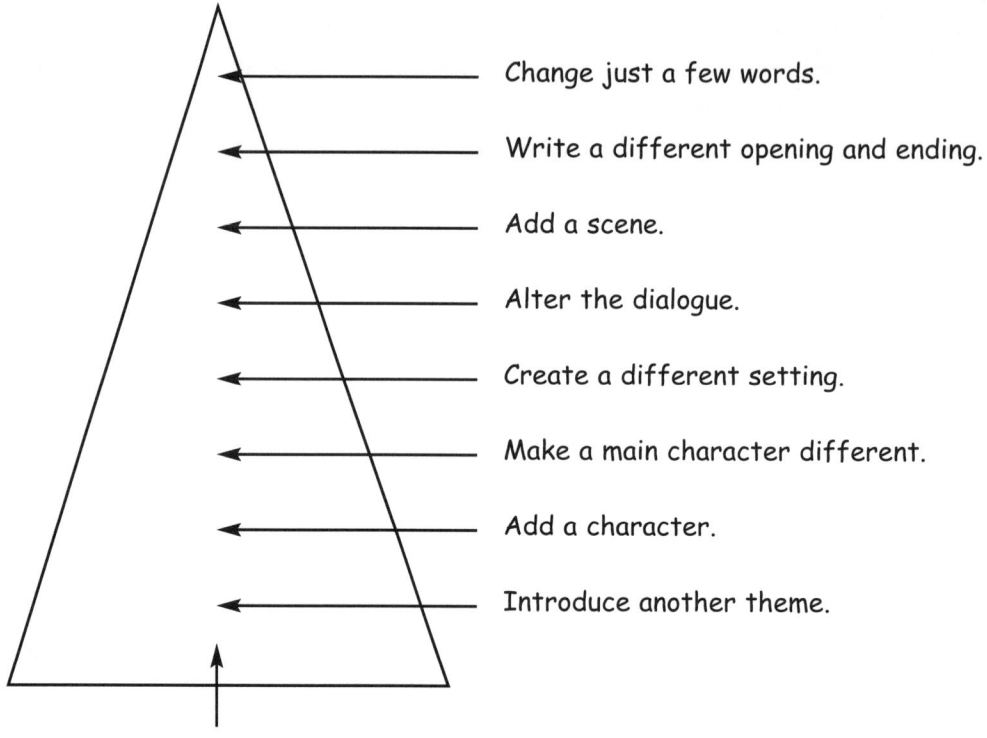

Change just a few words.

Write a different opening and ending.

Add a scene.

Alter the dialogue.

Create a different setting.

Make a main character different.

Add a character.

Introduce another theme.

Make a new story keeping only the original title.

Storylines and the mythic structure of stories

At their deepest level, most if not all stories share the structure that we encountered earlier in the form of the 'learning journey'. Contemporary Fantasy, Science Fiction and Horror stories make these 'roots of story' accessible – which they need to be before they can become personally relevant. Some exploratory activities follow in the next section.

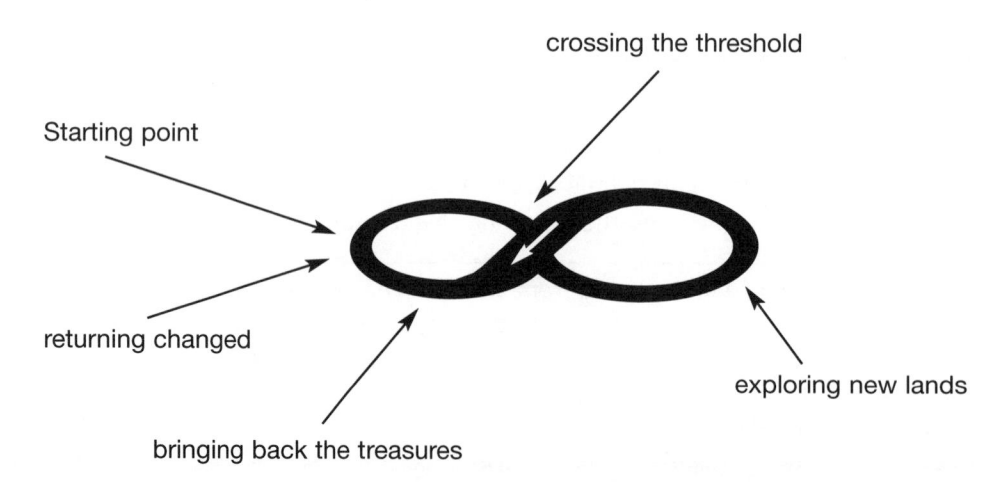

Starting point

crossing the threshold

returning changed

exploring new lands

bringing back the treasures

◆ Story ingredients

In my mind, story ingredients are smaller than themes but larger than motifs. A motif is a constituent feature of a story that helps to define and describe the genre: a crumbling castle perched on top of a sheer cliff and set against the backdrop of a lightning-torn sky is a motif – you know that this story is likely to be gothic Horror. Humour is a thread that might run through the story, part of the 'flavouring' of the tale, so to speak. Motifs can pick out the humour, of course – the vampire might have leapt from the castle battlements in his pyjamas – but the notion of 'humour' is not specific to Horror stories; it can be found throughout fiction.

Ingredients commonly found in stories include:

- problem
- secret
- conflict
- danger
- humour
- mystery
- treasure (something precious)

Once children are aware of the idea of ingredients, you can build them into a number of storymaking activities.

Story recipes

Make up story recipes as part of your own preparation for writing, or to review a story that's already in existence. Here's an example made from *The House That R'Ork Built:*

- Take two inquisitive boys, an autumn evening and an isolated farmhouse.
- Add two large spoonfuls of mystery, a dash of humour and increasing quantities of excitement as you bring the mixture to the boil.
- Make sure the problem is hot before adding the spice of danger and plenty of action towards the end.
- Throw in a dash of gore, spice up with danger and include a surprise twist as you remove from the heat.
- Serve with a little pickle and plenty of relish.

◆ SECTION FOUR

Ingredients and storylines

Because we naturally like to contextualise things, scattering ingredients along a storyline can throw up lashings of ideas. In the example below the size of the circle indicates the importance of the ingredient at that point in the story.

Strong first sentence

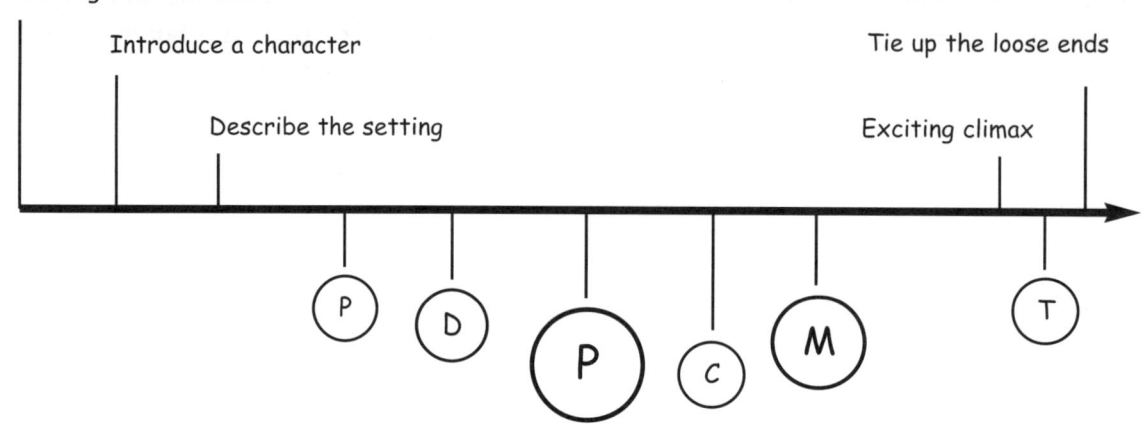

Introduce a character

Describe the setting

Tie up the loose ends

Exciting climax

P D P C M T

So – problem, danger, bigger problem, conflict, substantial mystery and a treasure just after the climactic conclusion but before the resolution and ending. The pattern can be varied endlessly.

Ingredients and story trees

See p.145 for more about story trees. The same idea of flexibility within a structure applies here, though in a more sophisticated way.

STORYMAKER CATCH PACK - USING GENRE FICTION AS A RESOURCE FOR ACCELERATED LEARNING

As in the storyline version, here you can vary the size of the circles depending upon the importance of the ingredient at that point in the story.

> **Tip**: Work at a table and use circles of card for the ingredients. Have children move the ingredient circles around to create a broad structure for a story. Use motif cards (see 'Story cards', p.139) to add further details.

Ingredients and maps

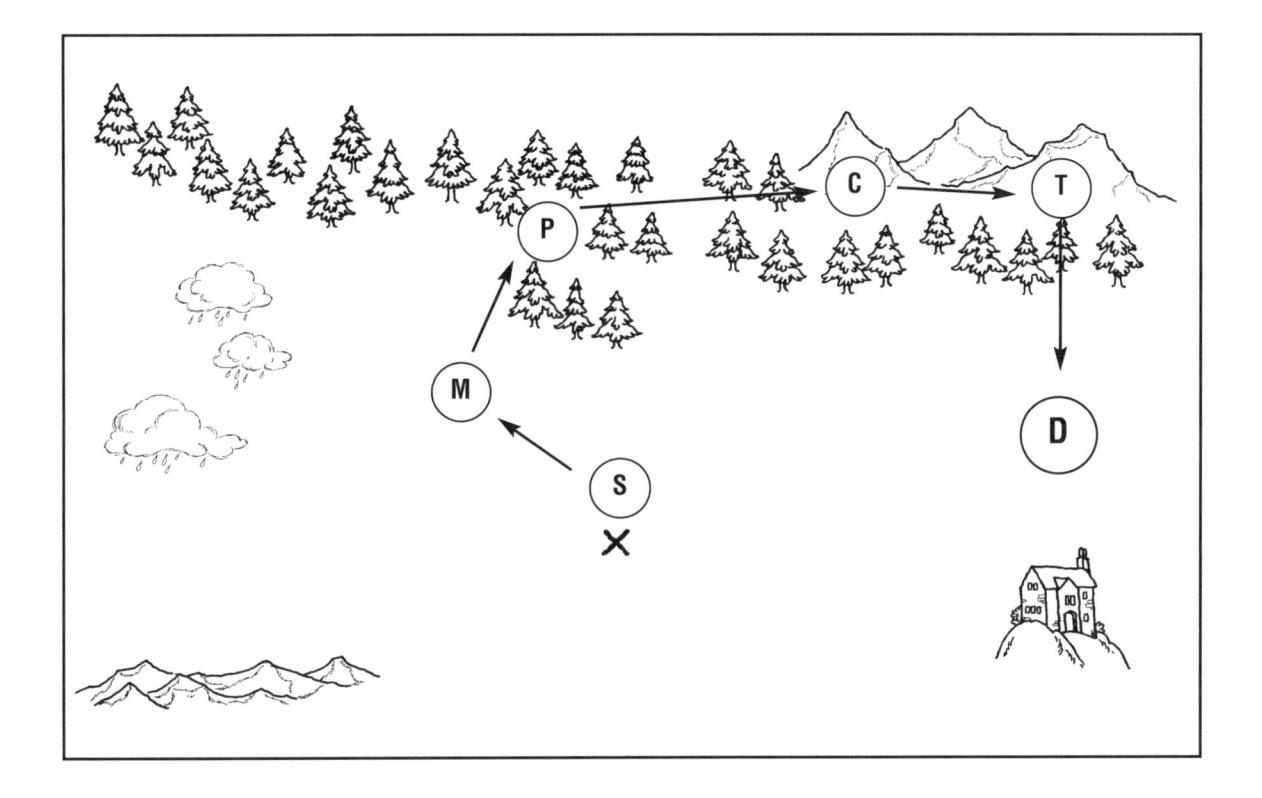

Again, you can work with motifs to help contextualise the ingredients. Place ingredient circles around the map and then annotate them to create a quick and easy story plan.

◆ SECTION FOUR

Ingredients and picture exploration

See p.55 for the process of picture exploration. Add ingredient circles to stimulate further questions.

Mixing ingredients

Continuing our recipe analogy, mix two ingredients together and use them with any of the above techniques.

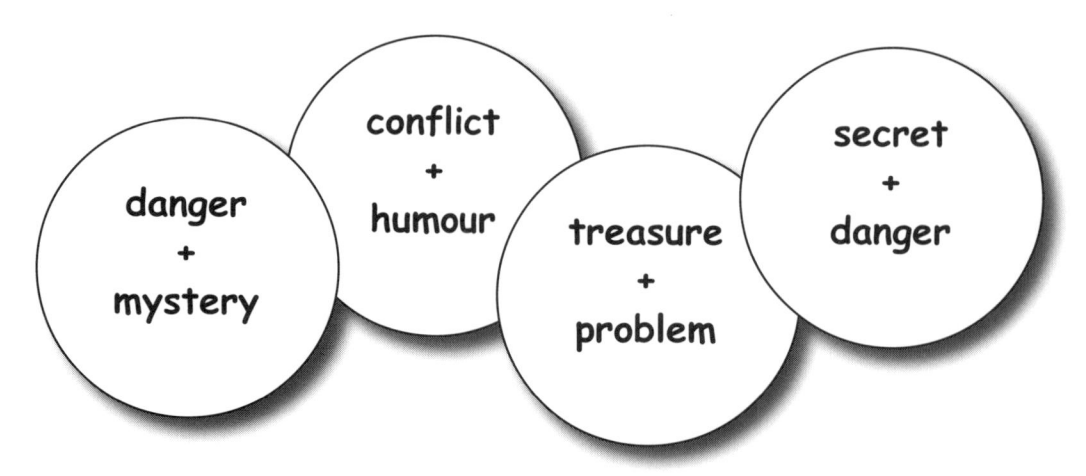

- danger + mystery
- conflict + humour
- treasure + problem
- secret + danger

Ingredients and themes

Choose a theme as the basis for the story and drop in a few ingredients and perhaps a motif or two, and see what happens.

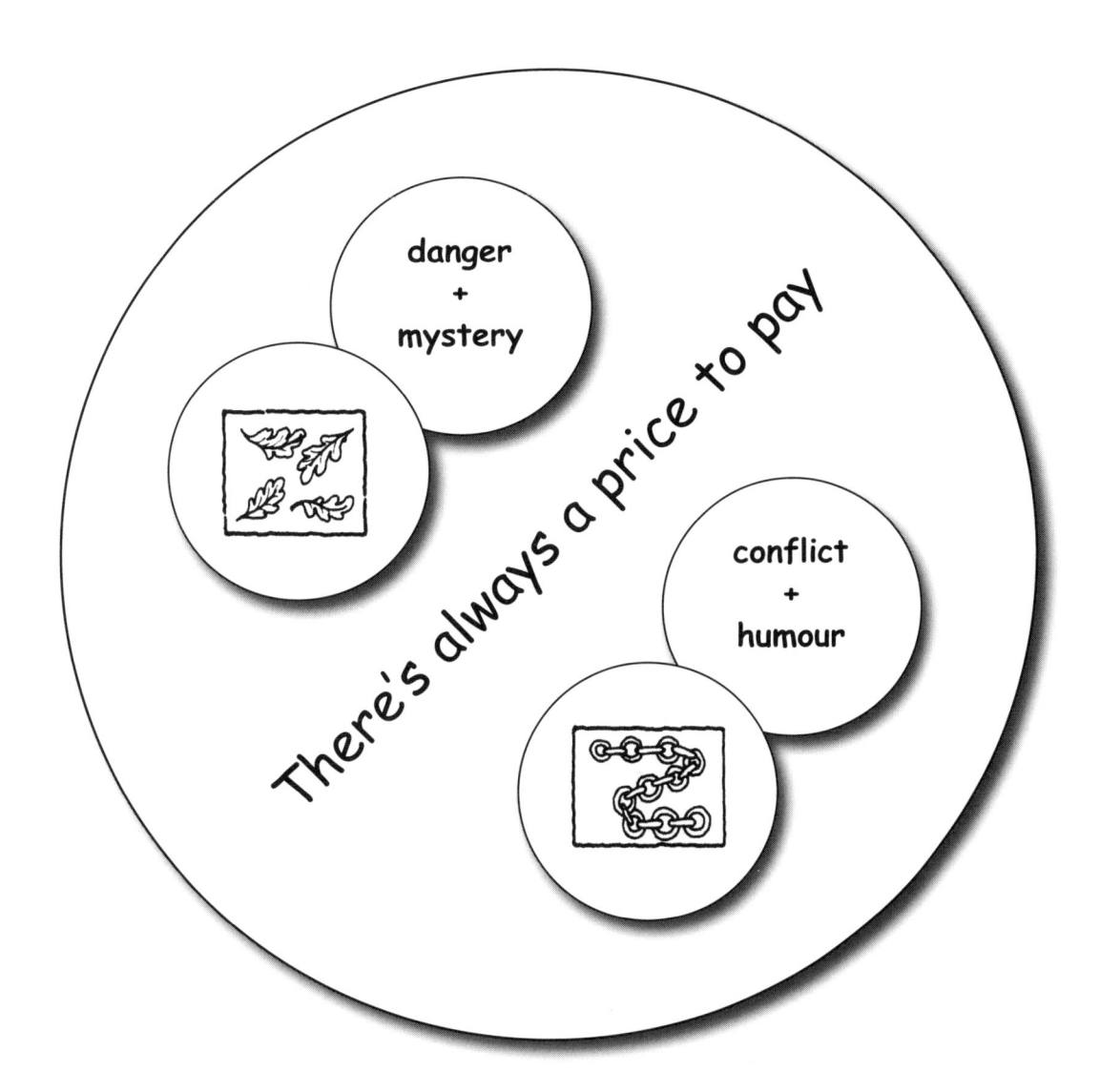

There's always a price to pay

- danger + mystery
- conflict + humour

Mix and match

The best way to encourage children to adopt the creative attitude is to display it yourself. My hope is that you won't just go 'by the book' when using *StoryMaker Catch Pack*: the trouble with going by the book is that it's usually somebody else's book. Feel free to adapt the storymaking games as you like. Put them together in new combinations and see what works for you. Overleaf are some mix-and-match grids so that you can make a start with this. Which games work best together in any grid? Then combine games from different grids.

SECTION FOUR

	Picture Exploration	Mix & Match Senses	Lensing	Fantasy Grid	Six Big Important Questions	Twenty Questions	Venn Diagrams	Nameplay	Design-a-Monster	Add-a-Bit
Add-a-Bit										▓
Design-a-Monster									▓	
Nameplay								▓		
Venn Diagrams							▓			
Twenty Questions						▓				
Six Big Important Questions					▓					
Fantasy Grid				▓						
Lensing			▓							
Mix & Match Senses		▓								
Picture Exploration	▓									

180

STORYMAKER CATCH PACK - USING GENRE FICTION AS A RESOURCE FOR ACCELERATED LEARNING

A BAGFUL OF STORY GAMES

	How Tall, How Strong?	Monster Maker	Monster As Metaphor	Character Grid	Thumbnails	Diamond Ranmking	Living Graphs	Context Sentences	Connective Prompts	Fortune Cookie Phrases
How Tall, How Strong?	�©									
Monster-Maker		▓								
Monster as Metaphor			▓							
Character Grid				▓						
Thumbnails					▓					
Diamond Ranking						▓				
Living Graphs							▓			
Context Sentences								▓		
Connective Prompts									▓	
Fortune Cookie Phrases										▓

◆ SECTION FOUR

	Consequences	Odd-One-Out	Personas	Gathering Treasures	Ideas Wheel	Story Circles	Start Anywhere	Story Maps	Jigsaw Town	Story Tray
Story Tray										
Jigsaw Town										
Story Maps										
Start Anywhere										
Story Circles										
Ideas Wheel										
Gathering Treasures										
Personas										
Odd-One-Out										
Consequences										

A BAGFUL OF STORY GAMES

	Story Tree	Mystery Mapping	Concept Maps	Other Worlds	Deeper Structure of Stories	Story Structure Grid	Melange of Motifs	Storylines
Story Tree								
Mystery Mapping								
Concept Maps								
Other Worlds								
Deeper Structure of Stories								
Story Structure Grid								
Melange of Motifs								
Storylines								

◆ SECTION FOUR

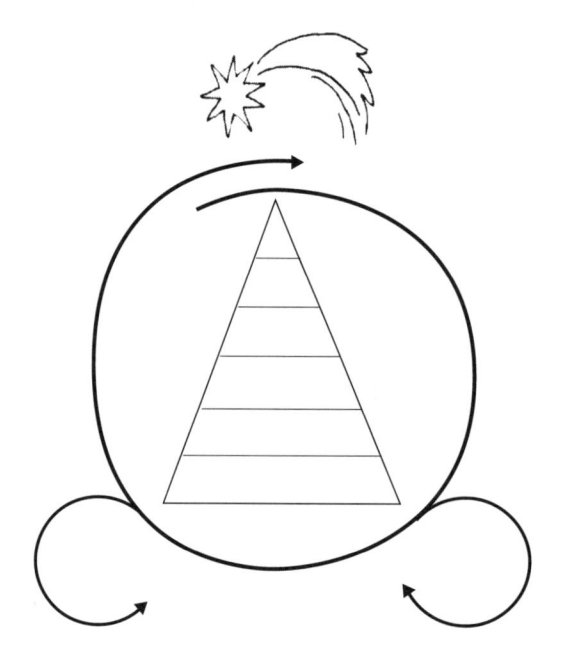

Section Five

Reviewing, evaluating and planning creative work

> Stories are people's hearts in other people's hands.
>
> *Arabic proverb*

Overview of Section Five

Page	Activity	Story element	ALPS StoryMaker reference	Accelerated learning & thinking skills link
187–196	The Story so Far; Looking-Back Time; Four Areas for Assessment, Evaluation and Planning; the 7/10 problem	All	The Story Process	Reviewing; self-evaluation; independence of judgement; summarising; transferring skills
196	Tiny Changes	All	Tips for Good Practice	5Rs; self-motivation
198	The 3:1 Ratio for Evaluation	All	What Have I Done?	As above
199	Stepping up to Mastery	All	What Have I Done?	The AL cycle; development of nonconscious competence; review and reiteration; transfer of skills; innovation
201	Writer's Pie	All	Countdown to a Story	As above
205	Attainment and Achievement	All		Consolidation of above

Section Five

Reviewing, evaluating and planning creative work

◆ The story so far

While it is a mistake to compose and edit a story simultaneously*, most experienced writers review their work in progress a number of times. This 'connects the creative learning', as it were; it gives the author a chance to refresh her memory, consolidate her thoughts, and allows the opportunity for more ideas to pop into mind. The subconscious is constantly preprocessing information as creative writing occurs. It is not just a question of ideas becoming conscious and then being expressed. As the ideas are expressed they feed back into the subconscious mind and act as further fuel to the fires of the imagination. True creativity is an ongoing positive feedback loop.

> * When creative writing is going well, the author is in a state of 'flow' (a term coined by Dr Mihaly Csikszentmihalyi, an authority on adolescent development). The artist brain and the logic brain are in balance and working together. The story is being composed creatively, insightfully and yet with a light touch of logic as the sentences are put together without great struggle or effort.
>
> However, if a writer attempts to correct and improve work as this happens, the flow is disrupted: writing time and looking-back time clash. Creativity is subsumed by concerns over technical accuracy, neatness, etc., and the act of writing becomes increasingly frustrating, more difficult and less productive.
>
> Some schools use editor caps or editor badges to avoid this. If a child wants to edit work, in the proper sense of the word, she must come out and collect a cap or badge to get into that role. The editor cap/badge serves the same function of kinaesthetic anchor as the story stone does for having ideas in the first place (see p.68).

Use 'The story so far' as a technique to encourage children to pause and take stock. This activity is especially useful if a young writer has not planned his work at all or very thoroughly, since it evokes the phenomenon of 'How do I know what I think until I see/hear what I say?' The very act of articulating work done clarifies those ideas and can lead to further insights.

◆ SECTION FIVE

The activity might simply take the form of a checklist of questions. The child can simply tick off the items he's considered, or use a variation of Alistair Smith's 'traffic lights' technique for checking understanding. Mark an item with *red* felt pen if you have not done it. Use *orange* if you have reviewed the item and know you need to do some more work on it. Use *green* if you have reviewed the item, and either you're already happy with it, or you've done some more work and now you're satisfied with it.

So have you…

- opened with a really strong sentence? (*green!*)
- set the scene using details of sight, sound, touch, etc.? (*orange*)
- introduced at least one important character? (*green!*)
- mentioned the story's main problem? (*red*)

These checklists can be put on laminated cards and made as brief or extensive as you like, depending upon where in the writing process you want the child to look back.

> **Look back…**
>
> Have you –
> - opened with a really strong sentence? ○
> - set the scene using VAK? ○
> - introduced an important character? ○
> - mentioned the story's main problem? ○
> - used a story ingredient – mystery, danger, etc? ○
> - decided that so far you're happy with your work? ○
> - decided what happens next in your story? ○

The ticklist box can be incorporated into a larger review sheet where the young writer has to summarise her work so far and affirm the specific points, and others, we've mentioned:

REVIEWING, EVALUATING AND PLANNING CREATIVE WORK

The story so far...

Summarise your story here. You can use pictures and diagrams to support what you write.

Then check off the items in the 'Look back' box.

Look back...

Have you –

- ◆ opened with a really strong sentence? ○
- ◆ set the scene using VAK? ○
- ◆ introduced an important character? ○
- ◆ mentioned the story's main problem? ○
- ◆ used a story ingredient – mystery, danger, etc? ○
- ◆ decided that so far you're happy with your work? ○
- ◆ decided what happens next in your story? ○

STORYMAKER CATCH PACK – USING GENRE FICTION AS A RESOURCE FOR ACCELERATED LEARNING

◆ SECTION FIVE

◆ Looking-back time

You'll remember that making a story involves three phases; thinking time, writing time and looking-back time. You might also recall me saying that when I look back over my work I have two questions in mind:

- What changes do I need to make in this work for it to be the best that it can be right now?
- What have I learned through doing this work that will make my next piece of writing even better?

There are a number of issues implicit in these questions:

- They are best generated by the writer and not by an outside authority.
- They must be asked with honesty and integrity, in the spirit of personal betterment rather than in any competitive or negatively judgemental way.
- Practice never makes perfect, only better and better.
- Good judgement comes from experience, and experience comes from bad judgement.
- 'Mistakes' are steps to more learning, and in this case more effective communication.
- Any piece of writing is a snapshot of an ongoing, highly complex, highly individual process. Any comparisons, judgements or conclusions will necessarily be simplistic.
- Looking back is also looking forward: assessment, evaluation and planning go hand in hand.
- The act of creative writing is 'structure-seeking' rather than 'rule-abiding'.
- Over-correctiveness and pedantry are the last refuge of the unimaginative.

When children ask these questions and *demand explicit answers* of themselves or you, they will be displaying a powerful learning behaviour. However, there is much that you can do to prepare children to look back in this way, and to allow them to look back more effectively.

◆ Four areas for assessment, evaluation and planning

It is a truism that both teacher and pupil are involved in that pupil's development, which depends upon a creative relationship between you and the work in question. I have found it useful to consider creative writing within these four areas:

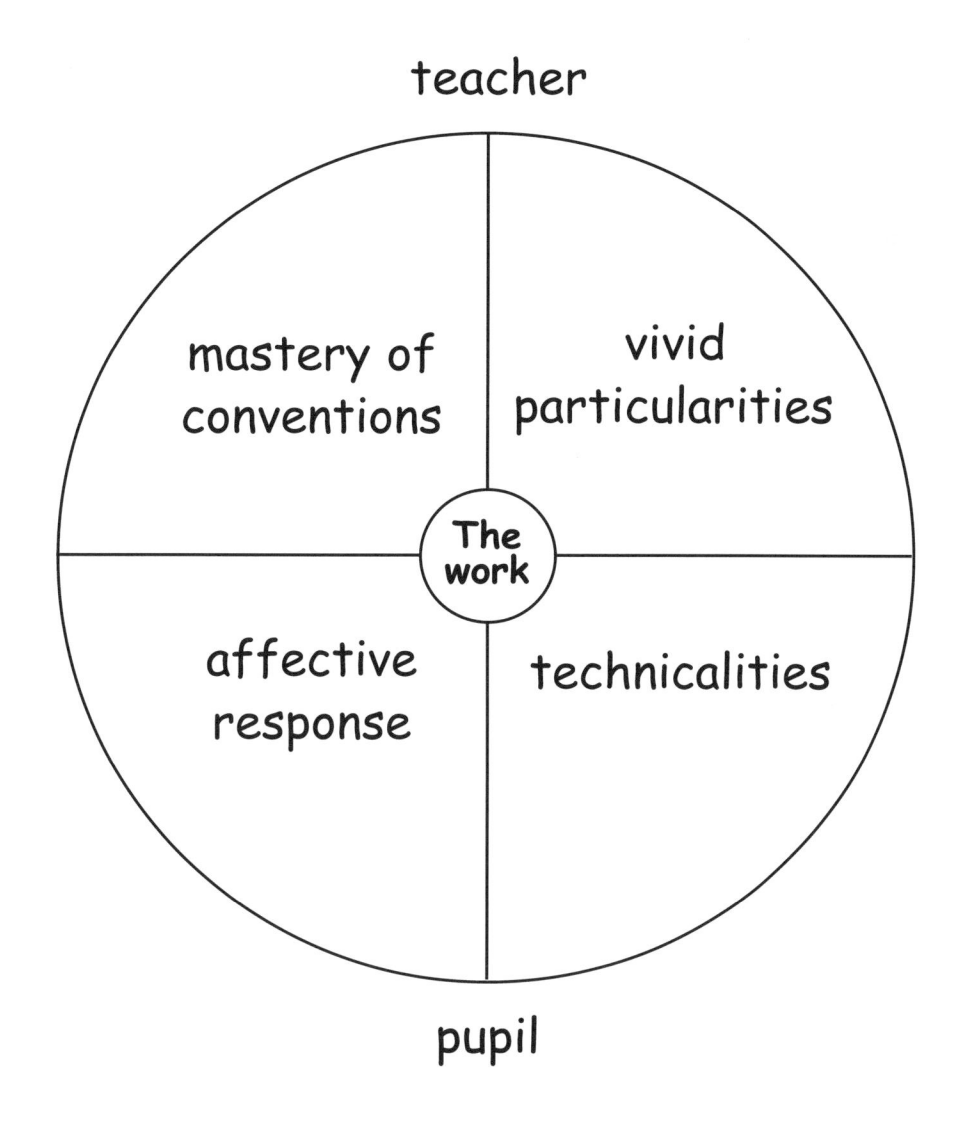

REVIEWING, EVALUATING AND PLANNING CREATIVE WORK

```
                    teacher

          mastery of    │    vivid
          conventions   │    particularities
                        │
          ──────────( The work )──────────
                        │
          affective     │    technicalities
          response      │

                    pupil
```

Naturally these four areas overlap, but for clarity we will look at them separately here.

Mastery of conventions

It is wisely said that you should know the rules before you bend them. Being unconventional works best when you have learned first how to be conventional – when, in fact, you have mastered the conventions. For our purposes there are two areas to consider:

- **Generic conventions** – simply put, these are the kinds of things you would expect to find in a story of a particular genre. And so, if a young author intends to write a Fantasy story and includes wizards, dragons, magic crystals, winged horses, etc., then she is demonstrating a fair degree of mastery of the conventions of Fantasy – in other words, the deliberate and effective use of themes, ingredients and motifs (see p.43). On the other hand, if the same story contains invaders from Mars and a zombie with a chainsaw, and these are not used with a deliberate intention to be unconventional, then I know that the writer has more learning to do in finding his way around the territory of Fantasy. (See 'Stepping up to mastery' on p.199.)

◆ SECTION FIVE

- **Narrative conventions** – these are more the conventions of the form and structure the writing takes, rather than its fictional content. Convention expects the writer to follow rules of syntax and grammar, to create a story that has 'a beginning, a middle and an end'. We would also anticipate that the story is broken down into scenes and paragraphs, and that these follow on logically one from the other. We would expect the story to use the form of narrative prose, and not suddenly and for no (as it were) rhyme or reason to flip into verse – and so on. Clearly, the domain of narrative conventions interconnects with the area of technicalities (see below).

Vivid particularities

These are the details of content and style that lift the whole story from the mundane into the memorable. They are often to be found in descriptions of character or place, but really can crop up anywhere in the story. Vivid particularities can be quite independent of the technical or 'conventional' aspects of the work: often indeed they are quite unconventional. Let us suppose that one young writer, attempting a Fantasy story, included the zombie mentioned above. Let's also suppose that she spelt the word incorrectly as 'zombi'. But it so happened that this zombi visited his Mum every Friday and never failed to bring her a bunch of flowers – that is a vivid particularity which will linger in my memory long after the associated 'errors' are forgotten.

You may well find that once children are aware of the idea they will load up their stories with many such details – serious overkill, which they will moderate in time.

Technicalities

This is the most familiar domain of the traditionalist. Clearly, getting the technical details right is important – most significantly (for me) because our written work represents us to the world. We need it to look good because we want to look good. To publish is linked to the idea of 'making public', and I like to show myself at my best. Also, of course, technical accuracy aids clarity and effectiveness of communication; a comma can change the emphasis and meaning of a sentence quite radically.

However, I feel we need to bear in mind that technical details are an aid to communication, and training children to use technicalities of spelling, punctuation, etc., should always be done within the context of making the work as a whole more impactful. Technicalities should be given their due weight, and no more.

Affective response

An 'affect' is another term for a feeling. The creative process is an often profound emotional experience for the writer, and effective writing invariably stirs the feelings of the reader. The working principle here is:

intention – output – effect

REVIEWING, EVALUATING AND PLANNING CREATIVE WORK

If one of my pupils writes a scary story, and I am scared when I read it, then her intention is matched by the effect that the writing has on me. Her achievement involves mastery of convention, technical accuracy, probably a number of vivid particularities and, most significantly, the fact that the storymaking has been a rich emotional experience for the author.

I can appreciate her 'cleverness' in making me jump or shiver. I can justifiably comment on the ethos or attitude she has brought to her writing. And, because she is my pupil, I can feel pleased and proud with the hard work she has put into the story. All of this is part of the affective response attached to the writing, and all of it is valuable feedback in building up that young writer's confidence, enthusiasm and pleasure for the future.

When I explain these four areas of assessment and evaluation to children, I modify the terms:

Mastery of conventions	What kind of story?
Vivid particularities	Clear details
Technicalities	Building the language
Affective response	How do we feel?

It's handy to use simple icons to represent these aspects, and then use them to annotate children's work as part of your feedback:

What kind of story?	☐
Clear details	◇
Building the language	☆
How do we feel?	☺

I often combine such annotations with the technique of 'writing between the lines' (see overleaf).

Here I encourage children to write on alternate lines, leaving plenty of space for us to look back and make the story even better. A wide margin also allows for further annotations, in this case 'visual cues' referring to the area of evaluation of my comments.

The example above is brief, but it does illustrate that this approach is a creative dialogue between pupil and teacher which shows much more of the process of storymaking, rather than just the pupil's finished product with the teacher's corrective marking.

◆ SECTION FIVE

A variation of the idea takes the form of what I call 'annotated notebooks'. Here I tell the children that they will write the story on the right-hand pages, while the left-hand pages will be used for thinking time, creative note-making during writing, and for looking back. There is an example in my book *What's the Story?* (see Bibliography).

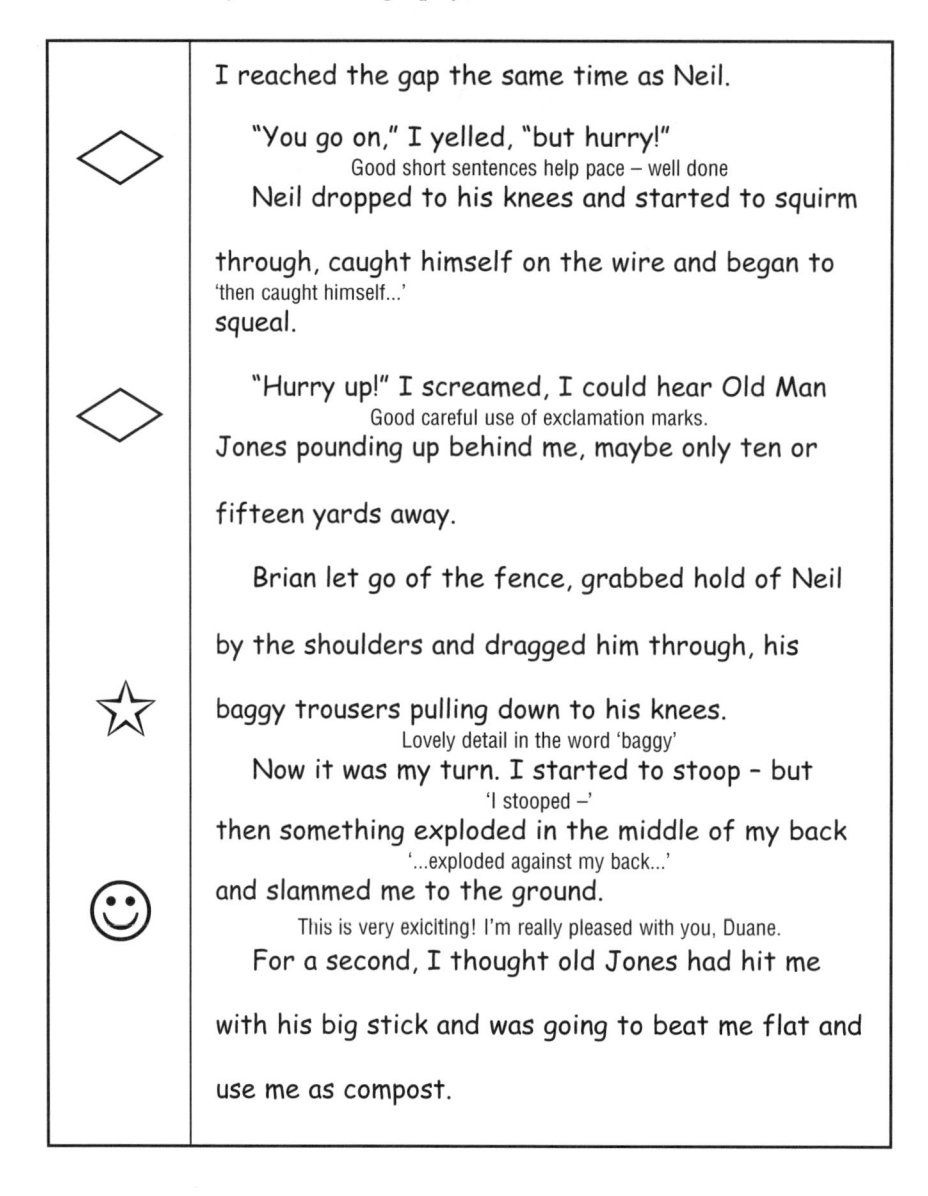

◇ I reached the gap the same time as Neil.

"You go on," I yelled, "but hurry!"
Good short sentences help pace – well done
Neil dropped to his knees and started to squirm

through, caught himself on the wire and began to
'then caught himself...'
squeal.

◇ "Hurry up!" I screamed, I could hear Old Man
Good careful use of exclamation marks.
Jones pounding up behind me, maybe only ten or

fifteen yards away.

Brian let go of the fence, grabbed hold of Neil

by the shoulders and dragged him through, his

☆ baggy trousers pulling down to his knees.
Lovely detail in the word 'baggy'
Now it was my turn. I started to stoop – but
'I stooped –'
then something exploded in the middle of my back
'...exploded against my back...'
☺ and slammed me to the ground.
This is very exciting! I'm really pleased with you, Duane.
For a second, I thought old Jones had hit me

with his big stick and was going to beat me flat and

use me as compost.

◆ The 7/10 problem

The 7/10 problem is a side issue to our main topic of discussion, but worth mentioning here, I feel. I recall on many occasions marking children's English exercises and putting the score at the bottom. Let's suppose I had asked the group to underline the adjectives in a batch of ten sentences. Andrew scores 7/10. Not bad, but what have I learned (and what has Andrew learned) about his understanding of adjectives? Can I reasonably conclude that 'Andrew is quite competent at spotting adjectives'? And what does that mean? I know there was more than one adjective in some of the sentences. Did Andrew spot them? Did he fail to underline them because he assumed I wanted only one adjective to be picked out per sentence? Was there anything different about the sentences where Andrew underlined the wrong word? What about adjectival phrases? Did Andrew understand the concept of 'adjective' sufficiently to realise that the descriptive function can be spread across a number of words? And what strategies, specifically, do I have in mind to improve Andrew's understanding of adjectives, apart from giving him more of the same sort of exercises?

I have to confess that the 7/10 problem (another example of the 'illusion of precision') haunted me for years. My approach now is to:

- relate individual learning experiences as far as possible to the big ideas at the heart of the subject
- ask pupils to explain what they understand about, in this case, adjectives, and what still puzzles them
- encourage them to realise than confusion is a necessary step on the road to 'fusion' (understanding)
- endeavour to apply their understanding in other contexts.

> **Tip: Story beads** – I have come across many children who are slaves to the tyrant of perfectionism. If they spell a word wrongly, they tear that page out of the exercise book and start all over again. Similarly, some kids insist on checking every word they're not sure about **at that moment**, thereby frequently interrupting the creative process of composition.
>
> In these cases I give out a certain number of glass beads (tailoring the number to the child) and explain that he can spend these beads as he chooses – giving me one bead each time he needs to check a word or makes an error and wants to start again. **But he must not go over budget**. So he must decide carefully which words and/or errors are the most serious, and tidy up the others at the end.
>
> You can work the technique the other way round. Give some beads to a child who doesn't seem to care about mistakes or checking spellings, and point out that she must spend this number of beads – but no more – during the course of writing and looking back. (See also 'Tiny changes', overleaf.)

The 'four areas for assessment and evaluation' model can also be used as a planning tool. Since looking back is a precursor to the thinking time of the next project, any evaluation tool serves to 'make the next piece of work even better'. You can link insights the children have when they've reviewed their work with techniques such as 'Countdown to a story' on the CD. I also offer children the 'Four areas for planning' template (see overleaf) and ask them to give me the answers to the questions.

The children themselves can take part in the construction of the template, choosing their own icons and questions/statements. The more they go through this process of reflective review and deliberate creative preview, the more they will internalise it and become more independent, creatively thinking individuals.

◆ SECTION FIVE

Four areas for planning

What kind of story?
- How do I know that this is a (Fantasy) story?
- What is the favourite Fantasy story I've read by another author? Why is it my favourite?
- How do the characters, settings and events in my story make it good Fantasy?
- How will the way, I write the story help to make it good Fantasy?

How do we feel?
- How do I want to make my readers feel as they read my story?
- Am I writing for a special person? How do I want to make him/her feel by reading my story?
- How do I intend to feel as I write my story, and when I have finished it?

Clear details
- What unique details of my characters can I bear in mind as I write about them?
- What special features of the story's settings and locations can I mention?
- As I write I can notice what I say, and decide sometimes to change my sentences to make them fresher and more original.

Building the language
- As I write I can think about how paragraphs each deal with a particular idea.
- I remember that I can change the length of sentences. This helps the pace of the story.
- As I write I will notice the job that particular words do for me, and how I might use other words that do a better job.

Note: A full-sized colour version of the template can be found on the CD resource.

◆ Tiny changes

The old conundrum asks, 'How do you eat an elephant?' The answer is, 'A little bit at a time.' So it is with making the learning journey. We fulfil our potential one small step at a time.

The educationalists Neil Postman and Charles Weingartner* maintain that true learning can best be measured *by behavioural changes in the learner*. These new and more resourceful behaviours have to be trained up – one step at a time.

> * In the only college book I ever kept – **Teaching as a Subversive Activity**. It's more relevant today than ever before. See Bibliography.

A useful technique for achieving this is 'tiny changes' and utilises what I call pledge cards. These small cards can be tailored to the individual child in terms of the area to be improved and the extent of the challenge. A pledge card is an agreement between you that the child *will do* one tiny

REVIEWING, EVALUATING AND PLANNING CREATIVE WORK

thing to make her work and performance better. This example focuses on the technicalities of writing in very specific ways, but you can ring the changes just as you like.

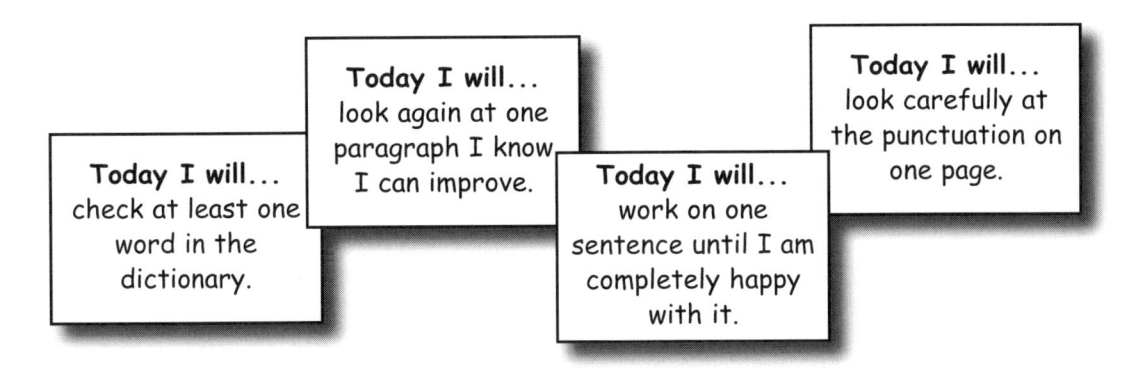

> **Today I will...** check at least one word in the dictionary.
>
> **Today I will...** look again at one paragraph I know I can improve.
>
> **Today I will...** work on one sentence until I am completely happy with it.
>
> **Today I will...** look carefully at the punctuation on one page.

- Once children become used to single pledge cards, invite them to take two, three, etc., per day. Step up the challenge.
- Have children produce their own pledge cards, spread across the four areas of evaluation (see p.193).
- Combine pledge cards with an 'Achievement tree'. Use a story tree template. Have four main branches, one for each of the main areas of evaluation. Split these further into smaller components of those areas. Stick pledge cards on the branches so that children not only pick their pledge, but can relate it to the Big Picture of achievement in creative writing.
- Award certificates of achievement, such as the one below. When a child has achieved so many pledges, give her a certificate to be proud of.

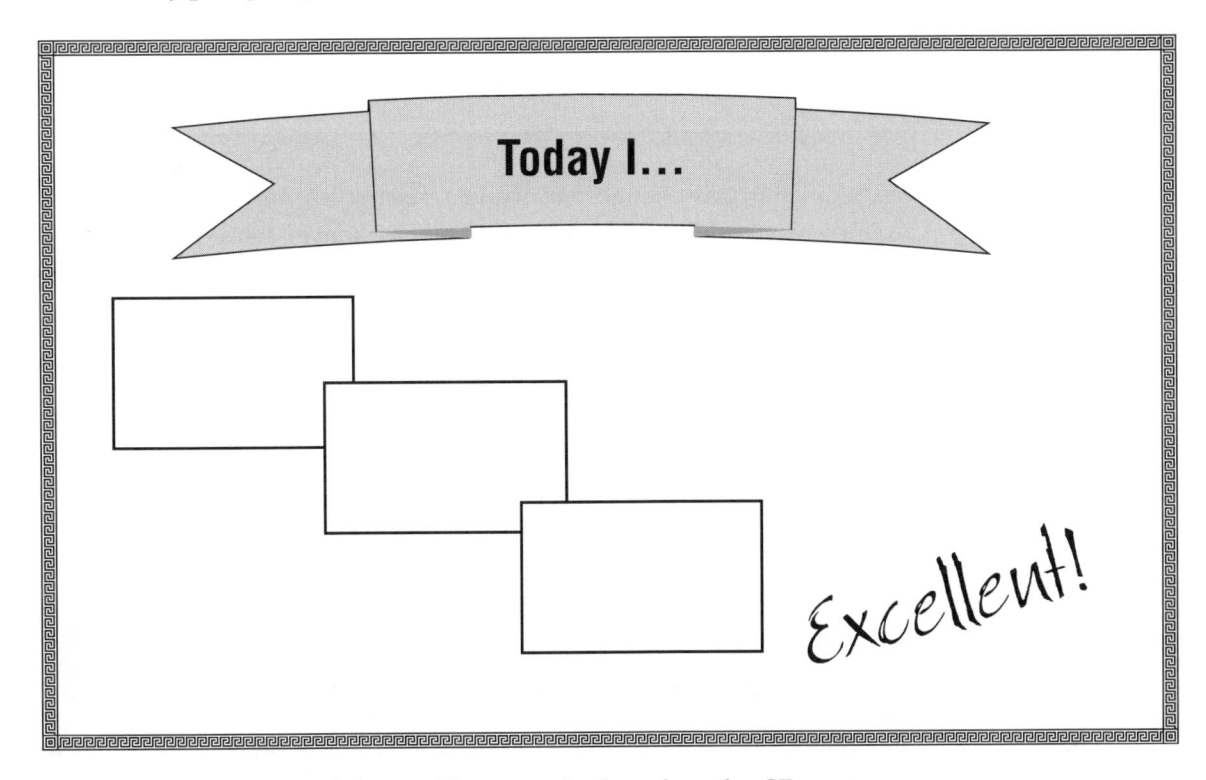

Today I...

Excellent!

Note: A colour version of the certificate can be found on the CD resource.

◆ SECTION FIVE

◆ The 3:1 ratio for evaluation

The most educationally valuable – and kindest – evaluative technique I have come across is the 3:1 ratio which offers learners *three points of praise and one area for improvement*. This approach makes use of some powerful insights:

- Corrective marking *per se* does not teach children the right way. In my youth my exercise books were filled with red crosses. I knew I'd done it wrong – but how do you do it correctly?

- The subconscious/artist brain processes positives by default and finds it harder to process negatives. If I say 'Don't think of pink elephants' the brain (consciously and/or subconsciously) creates the impression of pink elephants before the idea flips into a negative. Similarly 'Watch you don't trip over' not only states a negative but uses a visual reference (watch). If you're talking to an auditorily oriented child you may well increase the likelihood of a fall. So 'Watch you don't put your commas in the wrong place' needs to be reassessed.

- The 3:1 ratio uses the *pattern of three,* which is a powerful tool in the world of story (and the psychology of resourcefulness)*. Basically the pattern is this:
    - the first mention introduces the idea
    - the second mention makes the idea familiar
    - the third mention is anticipated (preprocessed) by the child, and the feelgood factor is already in place ahead of time.

The young writer is therefore feeling positive and buoyant when the 'one area for improvement' is mentioned. And note the emphasis here – not 'You've done something wrong' but 'Here's something we know you can do even better'.

> *Notice how many traditional fairy tales make use of the pattern of three.*

- The 3:1 ratio also exploits the 'tiny changes' principle. *Of course* learner-writers have lots of things they can improve upon, but how do you eat an elephant? I started to write creatively and for pleasure over thirty-five years ago, and I'm still learning. Our aim here is to equip children with an awareness and working knowledge of their mental/emotional toolkit and to offer insights into how they might use that toolkit even more effectively in the future, in the wider context of their lives.

As a teacher I might use the 3:1 ratio with children*, but the technique is even more effective when they use it for themselves. I have found children by and large to be very honest in assessing their own work, especially in an environment that supports the creative attitude and the ethos of achievement.

> *In some schools I've visited the same technique is used and called 'Three Stars and a Wish'.*

This is the template I give out: there's plenty of room to make notes, mind-maps, etc., and the visual cues are significant. A larger version of the sheet can be found on the CD resource.

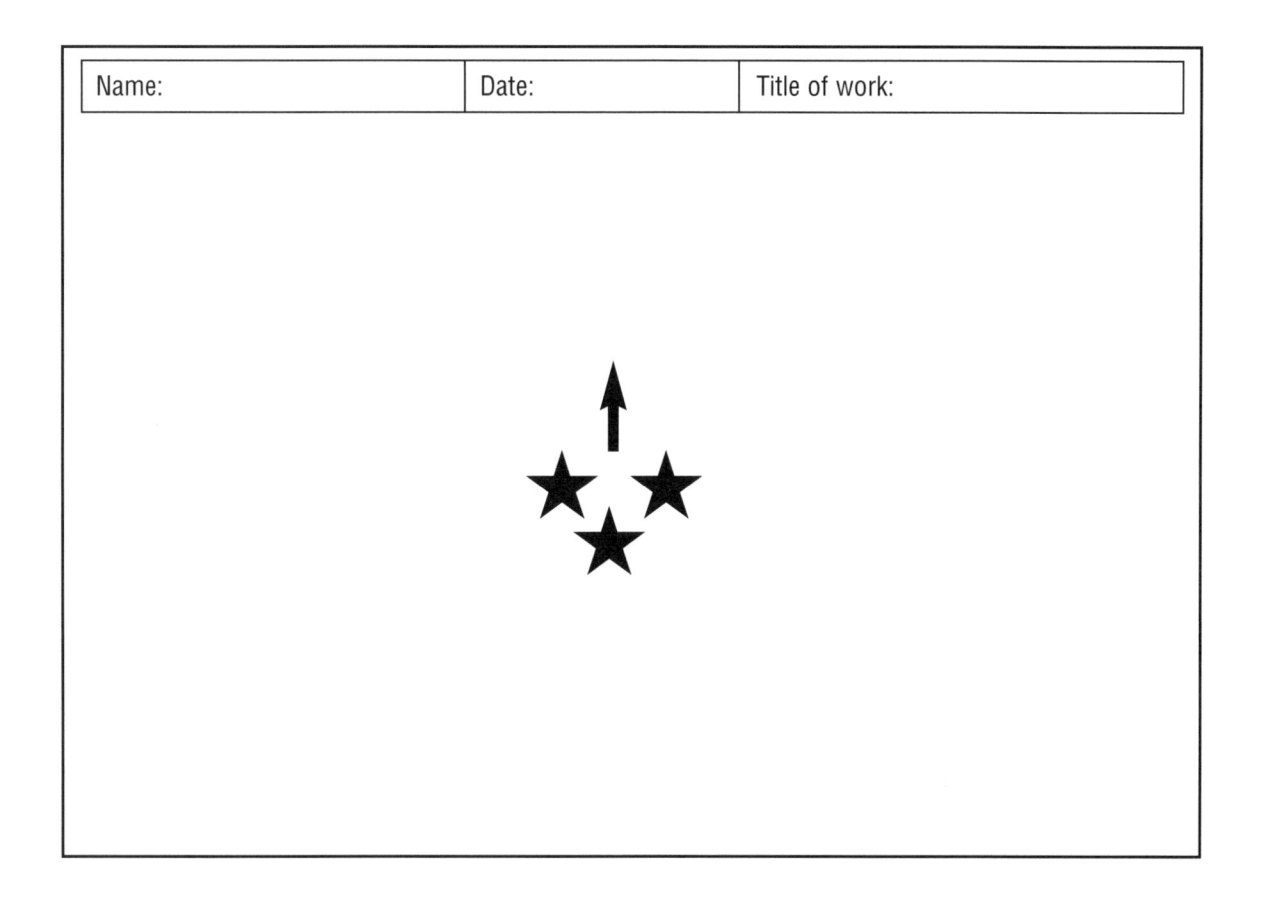

REVIEWING, EVALUATING AND PLANNING CREATIVE WORK

| Name: | Date: | Title of work: |

◆ Stepping up to mastery

Mastery of the many varied components of storymaking is part of the fixed goal of education – to allow children and young adults to be independent, creatively thinking individuals. That goal is necessarily process-centred: creativity isn't something you know, it's something you do, using content – knowledge, facts – as the fuel. And so, to achieve mastery of the skills, the 'raw material' that is knowledge must be put into a broader context.

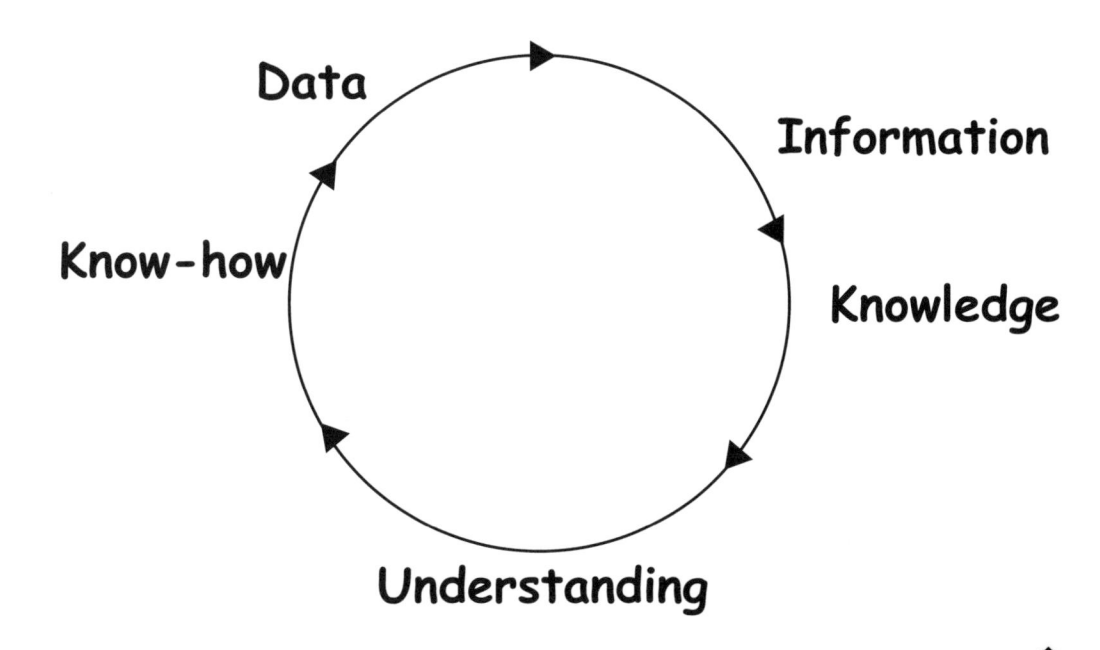

Data → Information → Knowledge → Understanding → Know-how → (Data)

◆ SECTION FIVE

The cycle runs from *data*, the bits and pieces that we throw on the fire of our imagination, through to *know-how* and beyond – knowing how to apply knowledge, ideas and skills in a new way across a range of domains. This process follows the golden formula of **awareness – understanding – control**, and can be achieved by having children reflect on the following steps:

[Name of the activity or idea]	
Reflection:	Step towards mastery:
I am aware of this idea.	awareness/knowledge
I understand this idea.	understanding/simple manipulation of knowledge
I have used this idea once.	first application
I have used this idea/practised this skill a number of times.	development of skill/know-how/ 'near transfer'
I have explained/taught this idea/skill to someone else.	review and reiteration
I have used this idea/skill in another lesson.	'far transfer'
I have used this idea/skill in some other part of my life.	
I have made the idea/skill better and more effective.	innovation
I have created a new idea based on what I have learned.	origination

Increasing Control →

Again I want to emphasise that once this whole process has been carried out within the safe environment of storymaking, it can be applied more comfortably in other areas. Implicit in this notion is the assumption that the culture of the school allows for such cross-referencing and encourages flexibility of skill use across the subject domains.

Stepping up to mastery also requires a strategy or game-plan for going through the stages outlined above. This will involve self-belief, confidence, determination and what have been called 'The New 5Rs' (Resiliency, Resourcefulness, Responsibility, Reflectiveness and … um … oh yes, Remembering).

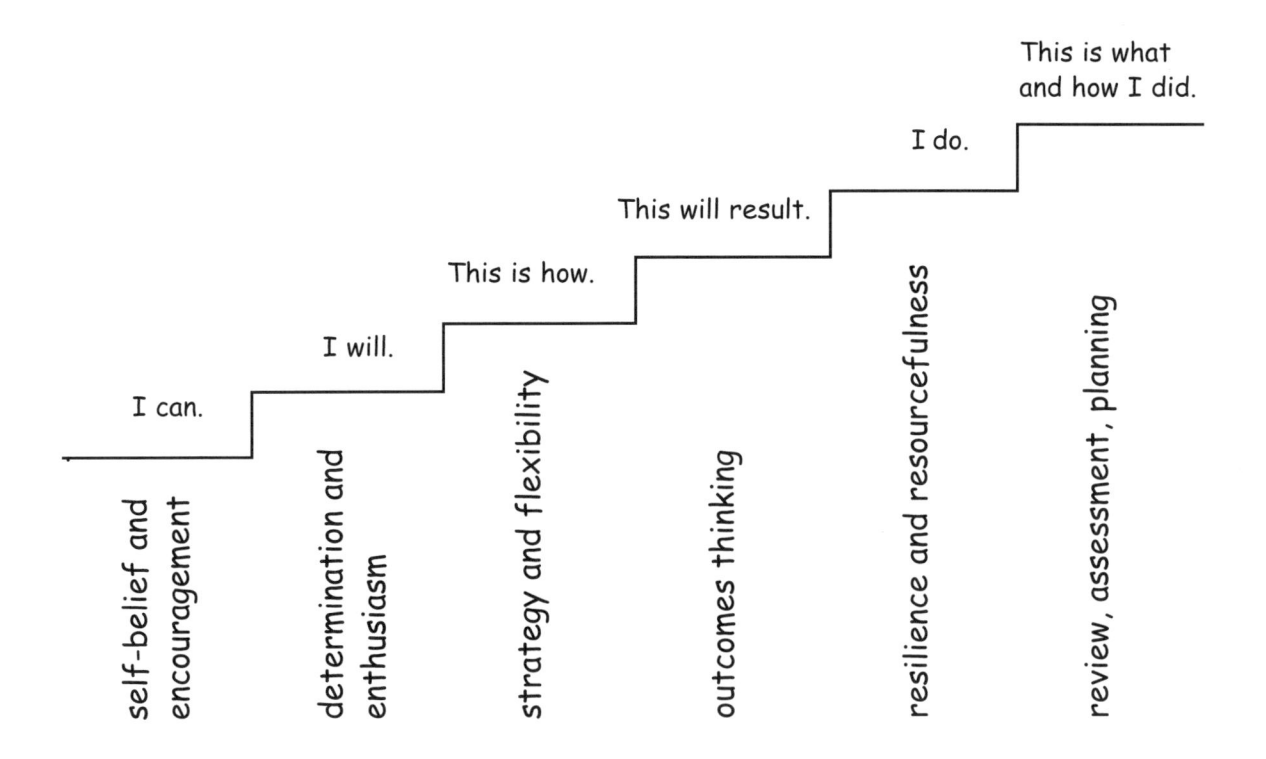

REVIEWING, EVALUATING AND PLANNING CREATIVE WORK

```
                                                      This is what
                                                      and how I did.
                                              I do.
                                  This will result.
                        This is how.
              I will.
    I can.
```

self-belief and encouragement | determination and enthusiasm | strategy and flexibility | outcomes thinking | resilience and resourcefulness | review, assessment, planning

The realm of storymaking not only accommodates this model but *actively generates it* as a byproduct of the activities offered throughout this book.

◆ Writer's pie

It is important that the children themselves understand their journey towards mastery and take the helm, as it were, in getting there. The ideas and strategies in this section should not simply be imposed upon young writers regardless of any confusion or lack of support: the creative attitude embodied in the 'IDEAS NOW' acrostic (p.34) should be clearly in place in order for children to engage meaningfully in the development of their abilities.

In line with the goal of making children self-determining, flexible and resourceful in their lives, they should play an active part in the assessment of their own performance. 'Writer's pie' is a useful activity in this regard, especially since it sidesteps the 'illusion of precision' mentioned earlier.

- Decide on the areas of work that you want a child to assess and make sure she understands what they mean. So, for example:

◆ SECTION FIVE

Area to look at...	This means:
story ingredients	● Has my story got a main problem? ● Do the characters solve it? ● Are there 'smaller' problems to be solved on the way? ● Did I have conflict between the characters? ● Did I think about using mystery, danger, etc. – and did I include any of these?
planning	● Do I feel that I did my 'thinking time' thoroughly enough? ● Did I write down any ideas of what the story would be about?... etc.
characters	● Did I think about what my characters were like on the outside and 'on the inside'? ● Did I put in at least one special detail for each main character in my story?... etc.
description	● Did I try to describe for my readers some of the sights and sounds of the places I used in my story? ● Could I see the story settings in my mind's eye as I wrote? ... etc.
vivid details	● As I look back at my story now, can I pick out any special details that will help me to picture and remember my story clearly?
spelling	● Did I avoid using any words in my story because I couldn't spell them? ● Did I check any words I wasn't sure about?
punctuation	● Did I check any punctuation I wasn't sure about? ● Do I understand why I have used these punctuation marks in my story?
purpose	● Did I think about why I wrote this story? – Have I thought of any other reasons since? ● Have I thought about what this story has taught me about being a better writer?

These are not the only questions you/the writer might ask, of course; but their purpose is to clarify the area of assessment and also to give the child the opportunity to *look again* at his work, and perhaps to make some corrections that will impinge upon his final evaluation. Obviously you can divide the writer's pie into as many or as few slices as you like, depending upon the challenge you want to present to the child. The template gives you and the writer the chance to revisit aspects of storymaking that you touched upon some time ago, as well as deepening understanding of recently-introduced elements.

● Once you have decided on the areas you wish the writer to review, prepare a template like this:

REVIEWING, EVALUATING AND PLANNING CREATIVE WORK

purpose   story ingredients

punctuation   planning

spelling   characters

vivid details   description

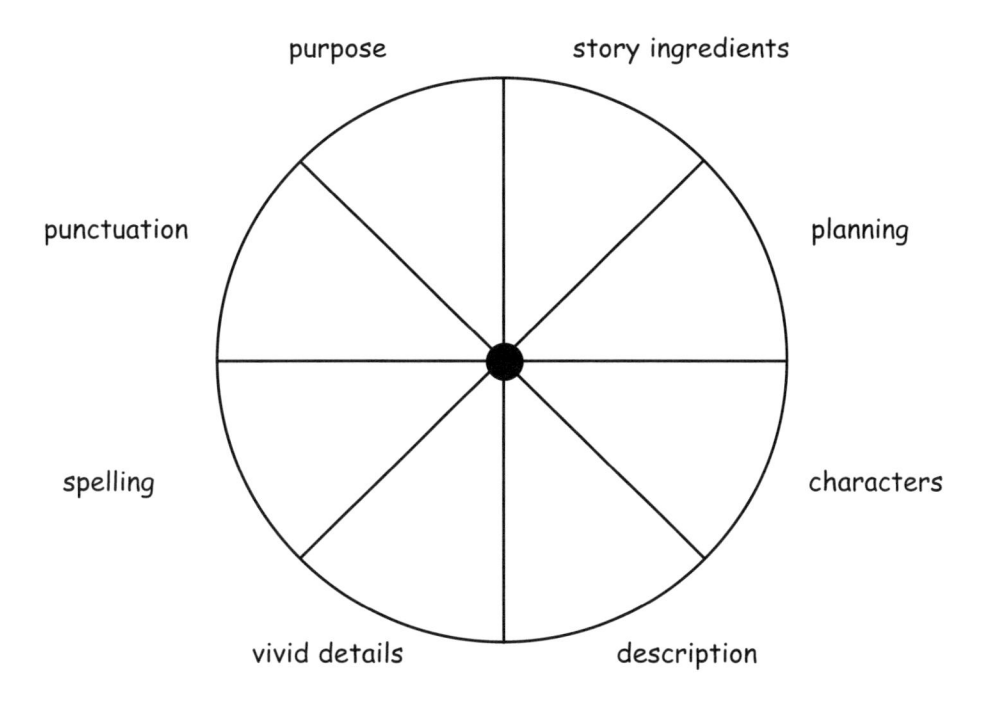

- Explain that you would like the writer to make a mark in each segment as a judgement of how well he feels he's done in that area, based on the questions both of you have asked – the closer to the rim of the circle, the more he thinks he's accomplished. Most children are pretty honest with themselves and will come back with what they feel is an accurate assessment.

- A variation of the activity is to have the child place counters on a writer's pie template on a tabletop. Through further review, discussion and your feedback he may change the positioning of some of the counters after a reassessment of his work. The aim is to create a well-rounded writer.

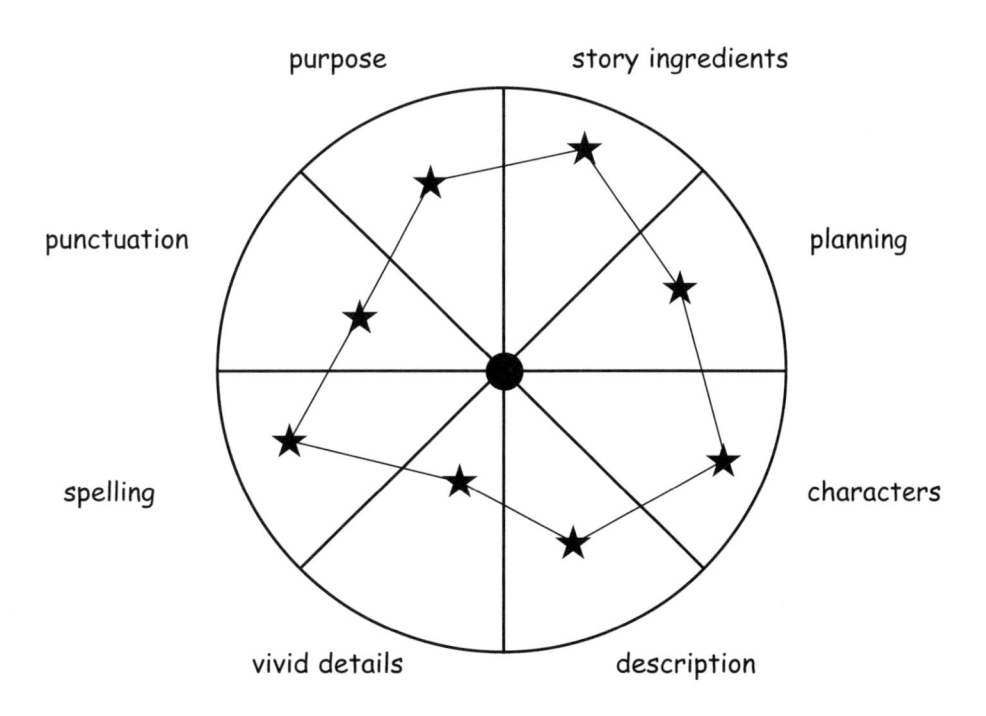

purpose   story ingredients

punctuation   planning

spelling   characters

vivid details   description

STORYMAKER CATCH PACK – USING GENRE FICTION AS A RESOURCE FOR ACCELERATED LEARNING

◆ SECTION FIVE

- A refinement of the activity makes use of the 'Stepping up to mastery' stages, and involves the writer and yourself in mediating performance in more detail. A simple version of the scale might look like this:

1	I don't understand this idea and I haven't used it.
2	I think I understand this idea and I tried to use it a bit.
3	I do understand this idea and can explain it clearly to someone else.
4	I have used/will use this idea in other stories/kinds of writing.
5	I know how to use this idea in other subjects in school.
6	I know how to use this idea outside school in other areas of my life.

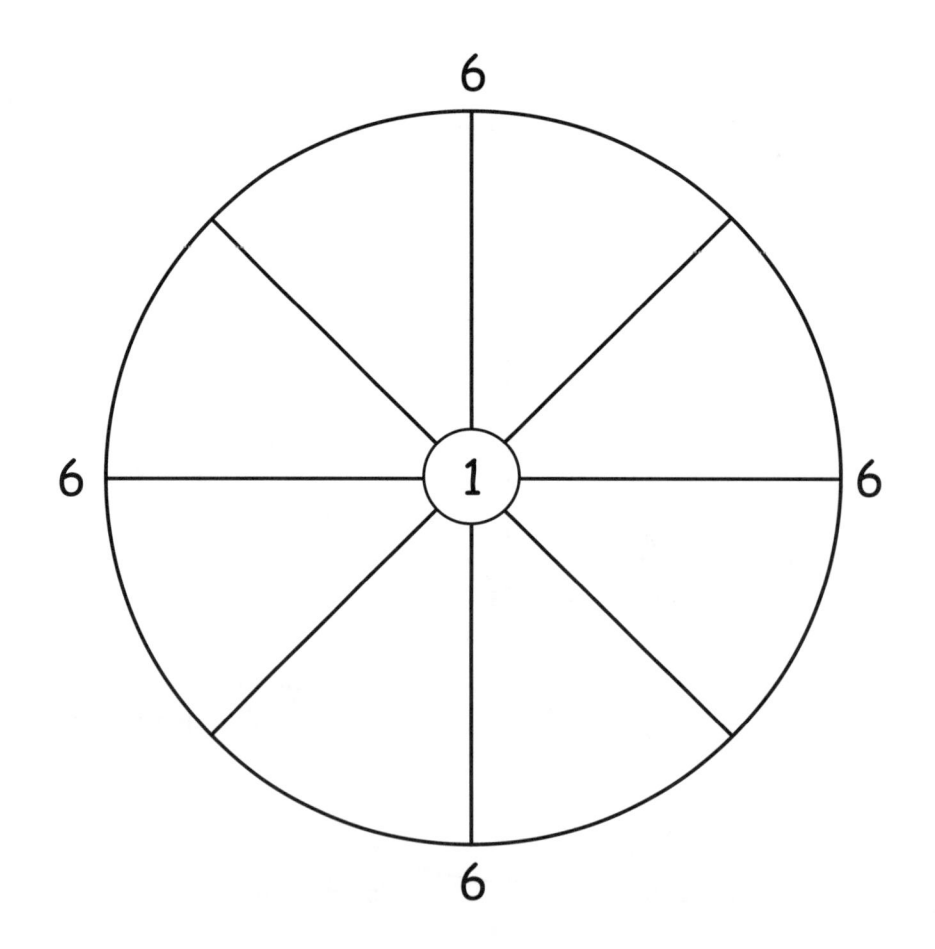

REVIEWING, EVALUATING AND PLANNING CREATIVE WORK

◆ Attainment and achievement

These two things are different and sometimes get confused. The attainment is what we receive at the end of a process: the achievement is everything we've done to reach that point. In the case of an Olympic athlete, he might enter the 100 metres sprint and win a bronze medal – that's what he has attained. His achievement has been years of dedication and discipline, hard work, self-belief, overcoming doubt and many obstacles. He might have pushed himself to his limits to get that bronze. And supposing he had come fourth or even last, his overall achievement would have been no less.

The 'modern' educational system is geared towards levels*, targets and attainment tests. Let's suppose Anika, a bright and confident girl, attained Level 5 in her literacy test and, she is the first to admit, managed it easily. Duane, on the other hand, reached Level 3 after a huge effort, during which time he excelled himself often. Whose achievement is the greater?

> * During an author visit once a little boy asked me what level you need to reach to be an author. I told him 'the level of happiness'. Luckily he was still childlike enough to understand.

The ethos at the heart of *StoryMaker* encourages and celebrates achievement, because achievement is about attitude and endeavour, while attainment deals only with outcomes and the finished product. Within the context of creative writing, we have all heard of authors whose books were rejected time and time again. (I speak from personal experience!) Undoubtedly there are many wonderful manuscripts out there that will never be published. Their authors have attained nothing publicly, but their achievement cannot be denied.

Pyramid diagram: tip labeled ← **Attainment**; body contains "years of", "Resiliency", "Responsibility", "Resourcefulness" with ← **Achievement** pointing to the body.

STORYMAKER CATCH PACK - USING GENRE FICTION AS A RESOURCE FOR ACCELERATED LEARNING

Bibliography

Note: The dates of publications refer to the editions I used. S.B.

Abbott, J. and Ryan, T.   *The Unfinished Revolution*. Network Educational Press, 2000.
Aftel, M. *The Story of Your Life: Becoming the Author of Your Own Experience*. Simon & Schuster, 1996.
Alexander, M. *The Earliest English Poems*. Penguin Classics, 1970.
Bandler, R. *Using Your Brain for a Change*. Real People Press, 1985.
Bowkett, S. *Dinosaur Day*. Heinemann, 1996.
Imagine That! Network Educational Press, 1997.
Roy Kane – TV Detective. A. & C. Black, 1998.
Self-Intelligence. Network Educational Press, 1999.
ALPS StoryMaker. Network Educational Press, 2001.
What's the Story? A. & C. Black, 2001.
Briggs, K. *A Dictionary of Fairies*. Allen Lane, 1976.
Buzan, T. *Use Your Head*. BBC Books, 1993.
Cameron, J. *The Artist's Way*. Pan Books, 1994.
Campbell, J. *Myths to Live By*. Souvenir Press, 1995.
Castle, M. (ed.) *Writing Horror*. Writers' Digest Books, 1997.
Chetwynd, T. *Dictionary of Symbols*. Aquarian/Thorsons, 1982.
Claxton, G. *Wise Up: Learning to Live the Learning Life*. Network Educational Press, 2001.
Covey, S. R. *The Seven Habits of Highly Effective People*. Simon & Schuster, 1999.
Crossley-Holland, K. and Paton Walsh, J. *Wordhoard*. Puffin, 1972.
Czerneda, J. E. *No Limits: Developing Scientific Literacy Through Science Fiction*. Trifolium Books, 1999.
Devereux, P. *Stone Age Soundtracks*. Vega, 2001.
Dilts, R. B. and R. W. and Epstein, T. A. *Tools for Dreamers: Strategies for Creativity and the Structure of Innovation*. Meta Publications. 1991.
Dilts, R. B. and Epstein, T. A. *Dynamic Learning*. Meta Publications, 1995.
Dixon-Kennedy, M. *Celtic Myth and Legend*. Blandford, 1996.
Egan, K. *Teaching as Story Telling*. University of Chicago Press, 1989.
Ekwall, E. *The Concise Oxford Dictionary of English Place-Names*. Oxford, 1981.
Gardner, H. *Frames of Mind: The Theory of Multiple Intelligences* (second edition). Fontana, 1993.
Ginnis, P. *The Teacher's Toolkit*. Crown House Publishing, 2002.
Harris, C. *The Elements of NLP*. Element Books, 1998.
Hickman, D. E. and Jacobson, S. *The Power Process: An NLP Approach to Writing*. Anglo-American Book Company, 1997.

◆ BIBLIOGRAPHY

Huber, C.	*Suffering is Optional*. Keep It Simple Books, 2000.
Jackson, S.	*The Haunting of Hill House*. Corgi Books, 1977.
Jones, G.	*Killing Monsters: Why Children Need Fantasy, Super-Heroes and Make-Believe Violence*. Basic Books, 2002.
Kelsey, M.	*Dreamquest: Native American Myth and the Recovery of the Soul*. Element Books, 1995.
King, S.	*On Writing*. Hodder and Stoughton, 2000.
Lucas, B.	*Power Up Your Mind*. Nicholas Brearley Publishing, 2002.
Mellon, N.	*The Art of Storytelling*. Element Books, 1992.
Melton, J. G.	*The Vampire Book: The Encyclopedia of the Undead*. Visible Ink Press, 1994.
Postman, N. and Weingartner, C.	*Teaching as a Subversive Activity*. Penguin Education Specials, 1972.
Propp, V.	*Morphology of the Folk tale*. University of Texas Press, 2001.
Rockett, M. and Percival, S.	*Thinking for Learning*. Network Educational Press, 2002.
Smith, A.	*The Brain's Behind It*. Network Educational Press, 2002.
Smith, A. and Call, N.	*The ALPS Approach*. Network Educational Press, 1999.
Tolkien, J. R. R.	*Tree and Leaf*. Unwin Books, 1972.
Voytilla, S.	*Myth and the Movies*. Michael Wiese Productions, 1999.
Yeats, W. B.	*The Celtic Twilight: Myth, Fantasy and Folklore*. Prism Press, 1999.
Zohar, D. and Marshall, I.	*Spiritual Intelligence*. Bloomsbury, 2001.

Index

Note: Items in **bold** type appear on the CD resource as interactive writing games or material linked to *Catch & Other Stories*. Most of the visuals in the book can be found as photocopiable templates on the CD, where this index is reproduced.

A

Abstract art – as a way of stimulating creative thinking 136
Accelerated Learning Cycle – a sound template for effective creativity; also linked with basic patterns of narrative structure 49
Achievement (as distinct from attainment) – the whole endeavour of the individual to make progress in the world: a celebration of the learning journey 205
Achievement, certificate of 197
'Add-a-bit' – a writing game for developing characters and/or motifs in fiction 97
Affective response – the 'feeling component' of creative writing 191
'Alphabet Roll' – choosing letters at random for creative wordplay 86
Alpha waves (*see also* 'Relaxed alertness') 21, 38, 52
Anchoring – a way of embedding a link or association in our own experience. See 'Story stone', for example 68, 127
Animations (Fantasy animations created by Russell Morgan and Chris Sellers)
Annotating children's creative writing 193
Application – the importance of self-determination in storymaking 51
Artist brain – right cerebral hemisphere 21
Artwork, Stella Hender (atmospheric black-and-white illustrations)
Artwork, Brian Towers (full-colour space, astronautics and fantastical worlds)
Attainment and achievement – distinguishing between the destination and the journey 205

B

Ben Leech – an excellent Horror writer of great wit and subtle good looks. See 'Pseudonyms' 49
Big Ideas in English – the core concepts and principles at the heart of the subject 37
'Big Picture learners' – *see* 'Story staircase' 46
Bisociations – creative linking 25, 64
Blocks to creativity 18
'Bottom–up top–down staircase' – *see* 'Story staircase' 47

Brag – Horror/SF tale
 • **audio**
 • **with author's commentary**
 • used as an example of 'storylines' 170
 • used with storylines to show sub-plot 172
Brain waves – electrical impulses of varying frequency produced in the brain, corresponding to different mental/emotional states 21
Burning – Science Fiction tale
 • **audio**
 • **with author's commentary**

C

Catch – Fantasy tale
 • **audio**
 • **with author's commentary**
 • *Catch & Other Stories* **menu page**
 • brief description of storylines 168
 • themes of the stories 45
 • linked with character types 90
Catch Minitales
 Menu page
'Character grid' – a template for generating and organising many characters within a genre 105
'Character pie' – a game for exploring the personality of fictional characters 93
'Character pyramid' – a visual organiser for consolidating information about characters in stories 93
Characters, quick tips for creating
Character types and stereotypes 88
Chunking – working with information on different scales and levels 93, 97
Comics 148
Compound words 84
Concentration 55
'Concept mapping' – a mind mapping technique applied here to the elements of a story 151
'Connective prompt' – a word that encourages a link between two ideas
 • used with the Six Big Important Questions 115
 • used with 'Lensing' 115
 • used with 'Parallel story' 117
'Consequences' – a quick, easy game for plotting that makes use of many story elements 120
'Context sentence' – a sentence taken out of its context and used to stimulate nosiness! 114
'Creative attitude' – basically, 'be nosy': notice things and ask questions 15
'Creative climate' – the classroom environment that supports and celebrates creativity 18
'Creative cycle' (*see also* Henri Poincaré's four stages of creative processing) 24
Creativity
 • blocks to 18, 49, 52
 • myths about 13
 • and 'Mediations' 140
 • stages of the creative process 23

INDEX

D

'Deeper structure of stories' – exploring the morphology and narrative structures of traditional stories and contemporary genre tales 156
Definition of Science Fiction and Fantasy 167
'Design-a-monster' – a coin-flipping game for creating 'monstrous' characters in Fantasy and Horror stories 90
'Diamond ranking' – a flexible sequencing tool 108
'Dice journey' – a fast moving plotting game using pole-bridging (understanding ideas better as you mutter them to yourself) 141
'Disney Strategy' – adopting different personas for different stages of the storymaking process 123
Dragon's Egg – Fantasy tale
- audio
- with author's commentary
- linked to the 'Writing pyramid' (the large- and small-scale structure of a story) 41

'**Dragonslayer**' – a word game to create names for Fantasy characters 87
'Dread of the blank page' – confidence, creativity and emotional resourcefulness 28
Dunne, Richard – mathematician, educational thinker and trainer. *See also* 'Big Ideas in English' 37

E

Editor caps – put them on once the creative composition has been finished! 124
Education – 'to draw out'; to understand what sense children have already made of the world 15
Egan, Kieran – the power of stories 44, 103, 157
Empathy 101
Encouraging language – 'en-courage', to give courage to 17
Evaluation – 190, 198

F

Fairy tales and folk tales – in the context of symbol and the deep structure of Story 156
'Fantasy grid' – a visual organiser for exploring genre. (*See also* 'Bisociations', 'Story stone' and 'Zigzag story'.) 64
Fantasy character grid – a visual organiser for inventing and sequencing many characters 105
'Feelie bag' – a kinaesthetic game for storymaking 144
'Five Rs' – Resiliency, Resourcefulness, Responsibility, Reflectiveness, Remembering (emphasising the difference between a teacher-led, content-driven curriculum and one that is child-centred and process based) 200
Forever Man, The – Fantasy tale
- audio
- with author's commentary
- motifs explored 44

'Fortune cookie phrases' – a grid of general statements that invite you to supply the details 117
- used with storylines 118
- used with 'Story ingredients' 119
- used with proverbs 120

'Four areas for assessment, evaluation and planning' – an ideas-rich domain for feedback of written work and previewing subsequent projects 186

G

'Gathering treasures' – spatial and kinaesthetic anchoring to develop emotional resourcefulness 125
'Gee whiz data' – fascinating facts for capturing interest and opening doors into topic areas 43
Goals – as part of a model for creative thinking 14
Gurney – Horror tale
- audio
- with author's commentary

H

Hidden curriculum – the wealth of information about the world that children learn at school, which is not formally taught 14
House that R'ork Built, The – Science Fiction/Horror tale
- audio
- with author's commentary
- used as an example of a 'story recipe' 175

'How tall, how strong?' – mediating between binary opposites
- with reference to characters 99
- with reference to settings 141

I

'Idea-as-hero' – the underpinning concept of some SF stories 167
'Ideas cascade' – a simple association game 127
'Ideas now' – an acrostic for remembering the creative attitude 34
'Ideas wheel' – a visual organiser used for making creative connections at different levels of storymaking 128
Illusion of precision – a misleading impression of accuracy: *see* for example the '7/10 problem' 190
Ingredients – general elements in stories, larger than motifs but smaller than themes. See 'Story ingredients' 43, 173
Intelligence – our capacity to handle information 16
Interpretation (and 'mind-reading') 95

J

'Jigsaw town' – a fictionalised setting featuring real and imagined locations 143

K

Kennings – short descriptive poems 86
'Knowledge pyramid' – a visual organiser for making sense of factual information 41

L

'Ladder to the Moon' – the hierarchy of stories from backyard gossip to creation myths, illustrating that the 'earthy' and everyday is connected to the cosmic; demonstrating that stories link our most ordinary experiences to our fundamental senses of purpose in the universe 30
'Learning arrow' – progress from conscious incompetence to non-conscious competence 24
'Learning journey'– ∞ – an ongoing Accelerated Learning cycle, used also as a metaphor for developing skills in storymaking 47
'Lensing' – perceptual filtering as a stimulus to creative thinking 61
Linguistic intelligence – and the Big Ideas in English 37
'Living graphs' – graphs that encourage active interpretation of data 108
Logical-sequential learners – learners who like to see the logical links between small bits of the bigger picture 40
Logic brain – left cerebral hemisphere 20
Looking-back Time – the two fundamental questions for reviewing creative work 38, 190

M

Major characters 169
Manipulating information – the basic activity of the mind that makes sense of the world and which is the essence of creativity 22
Mastery – the link between authority and authorship 24, 199
Mastery of conventions – *see* 'Four areas for assessment, evaluation and planning' 191
'Meaning-making' – the natural tendency for the brain to make sense of the world 23
'Mediations' – finding 'the middle ground' between two extremes 140
  • between binary opposites 99
  • in two dimensions for characters 105
'Merlin technique' – looking at a problem in different ways for creative exploration 26
Metacognition – thinking about thinking 16
Metaphor –
  • the metaphor of 'the story' and emotional resourcefulness 48

'Mix-and-match senses' – and the phenomenon of synaesthesia 59
Monster as metaphor – how monsters represent varieties of fear in the human psyche 103
'Monster-maker' – exploring the origins and nature of monsters in genre fiction 102
Motifs – constituent features of stories, often used for defining and describing the genre 43, 65
  • as distinct from themes, elements and ingredients of a story 164
  • used with storylines 171
'Mystery mapping' – a speculation and problem-solving activity 147
'Mythic journey' – the basic structure of our most profound stories. Also see the 'Learning journey' 174

N

Nameplay – creative wordplay to make up character and place names 81
Nanoman – Science Fiction tale
  • **audio**
  • **with author's commentary**
  • as an example of using 'Living graphs' 110
  • as an example of using 'Concept maps' 151
  • as an example of using a story structure grid 160
Neurological levels – Robert Dilts' model of the levels of experience that structure our lives. (Compare this model with the Ladder to the Moon.) 47
NLP – Neuro Linguistic Programming – the art and techniques of modelling excellence by 'training the neurology' through language 33
'Nosiness' and metacognition 16

O

Odd-one-out – a quick, creative thinking game using reasoning, interpretation and discussion
  • used with the 6×6 Fantasy grid 122
'Other worlds' – a basic pattern in traditional and contemporary stories 154

P

'Parallel story' – mapping and making changes to an already existing story 173
Pattern of Three – a powerful storytelling technique, *see also* the Three-to-one Ratio for evaluation 198
Personas – assuming different roles for different phases of the writing process. See 'The Disney Strategy' 123
Philosophical enquiry with children 99
'Picture exploration' – a core activity for raising awareness of a range of thinking skills 55

◆ INDEX

Planning, quick tips for stories
Pledge cards – see 'Tiny changes' 197
Poincaré, Henri – and the stages of the creative process 23
Pole-bridging – muttering your understanding; articulating 'in flow' as you create 68, 118
Preprocessing – subconscious anticipation and information gathering prior to conscious action 126
'Princess of the Stars' – a game for creating 'descriptive names' of Fantasy characters 88
Product and process – achieving a balance in teaching and learning 51
Proverbs – generalised 'life tips' that can be turned into themes 120
Pseudonyms – role-play as a way of modelling resourceful behaviours 49

R

Redrafting – (this does not mean writing it all out again more neatly with the spellings corrected!) 33, 38
Reframes – modifying the structure of perception 25
Relaxed alertness, as a learning state 38

S

Scaffolding – as an educational concept: supporting learning until a child becomes an independent thinker 97
Seed thoughts – small ideas that grow subconsciously into something bigger. We don't call it 'planting suggestions' for nothing! 128, 164
'7/10 problem' – the dilemma of getting, say, 7/10 in a test – an illusion of precision 194
She Bites – Horror tale
- **audio**
- **with author's commentary**
- and the 'Merlin technique' 26

Six Big Important Questions – Where? When? What? Who? How? Why? – applied to storymaking 70
Space Art – Science Fiction artwork by Brain Towers
- **activity involving observation, deduction, speculation**

Spirituality – our capacity to wonder about ourselves and the larger universe. It is one of our levels of being 113
'Start anywhere' – a technique for translating the qualities of any object into a character 132
'Stepping up to mastery' – turning data into know-how systematically by a number of small tasks 199
Story cards 139
'Story circles' and the morphology of stories 130
'Story darts' – a variation of the 'Ideas wheel' game 129
'Story ingredients' – general components of stories, such as danger, mystery, conflict 175
- with storylines 171

Storylines – linear mapping of story structure 169
'Story map' – visual organisers for plotting and visualisation of settings 136
'Story mobiles' – story mapping in 3D 145
'Story so far' – a progressive reviewing technique 187
'Story staircase' – a visual organiser connecting the general with the particular. (*See also* 'Themes, ingredients and motifs'.) 46
'Story sticks' – stories constructed in 3D using mailing tubes 145
Story stone – an anchoring and visualisation technique that trains the user to access a state of 'relaxed alertness' (the Alpha state) at will 68
Story structure grid – exploring the functions of characters, settings, motifs, etc., in a story 160
'Story tray' – story mapping in 3D 144
'Story tree' – a sophisticated mind-mapping technique that explores many options for plots 145
'Story wheel' – a close cousin of the 'Ideas wheel' but operating at a deeper level, incorporating basic structural elements of a story 157
Strategies – menus of techniques and activities, as part of the creative attitude 15
Submodalities, exploring – noticing sensory impressions in fine detail 59
Sub-plot – a narrative 'loop', action-on-the-side, that connects with the main plot of the story 172
Synaesthesia – perceiving/describing one sensory impression in terms of another; 'the colour of sound', etc. 59
'Systematic daydreaming' – a sustained state of 'relaxed alertness' 38

T

Themes – the underpinning concepts and concerns of stories 43
- in *Catch & Other Stories* 44, 159

Thinking 'tools' – useful metaphor in metacognition 16
Three-to-one Ratio for evaluation – three points of praise and one area for improvement 194
'Thumbnails' – brief sketches of people, places, etc.
- 'Character thumbnails' 107

'Tiny changes' – mastering skills through incremental commitments 192
Titles
'Topic tree' – using the story tree template as a visual organiser for factual information 146
Trying hard, as opposed to working hard 24, 69

'Twenty questions' – a quick-fire game for review, logic and questioning skills 77
'Two Big Important Questions' (for redrafting and forward planning) 190
'Two Travellers' (artwork by Stella Hender)

V

Venn diagrams – a visual organiser for classification and mapping relationships between items 80
Visualisation 143
Visual organisers – schematic ways of representing information 28
Vivid particularities – memorable details in creative writing: *see* 'Four areas for assessment, evaluation and planning' 191

W

'What's the problem?' – a technique for generating a story. *Also see* 'Mystery mapping' 149
'World inside' – a way of mapping the thoughts inside a character's head 95
'World of the story'
'Writer's pie' – an evaluation tool that includes many components of creative writing 201
Writing process 38
'Writing pyramid' – a visual organiser showing the different levels or 'chunks' that compose a story 39

Z

'Zigzag story' – a game for generating a basic storyline in a few minutes 66

Other NEP Publications

THE SCHOOL EFFECTIVENESS SERIES

Book 1: *Accelerated Learning in the Classroom* by Alistair Smith
ISBN: 1-85539-034-5

Book 2: *Effective Learning Activities* by Chris Dickinson
ISBN: 1-85539-035-3

Book 3: *Effective Heads of Department* by Phil Jones and Nick Sparks
ISBN: 1-85539-036-1

Book 4: *Lessons are for Learning* by Mike Hughes
ISBN: 1-85539-038-8

Book 5: *Effective Learning in Science* by Paul Denley and Keith Bishop
ISBN: 1-85539-039-6

Book 6: *Raising Boys' Achievement* by Jon Pickering
ISBN: 1-85539-040-X

Book 7: *Effective Provision for Able and Talented Children* by Barry Teare
ISBN: 1-85539-041-8

Book 8: *Effective Careers Education and Guidance* by Andrew Edwards and Anthony Barnes
ISBN: 1-85539-045-0

Book 9: *Best behaviour and Best behaviour FIRST AID* by Peter Relf, Rod Hirst, Jan Richardson and Georgina Youdell
ISBN: 1-85539-046-9

Best behaviour FIRST AID
ISBN: 1-85539-047-7 (pack of 5 booklets)

Book 10: *The Effective School Governor* by David Marriott
ISBN 1-85539-042-6 (including free audio tape)

Book 11: *Improving Personal Effectiveness for Managers in Schools* by James Johnson
ISBN 1-85539-049-3

Book 12: *Making Pupil Data Powerful* by Maggie Pringle and Tony Cobb
ISBN 1-85539-052-3

Book 13: *Closing the Learning Gap* by Mike Hughes
ISBN 1-85539-051-5

Book 14: *Getting Started* by Henry Leibling
ISBN 1-85539-054-X

Book 15: *Leading the Learning School* by Colin Weatherley
ISBN 1-85539-070-1

Book 16: *Adventures in Learning* by Mike Tilling
ISBN 1-85539-073-6

Book 17: *Strategies for Closing the Learning Gap* by Mike Hughes and Andy Vass
ISBN 1-85539-075-2

Book 18: *Classroom Management* by Phillip Waterhouse and Chris Dickinson
ISBN 1-85539-079-5

Book 19: *Effective Teachers* by Tony Swainston
ISBN 1-85539-125-2
Book 20: *Transforming Teaching and Learning* by Colin Weatherley, Bruce Bonney, John Kerr and Jo Morrison
ISBN 1-85539-080-9

ACCELERATED LEARNING SERIES
General Editor: **Alistair Smith**

Accelerated Learning in Practice by Alistair Smith   ISBN 1-85539-048-5
The ALPS Approach: Accelerated Learning in Primary Schools
by Alistair Smith and Nicola Call   ISBN 1-85539-056-6
MapWise by Oliver Caviglioli and Ian Harris
ISBN 1-85539-059-0
The ALPS Approach Resource Book by Alistair Smith and Nicola Call   ISBN 1-85539-078-7
Creating an Accelerated Learning School by Mark Lovatt and Derek Wise
ISBN 1-85539-074-4
ALPS StoryMaker by Stephen Bowkett   ISBN 1-85539-076-0
Thinking for Learning by Mel Rockett and Simon Percival   ISBN 1-85539-096-5
Reaching out to all learners by Cheshire LEA   ISBN 1-85539-143-0
Leading Learning by Alistair Smith   ISBN 1-85539-089-2
Bright Sparks by Alistair Smith   ISBN 1-85539-088-4
Move It by Alistair Smith   ISBN 1-85539-123-6

EDUCATION PERSONNEL MANAGEMENT SERIES
Education Personnel Management handbooks help headteachers, senior managers and governors to manage a broad range of personnel issues.

The Well Teacher – management strategies for beating stress, promoting staff health and reducing absence by Maureen Cooper   ISBN 1-85539-058-2
Managing Challenging People – dealing with staff conduct
by Bev Curtis and Maureen Cooper   ISBN 1-85539-057-4
Managing Poor Performance – handling staff capability issues
by Bev Curtis and Maureen Cooper   ISBN 1-85539-062-0
Managing Allegations Against Staff – personnel and child protection issues in schools by Maureen Cooper and Bev Curtis   ISBN 1-85539-072-8
Managing Recruitment and Selection – appointing the best staff
by Maureen Cooper and Bev Curtis   ISBN 1-85539-077-9
Managing Redundancies – dealing with reduction and reorganisation of staff by Maureen Cooper and Bev Curtis   ISBN 1-85539-082-5
Managing Pay in Schools – performance management and pay in schools
by Bev Curtis   ISBN 1-85539-087-6

VISIONS OF EDUCATION SERIES

The Unfinished Revolution by John Abbott and Terry Ryan   ISBN 1-85539-064-7
The Learning Revolution by Jeannette Vos and Gordon Dryden   ISBN 1-85539-085-X
Wise Up by Guy Claxton   ISBN 1-85539-099-X

OTHER NEP PUBLICATIONS

ABLE AND TALENTED CHILDREN COLLECTION

Effective Resources for Able and Talented Children by Barry Teare
ISBN 1-85539-050-7
More Effective Resources for Able and Talented Children by Barry Teare
ISBN 1-85539-063-9
Challenging Resources for Able and Talented Children by Barry Teare
ISBN 1-85539-122-8

MODEL LEARNING

Thinking Skills And Eye Q by Oliver Caviglioli, Ian Harris and Bill Tindall
ISBN 1-85539-091-4
Class Maps by Oliver Caviglioli and Ian Harris
ISBN 1-85539-139-2

OTHER TITLES FROM NEP

The Thinking Child by Nicola Call with Sally Featherstone   ISBN 1-85539-121-X
Becoming Emotionally Intelligent by Catherine Corrie   ISBN 1-85539-069-8
That's Science by Tim Harding   ISBN 1-85539-170-8
The Brain's Behind It by Alistair Smith   ISBN 1-85539-083-3
Help Your Child To Succeed by Bill Lucas and Alistair Smith   ISBN 1-85539-111-2
Tweak to Transform by Mike Hughes   ISBN 1-85539-140-6
Brain Friendly Revision by UFA National Team   ISBN 1-85539-127-9
Numeracy Activities Key Stage 2 by Afzal Ahmed and Honor Williams
ISBN 1-85539-102-3
Numeracy Activities Key Stage 3 by Afzal Ahmed, Honor Williams and
George Wickham   ISBN 1-85539-103-1
Teaching Pupils How to Learn by Bill Lucas, Toby Greany, Jill Rodd and
Ray Wicks   ISBN 1-85539-098-1
Basics for School Governors by Joan Sallis   ISBN 1-85539-012-4
Imagine That... by Stephen Bowkett   ISBN 1-85539-043-4
Self-Intelligence by Stephen Bowkett   ISBN 1-85539-055-8
Class Talk by Rosemary Sage   ISBN 1-85539-061-2